You Too Can Be Used by God!

Released In The Supernatural

By Dr. Guy Peh

**Unless otherwise indicated,
Scripture quotations are from
THE NEW KING JAMES VERSION.**
Copyright 1979, 1980, 1982 by Thomas Nelson,
Inc., Publishers.

ISBN 978-0-9817836-1-1

Copyright 2010, USA

Published by:
Reconciliation Ministries International Inc.
P.O. Box 763174
Dallas, Texas 75376
www.guypeh.com

Preface

As we travel the globe many people have asked me the question, "I am looking for answers to release God's gifts in me. Can you help me?"

This has been the vision God placed in my heart: to help people release the gifts God has placed in them.

This book will help you release the gifts of God in you.

May the Father use this book to help you become a vessel mightily used by Him in the Kingdom.

Continue to reach forward in Him!

Dedication

I want to dedicate this book to my wife, Ilke, for being such a "kingmaker", for all of her effort in helping me do what God has called me to do in the nations of the world.

Special thanks to Sue and Antinetta for their help with this project.

Table Of Contents

Chapter 1

The Release of the Spirit of Elijah

> *In every season of God's calendar there is an emphasis of the Holy Spirit.*

In every season of God's calendar, there is an emphasis of the working of the Holy Spirit. This is what some people in the body of Christ call *"a move of God."*

> *People who receive a word in the Spirit (from the Holy Spirit) have the grace to become a spear-head of a move of God in their generation.*

Those that will have eyes to see and ears to hear will have a revelation knowledge of what the Lord has prepared for those who love Him. Such a people will receive a word in the spirit and grace to become, at times, the spear-head of a move of God in their generation. In every major move of God, the Lord will use a man or a woman to lead their generation into revival.

> *Our ability to change and impact the generations is directly related to our ability to know what the emphasis of the Spirit of God is in a given season.*

The word, *"dispensation"*, is defined in Webster's dictionary as the *system of revealed commands and promises (from God) that regulates human affairs.* A dispensation of time is a period of time when God judges His people according to a certain set of moral standards of conduct.

People often associate dispensation with *cessationalism.* Cessationalism is the doctrine that believes that miracles stopped with the death of the last apostles of the early church. I want you to see dispensation from a different perspective. God is the God of dispensation. For instance, the Bible consists of two dispensations: the Old Testament dispensation, or *Old Covenant* and, the New Testament dispensation, or *New Covenant.*

A dispensation could also be described as a *word that has been given to you during a certain period of time in your life to govern that season of your life* – just like Abraham received a word to leave his country to go to a country he did not even know. Moses was told to go to Egypt to tell the pharaoh to let God's people go. Noah was told by God to build a boat on dry land and to warn his generation about the upcoming judgment of God.

> *When a dispensation turns into an instruction or an assignment given to you by the Lord, then, that dispensation becomes a word in the Spirit.*

Abraham received a word in the Spirit. Moses received a word in the Spirit. Noah received a word in the Spirit. The life of each one of these men of God was governed, at the season they received the word in the Spirit, by the Word they received... until its fulfillment.

To everything there is a season. A time for every purpose under heaven: a time to be born and a time to die; a time to plant, and a time to pluck out what is planted; a time to kill, and a time to heal; a time to break down and a time to build up; a time to weep and a time to laugh; a time to mourn and a time to dance; a time to cast away stones and a time to gather stones; a time to embrace and a time to refrain from embracing; a time to gain and a time to lose; a time to keep and a time to throw away; a time to tear and a time to sew; a time to keep silence and a time to speak; a time to love and a time to hate; a time of war and a time of peace.

~ Ecclesiastes 3 : 1 - 8

There is a time for every purpose under heaven. And... for the season you are living in, there is a word in the Spirit, or a dispensation, that governs your life. It is an instruction that comes from the Holy Spirit to govern your life for that season. That's why it's important for you to understand what season you are in and what God is saying in the Spirit for that season.

> *You have to know what season you are living in.*
> *Otherwise, you will be like*
> *someone living in the winter - wearing summer clothes;*
> *or someone living in the summer - wearing winter clothes.*

What happens to people like that? One of them will be very cold while the other will be very hot, because they are *out of season*. Such a person does not understand the word in the Spirit for the season. The word in the Spirit for those living in the winter is to get some warm clothes... or you are going to get cold! The word in the Spirit for those living in the summertime is to dress in lighter weight clothes... or you are going to be hot. In the same way, you must be dressed properly (spiritually-speaking) for each season of your life. That's why you need to understand what time it is in the Spirit.

> *If you don't understand the season you are in,*
> *you risk being a part of the "what's up crowd" – those who bounce*
> *back and forth from church-to-church and from*
> *conference-to-conference, looking for God and what He is doing.*

They are spiritually unstable because they don't understand the season of God in their life. They cannot grow spiritually because they don't understand the season they are in. It is so important for us to understand the season of God in our lives. Corporately, as leaders in the body of Christ, it's important for us to understand the *time* – so we can communicate it to the Church.

> *Heaven has a language.*
> *Heaven has a voice.*
> *Heaven has a protocol.*

> *Before God does anything on the face of the earth,*
> *God first announces it in the Spirit.*

There will be people, like Abraham, Moses and Noah, who will hear what God is saying and tell it to their generation. Then, there will be those who will criticize those who are saying what God shows them. Still others will not care if they are seeing or saying anything! The government (leaders) of God exists to release and declare His prophetic assignment (Ephesians 4 : 11 - 13): to tell the Church where we're heading, where we're going, and where we are, so that we can follow the leadership of the Holy Spirit. Whenever you have a word in the Spirit, God will give you the dispensation of grace needed to allow you to fulfill that season and that word.

> *Without a word in the Spirit for the season, you will not have the grace and power beyond your natural ability that is needed to fulfill the will of God for the season.*

Without a word in the Spirit for the season, you are going to get frustrated. No wonder… it is winter and you have on summer clothes! That's why you're feeling the cold! You are out of season. But if it is winter and you have on winter clothes, you're going to flow with the season, because you have the word in the Spirit. It is going to dress you up, and the grace of God is going to be in your life – empowering you to do God's will for that season.

Not only that… when you respond to the word in obedience to God, there will be 3 **manifestations of grace:**

- Grace for the *place* (power beyond your ability for your position), which is your position in the place.

- Grace for the *case* (power beyond your ability for your experience), which is your experience in the place.

- Grace for the *race* (power beyond your ability for your mission), which is your mission in the season.

When you have a word in the Spirit for the season and you understand what time it is in your life, you may go through hard or difficult times (like Moses in the wilderness or Abraham in war), but God's grace is going to be there to help you stand. You will see the victory of God because you will understand that God has put you in that place.

And having done all, to stand. Stand therefore.
~ Ephesians 6 : 13 - 14

Now, I said all that to say that I thank the Lord for all the past moves of God! It is important to us as the church to understand our past so we can prepare for the future. I don't want to take away from the past moves of God. I understand that God did different things at different seasons, but I don't want to live in the past. What I want to know now is: "What is the word in the Spirit for this generation, and what time is it?"

An "inheritance" is *receiving something that someone else has paid for. A "legacy" is what you pass to the next generation.*

We have received a great heritage from great men of God in great moves of God. From the ancient times of revival until now, there has been a restoration of the five-fold ministry – which constitutes the government of God. Because of the lives and ministries of great men and women of God and of the past times of revival, God's government has been restored and a foundation has been built.

The commitment of our spiritual fathers has now become our call to reach the next generation.

But the question is, "What legacy shall we pass to future generations?" What is the word of the Spirit for **this** generation?"

I believe that the word in the Spirit for this generation is *the release of the spirit of Elijah for the saints' movement... an army of believers being used by God.*

But to you who fear My name, The sun of Righteousness shall arise with healing in His wings. And, you shall go out and grow like stall-fed calves.

~ Malachi 4 : 2

Behold, I will send you Elijah the prophet before the coming of the great and dreadful day of the Lord, and he will return the hearts of the fathers to the children, and the hearts of the children to their fathers, lest I come and strike the earth with a curse.

~ Malachi 4 : 5

This was prophesied *before* Christ's First Coming. For more than 400 years after that Word was spoken, no prophetic word was given. There was 400 years of darkness with no prophetic light... 400 years of stillness with no prophetic voice. The move of God was dead. The people of God had become complacent and had drifted away from the purpose of God in their generation. Religion took over their lives, and God's children were desperate to see a visitation. Doesn't that sound like today within some parts of the church? We can see a prophetic parallel. It seems like some modern-day churches are in the same place.

> *Some churches have moved from*
> *the apostolic power of the Holy Spirit*
> *into the mechanics of religion*
> *and from demonstration into dignity.*
> *But there is always a remnant.*

Four hundred years of silence... dead religion. The earth needed an awakening... a revival. That is what everyone was waiting for. John the Baptist came in the power of the Spirit of Elijah. It was the buzz of the town. Everyone knew Elijah must come first. They were excited for Elijah to come because they knew that when he did... the Messiah would come. And then, after 400 years of silence, an angel came and appeared to Zachariah.

During the visitation described in Luke 1 : 13 - 17, Zachariah went into the temple to fulfill his priestly duty. While he was going about his duties, the angel said to him, "Your barren wife, Elizabeth, shall give birth to a son. He then will be called John and he will come in the power of the Spirit of Elijah." And just as the angel said... John the Baptist was born. John did not come to say, "Behold my ministry!" He came to prepare the way for the coming of the Lord. He was a voice crying out in the wilderness. He said that his ministry should decrease so that Jesus' ministry might increase. His ministry was to point out the coming of the Christ.

Do you believe that if there was a first coming, there will be a second coming? You better believe it, my friend, because Jesus is coming back! Jesus is coming back, and He's coming soon. He is a soon-coming King. Before the first coming, there was an Elijah who was released. John came in the *Spirit* of Elijah. And, may I suggest to you, if before the first coming there was a *John* who came in the power of the Spirit of Elijah, that before the *Second* Coming there will be a second John who will come in the power of the Spirit of Elijah. There will be a second John who will point-out the Messiah to the world – who will make the crooked way straight, and who will cause mountains to come down. And, this time, it's not going to be one man eating honey and locusts, standing in the wilderness. This time, the second John the Baptist, whom God is raising up before the second coming, is the Body of Christ... **the Church!**

> *The Church is going to rise in the power of the Spirit of Elijah in the last days – ordinary believers doing supernatural things.*

That's why God has restored the government of the Church: to equip the believers for the work of the ministry.

> *"Revival" is not a place where you go. It is not something you do. Revival is a person. His name is "Jesus".*

True revival always causes people to fall in love with Jesus over and over again. When every person gets a personal revival, then we will have a corporate revival.

John's ministry was to present Jesus to the world before the first coming of Jesus. Today, before the second coming of Jesus, the spirit of Elijah is coming upon the saints of God to present Jesus to the world again.

I hope you understand this! **You** are the Elijah generation!

The relationship between Elijah and Elisha is a prophetic parallel to the relationship between Christ and the Church. Elisha's name resembled Elijah's name; Christians' name resembles Christ's name. Elisha followed Elijah; Christians must follow Christ. Elijah gave his mantle to Elijah when he ascended; Christ gave his mantle to the Church when He ascended, and He gave gifts to the Church. Elisha did twice as many miracles as Elijah; Jesus said, *"Greater things shall you do because I am going to the Father."*

~ John 14 : 12

You are the Elijah generation!
You have been released in the supernatural.
You, too, can be used by God
as a forerunner of Christ for your generation!

Now when they drew near Jerusalem, to Bethpage and Bethany, at the Mount of Olives, He sent two of his disciples; and He said to them, "Go into the village opposite you; and as soon as you have entered it you will find a colt tied, on which no one has sat. Loose it and bring it and if anyone says to you, 'Why are you doing this?' say, 'The Lord has need of it,' and immediately he will send it here." So they went their way, and found the colt tied by the door outside on the street, and they loosed it. But some of those who stood there said to them, "What are you doing loosing the colt?" And they spoke to them just as Jesus had commanded. So they let them go. Then they brought the colt to Jesus and threw their clothes on it, and He sat on it. And many spread their clothes on the road, and others cut down leafy branches from the trees and spread them on the road. Then those who went before and those who followed cried out, saying: "Hosanna! Blessed is He who comes in the name of the Lord! Blessed is the kingdom of our father David that comes in the name of the Lord. Hosanna in the highest!"

~ Mark 11 : 1 - 7

For his triumphant entry into Jerusalem, Jesus told his disciples to untie and bring to Him a donkey that no one had ever sat upon. The word, "Christ", means, *anointed one*. This donkey did not have the experience to carry the anointing, but God chose to use it anyway. God was not looking for ability only; He was looking for availability. Many people today may feel inadequate to do the work of the ministry.

> *God is not looking for ability only.*
> *He is looking for availability.*

That's why God restored the government of the Church: the office of the apostle, prophet, teacher, pastor, and evangelist. He did it for the edification and the preparation of the saints, so we can go out in the spirit of Elijah and prepare the way of the Lord: preaching the Gospel – the good news – to the poor! Unfortunately, many people live below their potential and calling. Sometimes, we are tied up with the affairs of this world – with fear or even with religion. Just like Jesus sent the disciples to loose the donkey and to bring it to Him, some believers need leaders with apostolic anointing to loose them and release them into their calling.

> *You are a part of the Elijah company of the 21st century.*

Let me say it again:
You and your generation are the ones God is using and is going to use to open the blind eyes! You are the ones He is using and is going to use to open the deaf ears! You are the ones who are preaching the Gospel and the ones who are going to preach the Gospel! ***You are the second Elijah generation!***

Church leadership has received the *Elijah commission* to raise up sons and daughters in the faith so they can be released into the ministry. No matter how anointed a man of God is, one person cannot reach everyone. There are people that I will never be able to reach; but, there are people in each of our lives that we **can** reach.

> *Everybody must be somebody to somebody to be anybody.*

Did you get that? ...There are people whom you cannot reach, but there are people you **can** reach. That is why it is so important for Church leaders to walk in the Elijah commission: to raise up believers who know how to participate in world evangelism. The second coming of Jesus Christ is directly related to world evangelism. In Matthew 24, Jesus says that there will be wars and rumors of wars in the last days. There will be earthquakes, famines and floods. These are signs that the end is coming, but they are not the end. When will the end come? The end won't come until this Gospel is preached in all the world for a witness unto all nations. How will the Gospel be preached in all the world? This will be accomplished when the body of Christ is entirely activated into the great commission.

Jesus said, "Go into all the world and preach the Gospel to every creature. And, these signs will follow those who believe. In My name they will cast out demons; they will speak with new tongues; they will take up serpents; and if they drink anything deadly, it will by no means hurt them; they will lay hands on the sick, and they will recover."

~ Mark 16 : 15, 17 - 18

The leaders of the Church are responsible to raise up an army of believers and release them into global evangelization as they come under authority. Believers must receive teaching and training so they can be released to go into the world and do the work that many people who are in leadership cannot accomplish without the saints' participation.

Jesus said, "Most assuredly, I say to you, he who believes in Me, the works that I do he will do also; and greater works than these he will do, because I go to My Father."

~ John 14 : 12

There is such a thing as a *multiplication factor*. As leadership begins to walk in the power of this Elijah commission and they begin to release the saints into the work of the ministry, an anointing of multiplication will come upon the Body of Christ. It is my personal belief that the last spiritual movement on the face of the earth (before Jesus Christ comes back to this world at the second coming) is going to be the *Movement of the Saints*. I see no other way for the Church to accomplish the massive task of global evangelization that lies before us.

When I talk about the saints, I'm not speaking about leaders of some clerical religious order wearing long robes with big crosses around their necks making the sign of the cross and carrying candles. That's not what I'm talking about. When I talk about the saints of God, I'm talking about those who have been born again, cleansed and washed by the blood of Jesus... *these* are the saints of God. God is going to raise up the saints no matter their ages. I believe we will see young and old being used. We will see people of all ages with miracle ministries.

And it shall come to pass afterward that I will pour out My Spirit on all flesh. Your sons and your daughters shall prophesy, your old men shall dream dreams, your young men shall see visions.

~ Joel 2 : 28

> *If you have flesh,*
> *you are a target of the outpouring of God's Spirit,*
> *you are a target of revival.*

In the end-time revival, there will be an outburst of power as the Spirit of God descends upon the earth. Everybody will be used. The old men will be used. The young men will be used. The women will be used. The children will be used. A company of miracle-workers is here and is moving into action. The army of God will begin to march and they will keep marching until the end – the young with the old, with the grandpa, the grandma, the auntie and the uncles. **Everybody** will be used by God!

> *Every segment of the church population is going*
> *to be activated and released in the supernatural.*

It doesn't matter what your ethnicity, your education, your gender, your age, your economic status, or your zip code is. If you are born again, you have been released in the supernatural and you can be used by God.

For 400 years, the Israelites had been looking. For 400 years, they had been waiting for Elijah to come. They were eager for him to come. Can you imagine what that was like? They were a people living under the domination of the Roman Empire. They couldn't wait for Elijah to get there. You may think that it sounds like the Church today. We continually say that we can't wait for revival. We pray for revival. We say that we will take over our cities for God when revival gets here. Do you realize that when John the Baptist came in the Spirit of Elijah (which is a type of the move of God), the religious community did not recognize the move? He didn't come speaking their religious language. He didn't come wearing religious robes, and he didn't preach in or spend most of His time in the synagogue.

> *Don't try to put God in a box,*
> *because when revival breaks out, it's not going to*
> *look like what you think it's going to look like.*

They expected Elijah, when he returned, to be conformed to their religious ways. The religious leaders were wearing a priestly robe and were preaching in the synagogue. But he came wearing what? Camel skin clothing! Eating what? Locusts and honey! Preaching where? In the backside of the wilderness! And **that** was revival! The Pharisees said, "That's not from God! That's from the devil." Pharisaical people are still saying, "Oh, no! That's not from God. We've got to wait for Elijah. We've got to wait for the move of God."

Now after six days Jesus took Peter, James and John, his brother, led them up to the high mountain by themselves and He was transfigured before them. His face shone like the sun and His clothes became as white as the light. And, behold, Moses and Elijah appeared to them, talking with Him. Then Peter answered and said to Jesus, "Lord it is good for us to be here; if You wish, let us make here three tabernacles: one for You, one for Moses, and one for Elijah." While he was still speaking, behold a bright cloud overshadowed them and suddenly a voice came out of the cloud, saying, "This is my beloved son in whom I am well pleased, hear Him." And when the disciples heard it, they fell on their faces and were greatly afraid. But Jesus came and touched them and said, "Arise and do not be afraid." When they had lifted up their eyes, they saw no one but Jesus only. Now as they came down from the mountain, Jesus commanded them saying, "Tell the vision to no one until the Son of Man is risen from the dead." And His disciples asked Him, saying, "Why then do the scribes say that Elijah must come first?"

~ Matthew 17 : 1 - 10

Elijah must come first. I want you to see this. This is powerful. Why did the disciples say that Elijah must come first?

Jesus answered and said to them, "Indeed Elijah is coming first and will restore all things. But I say to you that Elijah has come already, and they did not know him but did to him whatever they wished. Likewise the Son of Man is also about to suffer at their hands."

~ Matthew 17 : 11 – 12

Even the disciples did not know that John was the one who was prophesied to herald the Messiah… until Peter, James and John went with Jesus up the mountain of transfiguration. When they saw the vision of Elijah, they got excited. They didn't even know that revival was **already there.** What they saw was awesome, and they were ready to go tell everyone Elijah was already there.

But, Jesus told them to tell the vision to no one. Can you imagine the conversation that must have ensued between Jesus and the disciples? "Come on, Jesus. Everybody is talking about this. Everyone is looking for Elijah. Why don't You want us to tell the people that Elijah is already here? Come on, man! We have got to tell them! We saw him with our own eyes. We saw him there talking to You and Moses. We want to go tell everybody that Elijah is here! For 400 years we have been waiting for this!"

Jesus' answer might have gone something like this: "Yes, Elijah must come first and restore all things. But Elijah is already here. The Pharisees did to him whatever they wanted to. And likewise, so the Son of Man will suffer in their hands."

In other words: The religious leaders of the day killed the move of God for which they had been praying for 400 years when it showed up in town! Herod beheaded John the Baptist. The religious leaders hated John the Baptist's message. They hated what he wore and what he ate. They didn't like his ministry style. They said that he was from the devil. But he was what they had been praying for… *for 400 years!*

I'm telling you, it's the same with the Church today. We have been waiting on "the end-time revival." We have been praying for it. We have been praying for God to move, for God to change our cities, for God to change our nations, for God to change the continents. But God is saying, "Listen, I have already released My Spirit. What has been released… has been released."

> *Smith Wigglesworth, evangelist and apostle of faith,*
> *said that he was not waiting for a move of God,*
> *but that he was going to move God.*

Wigglesworth said that God already moved 2000 years ago when He sent His son, Jesus Christ. Revival is not something you do. Revival is not a place where you go. Revival is not screaming from the top of your voice. Revival is not shaking. Revival is a person and His name is **"Jesus Christ"**. When you fall in love with Him… that's when you get revival.

> *We are waiting for a move of God,*
> *but God wants us to move like God*
> *by releasing the Christ in us… the hope of Glory.*

> *We are seeking God's hand,*
> *but He wants us to know His feet.*
> *In other words: He wants us to know His way.*

There is a calling on the life of every believer to operate in supernatural power. In the great commission, Jesus says that signs will follow those who believe in Him. The Spirit of Elijah is the agency of power in the scripture. That spirit is released on the earth to raise up believers in a forerunner ministry for Christ - like John the Baptist.

In Philippians 2 : 25, Paul referred to his disciple, Epaphroditus, as a "fellow soldier". Believers are soldiers in the army of God.

Paul said to Timothy, "You therefore must endure hardship as a good soldier of Jesus Christ."

~ 2 Timothy 2 : 3

Your people shall be volunteers in the day of Your power.

~ Psalm 110 : 3

The end-time move of God is going to be the movement of the volunteer army of the Lord.

> *We are at war as Christians. There is no neutral zone, and there is a good fight that needs to be fought.*

Paul said: "I have fought the good fight, I have finished the race, I have kept the faith."

~ 2 Timothy 4 : 7

Soldiers receive their training for the battlefield in a boot camp – before they are sent into a war zone. The unarmed soldier is useless in battle. The soldiers any country will want in their army are soldiers that are "armed and dangerous". They have weapons and know how to use them.

> *The church of Jesus Christ*
> *is not just a hospital… it is a battleship.*

We are an army with a hospital where people get healed and sent back into battle. It is in God's spiritual boot camp on earth where Christians are trained to become strong, obedient, disciplined, devoted, and awake. All of these are characteristics of a soldier. Many people come to church today just to receive from God with a "Give me… meet my need" type of mentality.

> *After a person comes into the Kingdom,*
> *there has to come a point in their lives where,*
> *after they have received ministry for a while,*
> *they begin to give ministry to those that need it.*

Reaching this point of ministering to others is the result of a person's spiritual growth.

We cannot be always learning and never able to come to the knowledge of the truth.

~ 2 Timothy 3 : 7

> *The Church is God's spiritual boot camp*
> *where saints are trained for the work of the ministry*
> *and sent into the harvest fields of the world.*

This training is for Christians in all spheres of society - including the marketplace.

For the weapons of our warfare are not carnal but mighty in God for pulling down strongholds.

~ 2 Corinthians 10 : 4

This means that we have weapons with which to conduct warfare, but to use a weapon, a soldier must go through weapons training. Today, every person operating in the five-fold ministry must have an apostolic mandate in their life so they can operate in the Elijah commission - which is to train and equip believers for the work of the ministry so that believers can be released into ministry.

> *Today, many in church leadership are called to be generals in God's army to raise up soldiers for Christ.*

In this book, we are going to study and discuss subjects that will help the average believer and leader operate in the supernatural and wage the warfare that is needed to win souls and display the championship quality of God in their lives for the end-time harvest. We are going to go through a spiritual boot camp so that you can become a soldier that is armed and dangerous. We are going to learn more about:

- **Encounters with the Supernatural**
  How I started my journey in the supernatural. 3 questions that every person who wants to be used by God has to answer.

- **Supernatural Thinking**
  To be used by God we need to have the right mindset and right thinking. For as a man thinks, so is he.

- **Authority**
  Most Christians know who the devil is and who God is, but they don't know who they are in Christ. Know your God given authority.

- **Walking in the Supernatural**
  Walking in the supernatural is necessary to experience the fullness of the power of God. It's important to understand the dynamics of the gifts of the Spirit, origins of sickness, and how to pray for the dead in order to be an effective minister of the gospel.

- **You Can Cast it Down and Cast it Out**
  The spiritual realm is as real as the natural realm. There is angelical activity and demonic activity. There is a supernatural dimension that supersedes your natural sight where God and the enemy operate. To be used by God to help people who are oppressed by demonic forces, you need to learn how to minister deliverance.

- **Use Me Lord**
  This is the heartbeat of someone that wants to be used by God.

Chapter 2

Encounters With the Supernatural

It is a good thing to learn from the experiences of others. Learning from other's voices can inspire you to, then, speak with your own voice. Many times, people around the world have asked me, "How did you start out in the ministry? How did God start to use you?" In this chapter, I want to share some experiences of my journey with the supernatural and some of my spiritual encounters.

The word, "encounter", means, *to collide with the unexpected.*

> *An encounter with God is a collision that bridges the gap between the natural and the supernatural.*

When you have an encounter with God, the spiritual meaning and significance can be that something is about to change. *Something is about to happen.* It may be the birth of a vision, the opening of a new door, the launching of a new ministry, or perhaps new steps that you need to take. My prayer is, as you read about my personal experiences with the supernatural and all the teaching and principles written in this book, that you will experience the power of God and the touch of Jesus Christ in a very real and powerful way.

I was not born into a Christian family. Christianity for me was something that I "did" by going to church once or twice a year on Christmas or Easter. My life from an early age was marked with many crises. At the age of 3, I found myself being raised by my grandparents. At the age of 13, I was being raised by an uncle. I never knew my biological father, and had a mother that was absent most of the time as I was growing up. Left abandoned at an early age, I was forced to take the leadership of my life into my own hands.

I endured a lot of challenges as a child and teenager. My life was marked with many painful emotional and physical experiences. There were times where my life was filled with hopelessness in a world that didn't seem to be fair. As a teenage boy, I developed a passion for sports and became an athlete. I spent a good part of my life in the sports world where I found acceptance, friends, and fun. I tried to fill the vacuum in my heart with basketball. But, God is a merciful God. During that time, God introduced me to a relationship with a strong Christian girl that He used to introduce me to the love of Jesus. And by the grace of God, I got saved.

I discovered the Kingdom of God. I went through different seasons, where God sent a variety of people to teach and mentor me. I had a hunger for the Word of God and began to study the

Bible. I discovered that God was a God of miracles. I began to notice unique signs and wonders when I prayed, which indicated to me that God wanted to use me. With a momentum of faith, zeal, and miracles, doors began to open and I began to preach in different places. My heart was stirred to learn even more, and I decided to get an education in the Word of God and to go to Bible school.

The call of God in my life and my personal spiritual development was a journey with different seasons. I had supernatural encounters that caused me to experience the power of God in a real and tangible way. I want to share some of those experiences with you.

The First Time I Saw God Do a Miracle Through My Prayers

People often ask me, "How did you start in the healing ministry? How did God start to use you?" It was, and is, a process.

When I got saved, my heart was stirred for miracles and the supernatural. In the part of the world where I was at that time, you could go into public hospitals (with the permission of the hospital), and pray for the sick. On the weekend, my friends and I would go to the hospital to preach the gospel and minister to the sick… praying for them.

I remember the first time I saw God's power touch someone. There was a man that was in a car accident. He had broken many bones in his body. He was in excruciating pain, and had not slept for many days. I preached the gospel to him and told him that Jesus Christ could heal him. He accepted Jesus Christ as his savior, and I prayed for his healing. Even before I finished my prayers, all the pain left his body, and he went into a deep sleep. I was amazed to see God move so powerfully through my prayers. I was on top of the world, and I felt that with my God, I could do anything. This created great zeal, excitement, and confidence. Everyone could see it on me.

In my journey in the supernatural and miracles, things were not always that glorious. I once went through a difficult time. I was depressed and discouraged. One day, I went to the hospital again to pray. I was told about a teenage boy that was very sick and was dying in a room. I went into the room and prayed for him. As I prayed for him, it was just as if my prayer killed him. He was lying down. Suddenly, after I prayed, he lifted his head, took a deep breath, and died. I prayed for him for 3 hours, begging God to raise him from the dead; but nothing happened.

I was so sad and disappointed. Inside, I felt like a balloon that was losing all its air. There was a feeling of deflation inside my spirit. All my joy, zeal, strength, and excitement left. Suddenly, a feeling of guilt came over me, and some thoughts of accusation began to cross my mind. I thought, "Perhaps if I hadn't prayed for him, he would still be alive. Perhaps I did something wrong."

After this event, I went through a season that was very difficult emotionally and spiritually. I felt depressed and discouraged. I lost my spiritual appetite for the things of God – my desire to pray and minister to the sick. One day while I was having a self-pity party, I heard the voice of the Lord. He asked me, "Who healed the man that you prayed for that was in a car accident the first time you went to the hospital?" I answered, "You did, Lord." And He said to me,

> *"If you are going to take credit when people don't get healed, then you should also take credit when they get healed."*

Suddenly, I had a revelation that my job was to pray, regardless of the outcome; but it's *God's* job to heal and to perform miracles. So I repented and was set free. A new energy and a new zeal came into my spirit. From that day, I have never been intimidated again to pray for a sick person, because I understand that it's my job to pray and that it's God's job to heal.

> *Many people today are limited by the potential outcome of their prayers.*

They are afraid and say, "What if nothing happens?" But, I will say to you, "What if something happens?" I want to encourage you, God wants to use you. Start where you are.

> *Don't wait for something big to occur. Start where you are, with what you have, and that will always lead you into something greater.*

It is not your job to *heal,* but it's your job to *pray.* God does the healing and the miracles. If they don't happen, don't get discouraged! Do not be afraid to pray for people. God will move through your prayers. You, too, can be used by God!

The First Time I Cast Out a Demon

As the Lord started to use me, I saw many people healed, but I had never prayed for someone for deliverance. Later in this book, we are going to discuss extensively on how to minister deliverance. But back then, I had no clue. One of my friends told me about his cousin that had lost her mind after her boyfriend took her to a cult where they practiced some form of eastern meditation. Her parents were desperate, as their daughter could no longer go to school, drive, or function normally. Something happened to her mind. My friend told them about how God was using me, and they asked if I could come and pray for their daughter.

We went to their house. When we got there, I met the girl. She seemed to be normal. I thought I would ask her how the problem started. The moment I asked about it, her face began to be contorted, her eyes grew menacing, and she started to growl like an animal. A voice of a man spoke through her, saying, "She's mine! She's mine! I am going to kill you!" I was so scared! I never had an experience with anything like this before. I looked at my friend and the girl's parents, and they were looking at me with a look that was saying, "Do something about it!" The girl started to move towards me. With fear in my head and faith in my heart, I looked at her and I said, "In the name of Jesus, I command you to come out of her now." The girl collapsed on the floor, the demon came out, and the girl regained her mind and became normal again. I was so amazed!

Since that day, I have never been afraid to minister deliverance. I have prayed for many people over the years and have seen the power of God setting them free. God wants to use you, too, to cast out demons. This is the ministry of the believer according to Mark 16. You, too, can be used by God to minister deliverance! Start where you are.

The First Time I Saw an Angel

Even though I had seen the Lord perform many miracles, I was not satisfied. Out of my desire to pursue and develop the call of God in my life, I went to Bible school. I was stirred by the Lord with a strong hunger and passion to seek Him. For years, I would fast the first 3 days of every month, and I went on many extended fasts of 21 days. I would pray for three hours every day... from 3 am to 6 am.

While I was in Bible school, I was living in a ten-story building, where my room was on the 5th floor. I shared a room with two other students. They slept on a bunk bed on the other side of the room. My bed was close to the door that led to the balcony off our room. No one could ever come through that door, because it was on the 5th floor of a ten-story building. That morning, I was getting ready to wake up to pray. I was between sleeping and waking-up. I really felt like what the apostle Paul described when he said, *"And I know such a man, whether in the body or out of the body I do not know, God knows."*

~ 2 Corinthians 12 : 3

I don't know if I was in the body or out of my body. (We will discuss with more details the concept of spiritual dreams and visions later in the book – in the chapter *Walking in the Supernatural.*)

I saw the door of the balcony opening. I saw an angel walking into the room. I was scared because I thought that I was dead! I had read in a book once, that the first thing that happens to a Christian when he dies is that he will see angels coming to escort him. This angel came to my bed and grabbed me by the arm. I am a big man, but I was like a feather in his hand. I didn't feel my weight pulling against his hand. He took me to the balcony, and we started to go up towards the sky. I looked down and the buildings were getting smaller – just like when you are in an airplane and you look outside.

When we reached the clouds, suddenly they changed into a movie screen. I saw people from around the world from different races in different conditions; some were suffering. I heard a loud voice that sounded like thunder saying, "Preach the Gospel to all these people."

The angel took me back to my room and left. I found myself back in my bed. I was breathing heavily. I looked at my roommates, they were sound asleep. I asked them the next morning if they had heard or seen anything in the night. They said they heard and saw nothing.

The next day, I was praying during my quiet time, and the Lord gave me the scripture out of 2 Corinthians 5 : 18: *Now all things are of God, who has reconciled us to Himself through Jesus Christ, and has given us the ministry of reconciliation.*

That's when I received the name and the vision of our ministry: Reconciliation Ministries International.

I wrote the vision down. Our vision is the world, our passion is for souls, and our mission is to equip believers and train them in the supernatural — reaching every appointed person through miracle crusades, training seminars, conferences, and church services.

I wrote the vision and even printed some brochures. Three months later, there was a guest speaker at the school — a real prophet of God. He picked me out of the crowd of over 1,000 students and prophesied exactly everything that God had already given to me. He finished the prophecy by saying, "You are an ambassador of Reconciliation." It was amazing and encouraging to receive a confirmation from God. Years later — today — I am walking in the reality of that prophetic word and vision. We have preached the gospel in over 60 nations.

I want to show you some biblical truths about angels, because sometimes people do not know what the Word of God says about angels and angelic visitations.

The word, "angel", means, *messenger.* Angels are ministering spirits.

Angels are… ministering spirits sent forth to minister for those who will inherit salvation.

~ Hebrews 1 : 14

We don't worship angels! We only worship God!
Let no one cheat you of your reward, taking delight in false humility and worship of angels.

~ Colossians 2 : 18a

There's a difference between angels and God.

Angels Are	Angels Are Not	God Is
immortal Psalm 148 : 5, Luke 20 : 36	eternal	eternal
powerful Psalm 103 : 20, 2 Peter 2 : 11, 2 Thessalonians 1 : 7	omnipotent (all-powerful)	omnipotent
knowledgeable (having an intellect) 1 Peter 1 : 12, Luke 24 : 4 – 7	omniscient (knowing all things)	omniscient
present in one place or another Psalm 91 : 11, Zechariah 1 : 8 – 11	omnipresent (present everywhere)	omnipresent

It is important for us to acknowledge, recognize, and understand the ministry of angels. Through the scriptures, we can see that angels have a purpose. Let's look at some of the tasks of angels.

They strengthen believers. (Luke 22 : 43)

They protect believers. (Psalm 91 : 10 - 11)

They are sent to answer prayers. (Daniel 9 : 21 – 23)

They rejoice when souls are saved. (Luke 15 : 10)

They minister peace and encouragement. (Daniel 10 : 12,
Acts 27: 3–25)

They minister to children. (Matthew 18 : 10)

They remind God's people of His love. (Daniel 10 : 10 – 11)

They deliver warnings. (Matthew 2 : 13)

They inform believers. (Luke 1 : 13 – 20)

Every child of God has an angelic dimension in his or her life.

I Saw the Dead Come Back to Life

Before I even had the opportunity to pray for a dead person, I used to have a lot of dreams about it. I had dreams about me praying for people that died, and they came back to life. I used to ask myself why I was having these recurring dreams. I talked about it with one of my mentors at that time. He told me that God was giving me a healing ministry. Later in this book, we will talk about how to pray for the dead. I want to share with you one of my experiences praying for a dead person.

I was preaching the gospel in Watonga, Oklahoma. On a Saturday morning, the pastor of the church where I was ministering had a heart attack and was pronounced dead in the emergency room of the hospital.

I got a phone call from an elder of the church who told me about the situation, and later, came to pick me up at my hotel to go pray at the hospital. When we got there, the doctor had already discontinued resuscitation attempts. In an attempt to revive her, they had given Sharon 20 electric shock treatments and oxygen... without result. She was dead for more than 40 minutes. A person that is dead for more than 40 minutes – even if revived – will become a vegetable, because of the low level of oxygen in the brain.

When given the opportunity, I went into the emergency room. I laid my hands on her and prayed for her in the name of Jesus. When I was praying in the emergency room, there was no special worship song playing through the speakers, but the Holy Spirit was present. Even though I didn't feel goose bumps or a "special" feeling, God proved that He can move in any situation, anywhere, even if there's no special church atmosphere. All we have to do is to be obedient. God miraculously raised Sharon from the dead with no brain damage! The story was reported on the news and in the newspaper. You can find the newspaper's account of the story at www.guypeh.com, on the testimony link.

I have shared some of my personal encounters in the supernatural, and some of my personal life with you to encourage you to believe and know that you, too, can be used by God! If God can use someone like me with no parents, a difficult childhood, no church background, and no spiritual inheritance... He can use you!

Sometimes people are afraid to step out and allow God to use them in the supernatural and the miraculous, because they have questions. I believe that everyone who wants to be used by God – directly or indirectly – needs to answer the 3 questions below:

Can I trust God? Can God trust me? Can I trust myself?

The first question we need to answer is:

1. Can I trust God?

Another way of asking this question can be, "Can I have faith in God?"

> *I define faith as, "Man's ability*
> *to believe and trust in the ability of God."*

The answer to this question is, "YES, you can trust God!"

> *God has a good track-record*
> *that demonstrates that He is trustworthy.*

His record reveals who He is, and what He is able to do.

The Bible is full of accounts of people in desperate situations that trusted in God's ability. As a result, they experienced the supernatural power of God in their lives. I am referring to people like David, Daniel in the lion's den, or the three Hebrew children who said, "Oh king, our God is able to deliver us," before they were thrown into the fiery furnace. The fire did not burn them. The lions didn't eat Daniel. Goliath didn't defeat David. David had a history with God. Through God's power, David was able to defeat a lion and a bear. This became a platform of confidence that helped him believe that God would give him the victory over the giant.

> *King Saul thought Goliath was too big to fight.*
> *David thought he was too big to miss.*

Some people are afraid to trust in God because trusting God sometimes requires a willingness to take a risk.

> *Faith and trust in God involves*
> *the concept of risk and reward.*

But without faith it is impossible to please Him, for he who comes to God must believe that He is, and that He is a rewarder of those who diligently seek Him.

~ Hebrews 11 : 6

> *Faith is taking the first step even when*
> *you don't see the whole staircase.*

You may say, "I don't have enough experience to obey God," but I will say to you:

> *Obedience to God will bypass experience.*

Start where you are. He will guide and order your steps.

Trust in the Lord with all your heart, and lean not on your own understanding; in all your ways acknowledge Him, and He shall direct your paths.

~ Proverbs 3 : 5 - 6

Sometimes people do not trust God because of fear. Do not allow the devil to rob your destiny through fear. Fear produces death, disease, and torment. Faith produces life, health, and peace.

> *You block your dream when you allow your fear to grow bigger than your faith.*

The next question that people should answer is:

2. Can God trust me?

Another way of asking this question can be, "Can God have faith in me?"

> *God does not want to crush us, He wants to make us whole.*

You can rest assured that God can trust you, because He loves you unconditionally. Love equals trust.

> *You can never do anything to earn more of God's love. God will never love you more than He loves you now.*

He demonstrated His unconditional love for you and for me when He sent His Son to die on the cross.

But God demonstrates His own love toward us, in that while we were still sinners, Christ died for us.

~ Romans 5 : 8

God sacrificed His most precious possession just for you. If you were the only person in this world, He would still have sent His only Son for you. To me, there is no greater demonstration of trust and love. The answer is that with the sacrifice of His only begotten Son, God trusted you with His anointing, His power, His miracles, and everything good.

> *God meant for every part of our being to be used to its greatest potential.*

Every good gift and every perfect gift is from above, and comes down from the Father of lights, with whom there is no variation or shadow of turning.

~ James 1 : 17

> *God doesn't ask you to be the best, just to do your best.*

The last question we need to answer is:

3. Can I trust myself?

Another way of asking this question can be, "Can I have faith in my own faith?"

> *Sometimes the only thing that will stop you from fulfilling God's call is YOU.*

Many times people have faith in the preacher's faith. They have faith in other people's faith. But they do not have faith in their own faith.

How often, today, people feel inadequate when it comes to ministry for different reasons: inferiority, fear, intimidation, religion, culture, past failures. Most people think that you have to be special to be used by God, but the scripture is very clear when it says, "I will pour out my Spirit upon all flesh." "All" means, *all.* You are part of that *all.* **You are special.**

> *If you wait until every hindrance is removed*
> *before serving the Lord,*
> *you will never attempt anything for Him.*

Sometimes people cannot have faith in their own faith because of past mistakes and failures. They have not been able to forgive themselves.

> *We all mess up sometimes.*
> *So why is learning to forgive yourself*
> *a lot harder than forgiving others?*

Just think about the apostle Paul; he was a murderer, and a persecutor of believers before he got saved. He had to forgive himself, and obey the call of God.

> *Love yourself, accept yourself,*
> *forgive yourself, and be good to yourself,*
> *because without you, the rest of us are*
> *without a source of many wonderful things.*

Don't look to the past, but look to the future.

If your past is stopping you from serving God, pray the prayer below:

God, You Are All I Need!

You are the only reason my life is worth living. You are my only strength in life. You, oh God, You won't let me go! You won't let me fall. You keep picking me up and setting me to my feet. I fail myself, but You haven't failed me once. You forgive me even though I can't forgive myself. You love me, though I can't love myself. You see me differently than I see myself. You see me with Your eyes. Help me to see myself through Your eyes.

Help me quit hearing myself tell me I'm a failure in everything I do. I know it's not true. I will never give up on You, God. You have blessed me with so much. It's because Your love is just so awesome, God, and You are all that makes life worth living. I can't motivate myself, but You are my motivation. I can motivate others because the motivation You give me is more than I can handle. Through me, let others see Your love. Let others see themselves the way You see them.

Life is far too precious for me to live for myself. I will always live for You, oh God. Never will I turn my back on You. Let me live my life for You. I won't give up on following You.

Use me God. Mold me God. Write on me God. You are the potter and I am the clay; form me to be used for You.

I only want to care about what You think about me. Open my eyes, God, and let me see You more clearly. You are my desire. You are my hope and dreams. God, you are awesome! In Jesus Name! Amen!

> *The promises of God in your life are not connected to your history, but they are connected to your destiny.*

Brethren, I do not count myself to have apprehended; but one thing I do, forgetting those things which are behind and reaching forward to those things which are ahead.

~ Philippians 3 : 13

Start where you are! To have faith in your own faith, you need to renew your mind and think the way God thinks about you.

For I know the thoughts that I think toward you, says the Lord, thoughts of peace and not of evil, to give you a future and a hope.

~ Jeremiah 29 : 11

> *Inward security produces outward stability.*

Chapter 3

Supernatural Thinking

To be used by God and to operate in the supernatural, we must embrace supernatural thinking. The way we think controls our entire life. Our thoughts shape our words, habits and character. They have the power to produce life or death. Our thoughts release God's ability in our lives, or they limit us from experiencing His absolute best. It's time to take control of our lives by taking control over our thoughts if we want to be used by God.

For as he thinks in his heart, so is he.

~ Proverbs 23 : 7a

> *Too many people have lived below*
> *God's ultimate plan for their lives long enough!*

Thoughts That Create Inferiority:

~   I can't!
~   I don't have enough!
~   My life is not that significant!

~   I feel small!
~   I feel inferior!
~   My opposition is huge!
~   My problem is bigger than me!
~   I am not up for the challenge!
~   That's just the way I am!
~   I am not smart enough!
~   I have to settle with what I have!
~   Whatever happens must be God's will!
~   I am limited by my financial status!
~   I am not smart enough!
~   If I only had the right surroundings!
~   It's too late!
~   You never know what the future holds!
~   I feel guilty!
~   I just can't stop blowing it!
~   It's impossible!

A psychiatrist once said, "You have low self-esteem, but don't let it bother you because it's common among losers."

> *Who decides whether you will be happy or unhappy,*
> *a loser or a winner? The answer is, "YOU do!"*

Life is what your thoughts make it. Our world is not made just of the circumstances that surround us. It is determined by the kind of thoughts we think.

> *People are just about as happy*
> *as they make up their minds to be.*
> *~ Abraham Lincoln*

"A man is what he thinks about all day."

~ Emerson

Walking in the supernatural and right-thinking go together. Change your thoughts and you can change your world. Change your thinking… change your life. Change your thoughts correctly and you will discover inner peace, happiness, personal power, and freedom to be used by God.

Be transformed by the renewing of your mind.

~ Romans 12 : 2b

Finally, brethren, whatever things are true, whatever things are noble, whatever things are just, whatever things are pure, whatever things are lovely, whatever things are of good report, if there is any virtue and if there is anything praiseworthy – meditate on these things.

~ Philippians 4 : 8

Don't waste your time complaining about the conditions of your life. Instead, honestly face the possibility that your thinking is wrong – that the problem lies within. It isn't because you lack ability, talent or toughness, but rather that your mental slant is filled with thoughts of failure. Your attitudes have become harsh, critical and unfriendly towards others. People, opportunities and victories are withdrawing themselves from you. Change your thinking. One great thought you must always hold if you want to be used by God is that you can attain a higher level for your life.

> *One of the chief functions of spiritual thinking is to reveal and release the possibilities of God in you.*

A medical doctor in Alabama said, "75% of my patients do not need the surgeon's knife or medicine, they need God". In short he was saying that much of the illness today is due to unhealthy thoughts which occupy our minds.

> *You can make yourself sick by wrong thinking, and you can make yourself well by right thinking.*

We need God's help in clearing away unhealthy thoughts and establishing a pattern of right thinking.

That you put off, concerning your former conduct, the old man which grows corrupt according to the deceitful lusts and be renewed in the spirit of your mind, and that you put on the new man which was created according to God, in true righteousness and holiness.

~ Ephesians 4 : 22 - 24

When you think unpleasant thoughts and experience emotions of anxiety, fear, apprehension, depression and disappointment, replace them with the pleasant thoughts and emotions of confidence, assurance, expectancy, joy and hope. Study your thoughts. Write them down and analyze them. Are they creative or destructive, positive or negative, critical or uplifting? Always remember that most depression is an *attitude of mind*. We become depressed because our thoughts are depressed. How do we change it? We change it by passing through our mind thoughts of faith. This must be done consistently and with great perseverance until it "takes hold". Faith, hope and love are stronger than depression fear and worry.

One of the greatest thoughts we can ever hold in our minds is the simple concept that God cares for us, He will see us through, and He is always with us and wants to use us. When these truths sink deep into our conscious and subconscious mind, they produce a great inner strength and freedom. They cause our faith to be placed in Him and an inner knowledge that everything will work out for the good.

> *Success is seldom achieved by people*
> *who contemplate the possibility of failure.*
> **~ William Feather**

Why should we contemplate failure? We have an incredible God to support us. He is more than equal to any crisis or difficulty in this world!

With God all things are possible.

~ Matthew 19 : 26b

Eye has not seen, nor ear heard, nor have entered into the heart of man the things which God has prepared for those who love Him.

~ 1 Corinthians 2 : 9

Most difficulties can be overcome by filling our minds with God's thoughts. That is how we gain His perspective and are able to use our minds correctly and positively rather than negatively. Instead of dwelling upon your troubles, affirm that God is helping you this very minute. Practice living with Christ; talk to Him. He is right there with you. Soon you will be flooded with a healing sense of peace. The old negative thought patterns that brought you down will pass away and all things — life, energy, vitality, purpose and a passion for living — will become new to you.

> *"You are not who you think you are,*
> *but what you think, you are."*
> ~ **Norman Vincent Peale**

What you think, what you have been thinking over a long period of time, and what you continue to think about will determine what you are and what kind of world you will live in. By adopting a certain frame of mind or way of thinking, we tap into an ability inside that has the power to lift and put us over. I am reminded of the story of a small black boy at a county fair. A man was blowing up balloons and letting them float up into the sky, the balloons were of all colors. "Do you suppose that black one will go as high as the rest?" the little boy asked. The man looked into the eyes of this young boy and said, "It's not the color on the outside that makes the balloon go high, it's what is on the inside."

Who is on your inside?

Christ in you, the hope of glory.

~ Colossians 1 : 27b

Consider the following people who chose to rise above their difficulties:

~ **Winston Churchill**, failed sixth grade. He was subsequently defeated in every election for public office until he became Prime Minister at the age of 62. He later wrote, "Never give in, never give in, never, never, never, never - in nothing, great or small, large or petty - never give in except to convictions of honor and good sense. Never, Never, Never, Never give up."

~ **Thomas Edison**, who invented the light bulb, was told by his teachers that he was "too stupid to learn anything." He was fired from his first two jobs for being "non-productive". As an inventor, Edison made 1,000 unsuccessful attempts at inventing the light bulb. When a reporter asked, "How did it feel to fail 1,000 times?" Edison replied, "I didn't fail 1,000 times. The light bulb was an invention with 1,000 steps."

~ **Albert Einstein**, a great scientist, did not speak until he was 4-years old and did not read until he was 7. His parents thought he was "sub-normal," and one of his teachers described him as "mentally slow, unsociable, and adrift forever in foolish dreams." He was expelled from school and was refused admittance to the Zurich Polytechnic School. He did eventually learn to speak and read, even to do a little math.

~ **Walt Disney** was fired by a newspaper editor because "he lacked imagination and had no good ideas." He went bankrupt several times before he built Disneyland. In fact, the proposed park was rejected by the city of Anaheim on the grounds that it would only attract riffraff.

The sun always outlasts the storm. Storms come and go, but the sun is always shining. This is a required way of thinking in order to live a supernatural life. Difficulties may cause us to fall or stumble, but with God's help, we shall arise. You might think you are defeated, but you are not. Get up! With God, you can overcome your difficulties and live the victorious life for which you were created.

Here are some things you can confess to help you have the right thinking. Right thinking will help you position yourself to operate in the authority that God has given you by the death, burial, and resurrection of Jesus Christ.

Confessions of Right Thinking

- I declare, "I can do all things through Jesus Christ who strengthens me."
- I eliminate "can't" from my vocabulary.
- I can do anything God's Word says I can do.
- I submit my thinking to the Word of God and my whole life is changing today.
- I will always have more than enough of whatever I need because God is my source. He provides me with enough money, time, energy, opportunities or whatever is lacking.
- Nothing is too difficult for God; therefore, I declare that nothing is too difficult for me today! He is the author and finisher of my faith.
- He is watching over His Word to perform it in my life; therefore, I expect something good to happen.

- I am no longer going to damage myself or those around me with thoughts of worry.
- My focus is on doing the will of God, winning souls, serving others and blessing people.
- I am secure. I have a special gift and treasure God has given me.
- There is a portion and a place in God's Kingdom reserved for me.
- All of God's promises are personally for me.
- I have a great life because God is my Father and He has chosen gladly to give me His Kingdom.
- I am significant. I bring value to those around me.
- I have a specific part in the Body of Christ. My life counts for something. The people in my life are better because of my relationship with them. I am a work of art.
- I am the workmanship of God. You have made me a work of art. I am fearfully and wonderfully made according to Psalm 139 : 14.
- I am not inferior to anything or anyone, because I am made in the image of God.
- I am in the royal family, and royalty destroys inferiority. I have His divine image, His divine breath, and I am endowed with His divine authority.
- I am as He is, in this life. I am not under man's opinion and judgment. I am only under God's.
- I am seated with Christ in heavenly places, and therefore, I see myself from His point-of-view. I am bigger than the mountains, taller than the trees, and more giant than the giants! I shall, by all means, go up and take possession of the Promised Land!

- I am unlimited in my ability to grow and change.
- I am not in bondage to my weaknesses.
- My hopes are up! I eliminate the notion of lowering my expectations.
- I expect ideas, favor, and wisdom to come to me. I look up, expecting to receive the best of what God has for me today.
- I will never again submit to the thought of, "I am not that smart" or "I can't figure it out." I am smart and I can figure it out.
- I will never again be intimidated by the "elite" mentality.
- I will never again think small. I was made in the image of a BIG God and now I think BIG thoughts.
- I give up giving-up.
- Opportunity comes to me, because I expect it to.
- I decide today that I will stop listening to the voices telling me to stay the way I am.
- God can work in my life regardless of my financial status. He is not limited by money; therefore, neither am I.
- I am being renewed on the inside by the Word of God, which will bring success in every area of my life.
- Success follows me. I prosper in my soul - in my mind. I fill my mind with the richness of God's Word and therefore it spills over into every area of my life.
- I refuse to take things personally. I will not absorb people's guilt or manipulation.
- Like Joseph, I will not allow my negative circumstances to determine my success or failure. I am a successful and prosperous man or woman because God is with me.

- I choose to stop comparing myself to others. This robs my soul of its health and well-being.
- I believe it's not too late for things to improve in my life and radically turn around.
- I accept in my heart and mind that God has a good future in store for me.
- I do not have to try to "get in" God's presence. I am already there through the blood of Jesus.
- Today, I stop beating myself up about all I haven't done or have done. I choose to live in the "now". I will enjoy the moment I am in and praise God in the midst of it.
- I rest in the fact that Jesus is my perfection. I don't have to be perfect; He already is, and I put my faith in Him.
- I take my eyes off of all I have done wrong and put my eyes on all God has done right for me.
- I expect favor today. Favor surrounds me like a shield. Doors are going to open for me that no one can close.
- God has made me righteous through Jesus' blood, therefore; my path is getting brighter and brighter every day.
- God has saved the best for last in my life and my latter days will be better than my former days, in Jesus' name.
- I put my faith in the blood of Jesus to forgive me if I have fallen, but also to empower me to be free from the things I'm struggling with.
- I stay attached to what God says about it, and I refuse to get offended.
- I will think "above" – beginning today. I choose to look down at life rather than look up at it. I see it from God's point of view.

- I'm bigger than my problem, bigger than the mountain, and bigger than any enemy I face today.
- Greater, larger, and more dominant is He that is in me than he that is in the world!
- I will not stay in a defeated, lonely, sick, depressed condition another day of my life.
- I focus on the inside. I know the thoughts of victory I am developing now will take care of my outside.
- God is at work in me, and He is bringing His will to pass in my life as I surrender my thoughts to Him. As I sow the Word of God in my heart and mind, God is watching over His Word to bring it to pass.

> *If you don't know who you are,*
> *the world is going to define you,*
> *your culture is going to define you,*
> *your circumstance is going to define you.*

Don't let your culture define you. Don't let your heredity define you. It is the blood of Jesus Christ that should define who you are.

Chapter 4

Authority

As a member of the end-time volunteer army, in order for us to be used by God we must understand the significance of authority as well as how to walk in the power of authority.

Let me ask you a question. Have you ever walked in a building; it could have been an office building or a hospital? Perhaps you saw a door. In front of that door there was a sign that read, "Access Restricted to Personnel Only" or "Authorized Personnel Only" or "Staff Only." To pass through that door you must have authority. Sometimes, to open such a door you must have a badge or identification card that you can slide through the security device to open the door. In the spiritual realm, it is the same. There are spiritual doors; behind those doors there's healing, blessings, and finances, etc. But there is a sign that says, "Access Restricted to Authorized Personnel Only." You can only have access to what is behind the doors by walking in your God-given authority. You walk in your God-given authority by knowing and living in the reality of what Christ has provided for us by His death on the cross. That's why as Christians, it is crucial for us to understand all the dynamics of authority and how it operates.

> *Some Christians are asking God for things*
> *that He has already provided,*
> *and then get mad and depressed because they*
> *feel like God is not answering their prayers.*

Imagine a Christian who is a new nurse working in a hospital. She needs to get into the Intensive Care Unit to take care of a patient in critical condition, but she gets to the door of the room where the patient is and the sign reads, "Access Restricted to Authorized Personnel Only." She does not know who she is, so she is afraid to use her badge to go into the room. She begins to pray with desperation and supplication and asks God to help her open the door so she can treat the critical patient, but God does not answer her prayer. As a result, the patient dies. She feels that God did not answer her prayer and she becomes depressed. Three weeks later, in her building orientation, she is told by the hospital manager that her staff badge allows her to open every door in the I.C.U. Then she realizes that she already had in her hands the key to open the door. She had the answer to her prayer before she even prayed. Many Christians are like that nurse.

> *Most Christians know who God is,*
> *most Christians know who Jesus is,*
> *most Christians know who the devil is,*
> *but most Christians don't know who they are.*

Who you are defines your heavenly identity. Your heavenly identity is the key to walking in authority and in victory.

Do you ever wonder why people sin? Why people do certain things? I think that it is due to an identity problem. Nobody sits in their home as a child of God and says, "Tomorrow I'm going to go sin against God." I think Christians fall into sin because they don't understand who they are in Christ.

Think about this. Adam had no desire in him to sin. That's why the devil didn't tempt him. He was full of his identity with the Father. He was created in the Father's image, and had no desire to disobey God because he knew who he was. It took someone who was close to him to get him to sin. I know there is a wrong teaching about woman been the seductress of man as a general rule, but that's not what I'm talking about here. I'm simply talking about the fact that Adam knew who he was and the devil did not confront him directly. Instead, he confronted Eve and deceived her. This is why it is so important for you to know **who you are.** If you don't, you can be deceived by the enemy. If you are going to walk in the authority of God, you're going to have to learn who you are in Christ.

There's a little story that I like that illustrates the importance of knowing who you are. It goes something like this: There was an elephant coming out of the forest. Three men were standing there watching: a Christian, a businessman and an intellectual guy. The businessman thought, "I wonder how much money I can make out of this elephant." The intellectual guy thought, "I wonder what the different parts of this elephant are and how he moves and lives." The Christian man thought, "I wonder what this elephant is thinking about me?"

> *If you don't know who you are,*
> *you will always have an inferiority complex.*

To be used by God, you must realize that the devil is a legal expert. If you're going to fight him, you need to know your rights and your authority. God placed two forms of judgment on Satan. First of all, his head was bruised. This happened when Jesus was on the cross. Secondly, Satan will face an end-time judgment... the lake of fire. My friend, hell was not made for humans. I know that many of you can think of individuals who need to go there, but it was not made for humans. Hell was made for the demons and for Satan, himself. God said that He desires that no one should perish. So, you've got to realize that, originally, hell is not the will of God for any of us, but many will choose to go to hell by rebelling against God and His Word.

> *"Power" is the ability to do something.*
> *"Authority" is power with permission.*
> *Authority is the ability and the right to do something.*

Recently we were traveling in the Middle East where there are about 1,000 miles of mountainous terrain. It is really remote – like a no man's land – but there are roadblocks and checkpoints set-up by the military in that region. We rented a van and were driving in that area when I saw this little, skinny soldier. He was really small, and he stood in the middle of the road and blew his whistle pointing to a truck that was approaching. That was a very interesting picture.

In front of us was a big truck that weighed tons. And that soldier probably weighed only about 70 kilos or 150 pounds. But all he had to do was stand, blow his whistle, and point… and each person stopped their vehicle. Technically, **the truck had power** – the ability to kill that soldier. But **the soldier had authority.** He represented the government. If a driver decided to run over him because he was only a little man, the government would call the armed forces and eventually, that person would stop! When that little soldier stood out there on that road, he represented the entire force of his government. You see, the truck had the power and ability to kill the soldier, but the soldier had the authority. You, as a child of God, have both power and authority with permission.

The devil has power, but he does not have authority.
Cancer has the power to kill, but it does not have authority.
Diabetes has power, but it does not have authority.

In order to understand authority and to be used by God, you've got to understand what authority is, and what it is *not.*

What Authority Is Not

1. Authority is not based on emotions or feelings.

Authority has nothing to do with emotions and feelings. In some churches, they think you have to sing three fast songs and two slow songs before they can get in the Spirit. There's a place for worship. There's a place for praise; it brings an atmosphere of

God's presence. But, most of the time, you are not going to have time to create an atmosphere to release the power of God in order to deal with the situations of life. Do you understand what I am trying to say? Like on your job, or on the road, or in your home at 2:00 a.m. when something bad happens. You need to be prepared to address that problem.

Think about Jesus walking down the street and a leper coming up to Him saying, "Lord, if You are willing, You can make me clean." (~ Matthew 8 : 2) Can you imagine Jesus replying, "Wait just a minute, Peter, give Me a couple of songs! No, not that one, not that one, either. Play the other one; I've got to feel the anointing. Okay, that's the right one! Get ready leper; the anointing is here!" Thank God that Jesus knew who He was and understood His authority so that no matter when He was faced with the needs of people, He was prepared to meet those needs.

Most of the time when situations arise, we do not have the time to get our emotions together. We either know who we are and what to do in the situation, or we don't. The anointing is not in the song. The anointing is not in the building. The Bible does not say, "Greater is He Who is in the song, in the building, or in the preaching." The Bible says:

He who is in you is greater than he who is in the world.

~ 1 John 4 : 4

A song is anointed because the person who sings the song is anointed. A church building is not anointed; it is those who are in the church building who are anointed. The power of God is inside of you.

Out of his heart will flow rivers of living water.

~ John 7 : 38b

> *Authority is not based on emotions or feelings.*
> *It is based on who you are in Christ.*

You may not feel like casting out a demon. You may not feel like praying for the sick. You may not feel like speaking the Word of God, but when you go ahead and speak it anyway, it's what is inside of you that ministers to others. It's not how you feel about the situation that matters, because authority is not based on emotions.

> *Worship creates an atmosphere of God's presence,*
> *but authority brings the atmosphere.*

2. Authority is not based on personality.

> *Authority is not based on personality or culture.*
> *It is based on who you are in Christ.*

Others confuse authority with personality. If authority was based on personality, then the anointing would be American or African. But it is not American, African, Latino, Asian or European. African people are loud and passionate – so are American people. But most people in the world are very reserved. If you go to Europe, the people are more reserved. But the anointing does not depend upon personality or culture. It comes from Christ. Some people have a lot of passion, but that doesn't necessarily mean that they have more authority or anointing than those who may be more reserved.

Authority is not determined by the volume in which you speak. It is based on who you are in Christ.

There is a difference between anointing and adrenaline.

Once, I was in Northern Europe holding a meeting. I was ministering deliverance to someone. I said, "Come out," and the interpreter said, "Ut". I asked, "What is that?" He said that "ut" is a translation for "out" or "come out" in our language. I said, "No, no, no, change that. It doesn't feel powerful." I said, "Come out," and again the interpreter said, "ut". But you see, the way it was stated has nothing to do with authority. Whether it's "come out" or "ut", if you know who you are in Christ, then the devil must flee. I didn't think that the "ut" was powerful enough, but the demon did… and came out.

3. **Authority is not based on seniority.**

Authority is not based on how long a person has been a Christian. Some people who are young in the faith don't know if they should attempt to minister the power of God to others. There are some who have been Christians for a long time – especially those with religious spirits – who discourage the young in-the-faith who say things like, "Young man, you have to be careful with your passion. I think you're pushing it a little bit. I remember back in the 60's when we started…."

> *Authority has nothing to do with how long you've been a Christian. It's based on who you are in Christ.*

It doesn't matter if you've been a Christian for two months, two years, or two decades.

> *You will never have more authority than what you were given when you got saved.*
>
> *You have all the power you need to have… right now! You have all the authority you need to have… right now!*

What takes time is growing and learning how to exercise the authority you already have. God is not going to give you more authority than He's already given you. The Book of Hebrews was written to third-generation Christians, who had grown immature, and the Books of First and Second Corinthians were written to long-time Christians who had become immature because of division and sin. But in Matthew 10 : 8, Jesus told the disciples to heal the sick, to cleanse the lepers, and to raise the dead. They were baby Christians. They had only been walking with the Lord for three-and-a-half years at the most, yet Jesus commissioned these baby Christians, instructing them to do the hard things.

4. Authority is not based on gender.

Just as authority is not based on how long you've been a Christian or on your personality, neither is it based on gender. It's not based on whether you're a male or female. Some say, "A woman has no authority. She is not a man." That is nonsense. There is this doctrine that teaches that a woman should be silent in the church. I know that there is a place for the man to have authority in his household and in the Kingdom. But listen... I was saved under the ministry of a girl who prayed and witnessed to me for six months. My question to you is this: "Is the Jesus in me feminine or masculine?" It is neither. It is spirit.

> *Authority is not based on gender,*
> *but on Jesus working through a person.*

My wife and I were doing some meetings. I asked her to pray with me for the people. As she hugged a woman, the woman began to manifest. My wife cast out the demon with authority and ministered to the woman through prayer and love. A minister of the gospel who was in the meeting told me at the end of the meeting that he understood that I had authority, but he was surprised and amazed to see my wife flow in her God-given authority. Many people may have the same perspective because of misunderstanding of scriptures, their culture or the wrong teaching they have received. They look at women as weak and incapable. It is important to understand that authority is not based on gender but on Jesus working through a person.

Authority in the Church

> *Once people come under authority, they will have authority whether they are male or female.*

The subject of submission is often misunderstood and used to push down women. There is a structure of government in the church. There is a pastor; there is a leader. But once people come under authority, they will have authority whether they are male or female. The Bible teaches husbands and wives to submit to one another in love. As they do so, God covers them. As we submit to church leadership, God covers us. It is *God* who is our covering – not a *person*. As we come *under* authority, we *have* authority, because God honors the principle of "submission". You cannot cover me.

For example: when Ilke and I travel in the Middle East, we are eleven hours ahead of America. There are hours when we are awake, but the people of our church in America are sleeping. Technically, our pastor cannot cover us at that time, but God covers us in relation to our submission to our church and our pastor.

> *You have authority because you are under authority.*

The centurion understood this. That's why he said:

For I also am a man under authority, having soldiers under me. And I say to this one, "Go," and he goes; and to another, "Come," and he comes; and to my servant, "Do this," and he does it.

~ Matthew 8 : 9

The centurion answered and said, "Lord, I am not worthy that You should come under my roof. But only speak a word, and my servant will be healed."

~ Matthew 8 : 8

Jesus had authority because He was under authority. The Bible says that He was God.

Let this mind be in you which was also in Christ Jesus, who being in the form of God, did not consider it robbery to be equal with God, but made Himself of no reputation, taking the form of a bondservant, and coming in the likeness of men. And being found in appearance as a man, He humbled Himself and became obedient to the point of death, even the death of the cross.

~ Philippians 2 : 5 - 8

Submission has to do with *obedience*. Authority has to do with obedience.

If you want to be used by God, you need to be under authority. You're under authority when you're obedient to the authority that God has placed over you. Jesus became obedient to God's authority to the point of death.

Therefore God also has highly exalted Him and given Him the name which is above every name, that at the name of Jesus, every knee should bow, of those on earth, and those under the earth and that every tongue should confess that Jesus Christ is Lord, to the glory of God the Father.

~ Philippians 2 : 9 - 11

> *There are two voices of authority: the external voice and the internal voice, external authority and internal authority.*

External Authority

You are under authority when you obey the *external voice* of authority. When we are born into this world, God begins to train us in the area of obedience. Two figures of authority are placed in our lives: our father and our mother. In most cases, they have genuine interest in us and love us. No parents are perfect, and there are some really bad parents. But that doesn't negate the fact that God, technically, wants to place a father and a mother in our life to be the first two figures of authority over us. Through them, we begin to learn obedience. As we grow up, more authority figures are introduced into our lives: school teachers, employers, pastors, etc.

> *There's a progressive training and a progressive revelation about learning obedience.*

Internal Authority

As we grow, the ultimate goal of God is to bring us into a place where we have learned to hear His voice and obey it; that's *internal authority.*

There Are 10 Rewards for Obedience.

1. **Prosperity** is a reward for those who are under authority.

This Book of the Law shall not depart out of thy mouth, but thou shall meditate therein day and night that thou mayest observe to do all that is written. For then thou shall make your way prosperous and thou shall have good success.

~ Joshua 1 : 8

When you walk in obedience – when you're under authority – you will be blessed with prosperity.

2. **Priority** is another reward for those who are under authority.

You become God's priority.

Therefore humble yourselves under the mighty hand of the God, that He may exalt you in due time.

~ 1 Peter 5 : 6

He will give you all you need from day-to-day if you live for Him and make the Kingdom of God your primary concern.

Seek first the kingdom of God and His righteousness, and all these things shall be added to you.

~ Matthew 6 : 33

It is God who exalts one and puts another down. When we are under authority, we become God's priority for promotion.

But God is the Judge: He puts down one, and exalts another.

~ Psalms 75 : 7

3.   **Heaven** is a reward for those who obey God.

Not everyone who says to Me, "Lord, Lord" shall enter the kingdom of heaven, but he who does the will of My Father in heaven.

~ Matthew 7 : 21

4.   Those who obey God **become His peculiar, special treasure.**

Now therefore, if you will indeed obey My voice and keep My covenant, then you shall be a special treasure to Me above all people; for all the earth is Mine.

~ Exodus 19 : 5

5.   **Healing** is a reward for obedience.

A lot of people are not healed because they are walking in rebellion – not because the preacher or the church isn't anointed. If you're not walking in obedience, if you're not under authority… you're in rebellion. This makes it hard for you to experience the healing power of God. We can pray and bind everything, but there's just something that is out-of-order.

God said: "If you diligently heed the voice of the Lord your God and do what is right in His sight, give ear to His commandments and keep all His statutes, I will put none of the diseases on you which I have brought on the Egyptians. For I am the Lord who heals you."

~ Exodus 15 : 26

6. **Blessings will overtake you** when you obey God.

This principle is a good way to preach prosperity.

Now it shall come to pass, if you diligently obey the voice of the Lord your God, to observe carefully all His commandments which I command you today, that the Lord your God will set you high above all nations of the earth. And all these blessings shall come upon you and overtake you, because you obey the voice of the Lord your God.

~ Deuteronomy 28 : 1 - 2

See, the ultimate goal of authority is to bring you to the place of hearing God's voice and obeying it. That's success my friend! Success is not about how much money you have in your bank account, or how big of a ministry you have. Success is hearing what God is saying and doing it.

7. **You will be blessed in all you do** when you obey God.

But he who looks into the perfect law of liberty and continues in it and is not a forgetful hearer, but a doer of the work, this one will be blessed in what he does.

~ James 1 : 25

8.   **A long life** is a reward for obedience.

Do you want a long life? When you are under authority… you will have one.

Children obey your parents in the Lord, for this is right. "Honor your father and mother," which is the first commandment with promise: "that it may be well with you and you may live long on the earth."

~ Ephesians 6 : 1 - 3

I know America is "the land of the free and the home of the brave," but the Kingdom of God has its own culture, and there are spiritual laws that, unfortunately, many people are not aware of. There are many people who are walking in rebellion: rebellion against authority, rebellion against their parents. They did not learn to respect their mother and father. Even believers come into the church and disrespect and disobey their spiritual fathers and mothers and the pastor whose authority they should be under. There is a lot of unnecessary casualty – or spiritual warfare – in the Church today because people are walking in rebellion.

9.   **Abundance** is a reward for obedience and willingness.

Do you want to live in abundance?

"If you are willing and obedient, you shall eat the good of the land. But if you refuse and rebel, you shall be devoured with the sword." For the mouth of the Lord has spoken.   ~ Isaiah 1 : 19 – 20

10. **Increased volume of God's voice** is a promise for those who obey Him.

Have you ever wondered, "How can that person hear God all the time? I've been trying to hear from God, and I can't hear anything!" The more you disobey God, the more you're not walking in submission and the more God's voice gets distant. Your heart gets calloused. It's not that God is not speaking to you... you just can't hear Him. You can't hear His voice because you're not close to Him. When my wife and I are in a crowd and she says, "Sweetie, where are you?" I will directly recognize her voice. I know her voice because I am intimate with her. Even though there is a crowd of people, the moment I hear her sweet voice... I know that she is the one calling me.

> *There are all kinds of voices:*
> *voices of confusion, voices of fear, voices of religion,*
> *voices of discouragement, voices of skepticism.*

My friend, if you don't stay close to God, if you're not under authority, those voices are going to overwhelm your mind and you're going to be a confused Christian. But, if you are staying close to God and pressing in with prayer and walking in obedience and in authority, then even in the midst of trouble, you can have the peace of God that surpasses all understanding. It will guide you and the voice of God will become increasingly distinct to you. It's amazing how God speaks.

For God may speak in one way, or in another, yet man does not perceive it. In a dream, in a vision of the night, when deep sleep falls upon men, while slumbering on their beds, then He opens the ears of men and seals their instruction.

                                        ~ Job 33 : 14 - 16

Sometimes I get prophetic dreams. Then, a couple of weeks after a dream, I see the confirmation of what God showed me in the dream. The spirit world is as real as the natural world. Religion wants you to believe that it's a bunch of traditional do's and don'ts. It's about relationship with God. It's not about duty. It's about delight. It's about devotion. So, as you walk into this, remember, my friend, authority is not having a shouting match with the devil.

Some of what is going on in church services sometimes is just a bunch of noise. What's going on in the body of Christ today? Why do I say it's a bunch of noise? I say that because I don't always see the fruit. I don't always see people healed. I don't always see people saved (not inclusively, because I know there is always a remnant). To me, if that isn't happening, then it is just a bunch of noise. Anybody can preach. But at the end of the day, people must be healed. At the end of the day, lives must be changed. At the end of the day, people must be saved. It's important to have an education, but people's lives are not necessarily changed because of it. Have you ever seen anybody pray for someone who said, "In the name of my Ph.D., I command you to be healed?" Of course not!

> *Authority depends on how much time you spend with God... how much you're trying to hear and obey what He is saying.*

That's the key to power. You can't buy it. You can't manufacture it. You can't try to fake it.

Why do we have churches today that are program-oriented only? It's good to have a plan, but we have many gimmicks because we don't walk in our God-given authority, so we operate with the mechanics of men. We have to create entertainment because we don't engage in intercession. We have a great reputation, but no repentance. We have dignity with no demonstration. We have playboys, but no prophets. That's what's going on in many churches today. Most of what you're hearing today is, "Oh, just send me *this*, and I'm going to get you out of *that*." "Get my three-step plan on how to do this." Yes, there is a place for teaching and instruction - a vital place. But, in the absence of personal devotion in the life of the believer, all of our programs become only a bunch of rituals with no power behind them.

> *God cares more about your soul than the things*
> *that you have, but we have it the other way around.*

Many people think this way: "I'm a successful Christian because I have a nice house and a nice car. Look at me. See how much I have!" There's nothing wrong with having a nice car and all the nice "stuff" because God has an orientation of success for you and He wants you to be blessed with all good things. But, He wants you to put His Kingdom first.

> *Our success should not only be measured*
> *by the amount of our possessions, but also by*
> *the quality of the life we are living.*

This is how we should measure our spiritual growth and progress in God. We should ask ourselves, "Do I have more power operating in my life today? Do I know God better today than I did yesterday? Am I confident in who I am because I know Him… because I know that He lives inside of me?"

We discussed what *authority* is and what it is *not*. I want to go into more detail on what it **is.**

What Authority Is

Authority is a legal reality. I am married to my wife, Ilke. Marriage is a legal reality. You're either married, or you're not. You can't say, "I feel like I'm married today." Nor can you say, "I don't feel like I'm married today." You're either married or you're not. It's not how you feel. It's an actual reality. Some people want to get into marriage; some people want to get out of marriage. But, if you're married, you're married… period. It has nothing to do with how you feel. If you said, "I do," you are married.

Another legal reality is your citizenship. You are either an American citizen, or you are not. You cannot say, "I don't feel American today." You either are one, or you are not.

> *You either have authority, or you don't.*
> *It is a legal reality.*

> *Authority is something that was in the hand of God,*
> *and He gave it to man.*

The Bible says, in Genesis 1 : 28, that God gave dominion to mankind over the earth. Now, mankind's disobedience on earth brought about what I call *shared authority*. When man disobeyed, he shared his authority with the devil. What do I mean by *shared authority?* Satan cannot do anything on the earth without human agreement. I'm going to repeat that. Satan cannot do anything on the earth without finding human agreement. He's a spirit. He needs a body through which to work on the earth.

> *Disobedience brought shared authority.*

Many places where you see evil manifestations, there are demonic forces at work. However, they need the participation of human bodies in which to operate. Some human was the recipient of the demonic revelation and acted on it. Disobedience brought this shared authority. Have you ever wondered why the devil did not tempt the bull? Why didn't he go to the baboon and say, "Go ahead and disobey God. Eat from the fruit of knowledge of good and evil and you will be like God"? He did not do this because monkeys do not have a free will, and man does. God has given mankind the authority over the earth and the choice of what to do with it. Therefore, Satan tempted mankind to sin in order to gain authority on earth.

> *Many times, the will of God or the will of Satan will be delivered into your life by human relationship.*

When God wants to bless you, He can send a man or a woman. When the devil wants to destroy you, he can also send a man or a woman.

> *Association brings manifestation.*
> *Relationships are the platform for spiritual warfare.*

God uses people… so does Satan.

The Old Testament is the story of how God brought the Seed of the woman (the Messiah) to the world through the nation of Israel. Why did Satan try to destroy Israel from the very beginning of that nation? It is because there was a battle for the Seed. Satan was trying to destroy the Seed because the judgment that was pronounced upon him after his successful temptation of mankind was that *the Seed of the woman would crush the head of the serpent.* God even took Israel into captivity at times to protect the Seed. So, the Seed came through the generations as Satan tried to destroy it, but, Satan was defeated by an act of humility called… *the cross.*

Be careful of arrogance when you walk in authority. Jesus had an opportunity to use the power of God for Himself, but He didn't. As a person who understands who you are in Christ, there will be a temptation to use your authority for your own pleasure. The devil tempted Jesus to jump from the pinnacle of the temple to prove who He was. The devil said:

If You are the Son of God, throw Yourself down. For it is written: "He shall give His angels charge over you." And "In their hands they shall bear you up, lest you dash your foot against a stone."

~ Matthew 4 : 6

What a great way to start a ministry! Can you imagine if it was advertised that a pastor was going to jump from the tallest building in the city and the angels of God were going to catch him? What a great publicity stunt! Do you think that would get the attention of the city? Wouldn't that have been a good way for Jesus to start? He did not think so. He did not want to use the power of God to show how strong He was. The biggest temptation for you, when God begins to use you in miracles, signs and wonders, will be to strike the rock with pride in your heart like Moses did.

> *The strength that comes from confidence can be quickly lost to conceit.*

Be careful of arrogance and pride. They are what brought Satan down. Arrogance, selfishness, comparisons, competition – all these things are the work of the flesh.

> *You cannot glorify self and Christ at the same time.*

When pride comes, then comes shame; but with the humble is wisdom.

~ Proverbs 11 : 2

> *People who place too much importance on their standing are generally too big for their shoes.*

The more God uses us, the more we begin to understand authority. The more we cry out to God, the more He trusts us, and the more we will see an increase of power in our lives. But, be careful. There will always be the temptation to let this go to your head. When people say, "Man, that was a powerful service!" Receive the compliment and be thankful but be careful to give God the credit and to thank Him for using you. Pride... I see it sometimes. Someone is given a position of authority in the ministry, and suddenly, they begin to treat people the wrong way. Our work is to cast care; God's work is to take care.

> *The people most preoccupied with titles and status are usually the least deserving of them.*

Pride is the only disease that makes everyone sick except the one who has it. Pride makes people look at others as "subject" to them. They begin to talk to people the wrong way.

> *When the "I" becomes dominant, the "spiritual eye" sees the entire world in a distortion.*

Have you ever seen someone who gets a promotion? They had been faithful to the church, on time, and willing to serve, but after receiving a promotion, you don't even see them in church anymore. What happened? They didn't really change. That nature was always inside of them. The money, the promotion, or whatever, only exposed what was already inside of their heart. So, learn how to pastor your own heart!

> *If you serve God only for the approval of men,*
> *you will lose the approval of God.*

One of the worst things that can happen to a Christian is when, the blessings of God begin to increase in their life, and their passion for God begins to decrease.

> *When you elevate the blessing over "the Blesser",*
> *the blessing turns into a curse.*

Some people have been cursed over a blessing! Be careful what you ask for.

> *Sometimes, it's not a question of whether or*
> *not God can give something to you, but whether*
> *or not you can handle what you're asking for.*

Statistics show that people that win the lottery are worse off 5 years after they won the lottery than they were before they won the lottery. It's not how much you can receive but how much you can handle.

> *If your output exceeds your input,*
> *your upkeep will become your downfall.*

Can you handle God using you to heal the blind... still come home and be a husband or wife... still come to church and treat people normally... and still have casual conversations with people without expecting special treatment? What has happened to some ministers in the body of Christ today? Unfortunately, as God starts to use them, they become too full-of-themselves. It happens far more often than it should. I was recently in Africa and I heard a story of a preacher who went to the same city where I was. He arrived in his own private jet, and the church sent a nice car – a Mercedes – to pick him up at the airport. He would not get into that car because he wanted a limousine to pick him up. That's sad, but true.

When Jesus made His triumphant entry into Jerusalem in Mark 11 : 1 - 11, it was His greatest public entry in a city. This was right before He was going to be killed. There were great religious elites there – Pharisees, Sadducees, and all kinds of people in leadership – but He asked for a donkey on which to ride. Think about that. *Jesus asked for a donkey.*

Can you imagine Jesus coming to your city? All the Church leaders would get together to try to decide who would pick Him up at the airport. There would be a big committee. The Catholic priests, the Protestants, the Non-denominationals would all be there. One pastor might raise his hand and say, "I think I should go pick up Jesus, because I'm more educated than the rest of you." Another pastor might say, "Hold it right there! How long have you been in the city? I have been here longer than all of you. I think I am the father of this city. If somebody needs to pick up Jesus… I'm the one." Others would argue that the privilege should be theirs based on the size of their churches. So, they get into this religious debate about who is going to pick up Jesus. Finally, they decide to e-mail Jesus or text message Jesus to find out who He wants to pick Him up. When Jesus gets the message saying they are all fighting over who should pick Him up, Jesus replies, "There's a donkey just outside the city. I want you to get that donkey to come and pick Me up." Can you imagine that? But that is what Jesus did.

The donkey Jesus rode upon into Jerusalem was not even experienced. The Bible says that no one had ever sat upon it before. The donkey was not experienced in carrying the anointing.

Jesus chose a donkey. Donkeys are known for stupidity and stubbornness, but Jesus wanted that donkey. When Jesus arrived in the city on the back of the donkey, people were lined up on both sides of the road, screaming, "Hosanna! Hosanna!" What if that donkey began to think, "Man, I have never received that kind of reception before! What happened? I think it was the grass that I ate yesterday. No, that couldn't be it; they can't see that. No, I think I know what it is! It's the stride in my walk." That would have been ridiculous, but don't we do that sometimes?

We are all just like that donkey. When God calls us, He finds us outside of the city... bound with issues. Nobody knows our name. God sets us free and calls us into the ministry. When God begins to use us – when the Christ in us begins to do miracles and lives are changed, and we are preaching good and the crowd is chanting and people are clapping and giving us compliments – we start to think that we have arrived. Then we start making special demands on others. It is true that people should respect those whom the Lord has anointed, but in today's world, we are sometimes taking this to the extreme. Some guest ministers make some outrageous demands. I understand that someone may have special needs because of dietary or health reasons, but to make demands for the sake of demands is not a Godly attitude.

One time I heard of a preacher who was ministering in Brazil that didn't want people to touch him because he said they had germs. The thought behind this kind of attitude is, "I love the ministry, but I can't stand the people." Can you see the pride in all of that?

Someone who walks in pride, my friend, is heading for a collision with a Mighty God. I don't know about you, but I don't want to be riding in a little car that is going to get into a collision with a semi-truck. You know which one will lose! When you see someone walking in pride, they're heading for a collision with the Living God. Humility is the secret to authority.

God resists the proud, but gives grace to the humble.

~ James 4 : 6

> *Humility is knowing who God is and knowing who you are and never mixing the two.*

Knowing God makes us humble; knowing ourselves keeps us humble.

True humility is not looking down on yourself but looking up to Christ.

If you are too big to be willing to do little things, you are probably too little to be trusted with big things. God wants great men to be small enough to be used. Humility is making the right estimate of yourself.

> *Sincere humility attracts.*
> *Lack of humility subtracts.*
> *Artificial humility detracts.*

Humility is a strange thing; the moment you think you have it, you have lost it. Too many people are humble and proud of it.

> *Humility is not denying the power you have.*
> *Humility is realizing that the power comes through you,*
> *not from you.*

Humility is a low road to new heights. The higher you want to go, the lower you must go. Do you want to be used by God? *Stay humble.* Do you want to have authority? *Stay humble;* be a servant. The reason for your powerful ministry and your anointing to pray for the sick is to serve *people.* It is not to serve *yourself.*

> *There must be purpose behind God's power in you,*
> *or it will destroy you.*

What is the Basis of Authority in the Life of a Christian?

1. Authority is based upon what Jesus did to the devil.

Casting out demons, praying for the sick, and believing for lives to be changed by God are all based upon what Jesus did to the devil. Jesus stripped the devil of his authority.

Having wiped out the handwriting of requirements that was against us, which was contrary to us. And He has taken it out of the way, having nailed it to the cross. Having disarmed principalities and powers, He made a public spectacle of them, triumphing over them in it.

~ Colossians 2 : 14 - 15

Jesus has dominion – supreme dominion – over everything. Everything was made by Him, through Him, for Him, and He is seated at the right hand of God.

The Lord said to my Lord, "Sit at My right hand, till I make Your enemies Your footstool."

~ Psalm 110 : 1

Jesus also destroyed Satan's work.

For this purpose the Son of God was manifested, that He might destroy the works of the devil.

~ 1 John 3 : 8b

The devil has used his power and the fire of hell to destroy many lives. The fire of hell may have burned your finances, your health, your marriage, and your family. You may feel like the fire truck came too late, and all that is left is ashes — that the fire has burned everything. But Jesus came to give you beauty for ashes. When you receive Jesus Christ as your personal Lord and Savior, He restores everything that the enemy destroyed.

People come to church messed up, broken up, disgusted, at the lowest points of their lives, and begin to listen to the teaching of the Gospel. Restoration begins to take place. God gives them beauty for ashes and the garment of praise for the spirit of heaviness. Jesus destroyed the works of the devil, and now, you have been called to reinforce that work which took place on the cross.

2. Authority is based upon what Jesus did for us.

Even when you don't feel like you are delivered, you need to understand that Jesus has delivered you. When you were born, you were born by the law of heredity. You were born in sin. You were in your grandfather's loins, and he was in his grandfather's loins before he was conceived. This goes all the way back to Adam. It's the law of heredity. So, when Adam sinned... you sinned.

The Bible says, "Through one man, sin entered the world, and death through sin, and thus death spread to all men, because all sinned."

~ Romans 5 : 12

You don't have to teach evil to little children. There's a sin nature inside of them. By the law of heredity, we are all born into sin. But, in the same way, when the Last Adam, Jesus, died on the cross, He took the punishment we deserved by the law of substitution. The opportunity is now available for us to get what He deserves. If you believe in Christ, the Son of the living God, by His death… you died. There was a divine exchange that took place on the cross. Jesus took our unrighteousness and gave us His righteousness. He took our poverty and gave us His riches. By the law of substitution, Jesus gave us beauty for ashes and the garment of praise for the spirit of heaviness. If you believe in Jesus Christ, God takes the righteousness of Christ and puts it in you. By the blood of Jesus, God erases your old life and gives you a brand new life.

> *There is not one thing in me*
> *that the Blood doesn't cleanse.*
> *~ Smith Wigglesworth*

~ Andrew Murray said:
The blood alone has done everything. He who once gave His blood for us will surely, every moment, impart its effectiveness. So perfect is the reconciliation, and so really has sin been covered and blotted out, that he who believes in Christ is looked upon, and treated by God, as entirely righteous. Trust Him to do this. Trust Him to open your eyes and to give you a deeper spiritual insight. Trust Him to teach you to think about the blood as God thinks about it. Trust Him to impart to you, and to make effective in you, all that He enables you to see. It is impossible for us to think too highly of, or to expect too much from, the power of Jesus' blood.

For He made Him who knew no sin to be sin for us, that we might become the righteousness of God in Him.
~ 2 Corinthians 5 : 21

By the law of substitution, "If anyone is in Christ, he is a new creation; old things have passed away; behold, all things have become new."
~ 2 Corinthians 5 : 17

> *Let God present you to your new self.*

To be used by God effectively, you need to know who you are in Christ.

> *Perceive yourself in Christ,*
> *just as God perceives you in Him,*
> *and you will look much better In Christ*
> *than you do outside of Christ.*

By the law of substitution, if you believe in Christ, when He died… you died. Paul said, *"I have been crucified with Christ; it is no longer I who live, but Christ lives in me."*
~ Galatians 2 : 20a

Jesus did something that had never been done before. That's why, in Him, you are somebody that never existed before. This is the miracle of transformation. You will not get God's best blessings as long as you live with a sense of condemnation, guilt, and unworthiness. Some people think they really do not deserve anything because of their problems, their weakness, or what they did 10 years ago. They have never gotten over it.

> *When He died… you died.*
> *When He was crucified… you were crucified.*
> *When He was buried… you were buried.*
> *When He was raised from the dead… you raised from the dead.*
> *When He ascended to the right hand of God…*
> *He took you with Him.*
>
> *That's your spiritual position with Him.*

By the law of substitution, you have been delivered. It really doesn't matter what you feel. Most people worry about the worst thing that can happen to them. The worst thing that can happen to you is *death*. Are you worried about dying? You shouldn't want to die now, but neither should you *fear* death.

> *He who lives to live forever, never fears dying.*
> *~ **William Penn***

The Bible says:

To be absent from the body is to be present with the Lord.
~ 2 Corinthians 5 : 8b

Don't be afraid to die if you're right with God.

> *Those who are prepared to die are the most prepared to live.*

I don't want to die now because I want to do more for God, but, I'm not afraid to die. The biggest challenge for many people is not to worry about dying. Accept the fact that when it's your time... you will go. The biggest challenge is not being able to *die* for Him, but being able to *live* for Him. You receive the power to live for Him through His death which has delivered you.

So many people are bound by their circumstance, Jesus has delivered you from your spiritual circumstance. He took you from the kingdom of darkness into the Kingdom of God, the Kingdom of Light.

Redemption did more than save us from hell. It put us back into the Garden – into a pre-Adamic fall adjudication. We have received dominion again. Our authority has been restored to subdue the earth, and we have been delivered. I have been delivered. I don't always look like it. I don't always feel like it. But I have been delivered. Christ will never go back on the cross. He will never die again. He did it once on the cross, and He said, *"It is finished."* ~ John 19 : 30

Even the apostle Paul said, *"For what I do is not the good I want to do; no, the evil I do not want to do this I keep on doing."* ~ (Romans 7 : 19 NIV) You may be struggling to do certain things right, but, I'm telling you that you have been delivered. Jesus has already paid the price for your freedom. So how do you begin to see that freedom manifest in your life? Begin to really study the Word and continue in the Word.

Why Do We Study the Word?

We study the Word for these reasons:
- To know more about God; to get acquainted with Him.
- To know who we are in Christ.
- To put the enemy out of commission in our lives.

> *When I know who God is and who I am in Christ,*
> *I can put the enemy out of commission in my life.*

The longer you live, the more you should get acquainted with what happened to you when you were born again. You've already been delivered, but the more you learn about who you are in Christ and the revelation of His Word, the more you will put the devil out of commission in your life. You do that by applying and practicing the truth that you have learned.

Before we were born again, there were certain things that each of us did that we didn't know were wrong. But as we came to church and studied the Word, we heard truth about those things.

It's when you discover the truth in those areas of your life, and embrace it, that you are set free. Jesus delivered us 2000 years ago, but we are just getting acquainted with our deliverance.

> *Our entire lives are a progressive revelation*
> *of who God is and what He has done for us.*

That's why we attend church. That's why we should not want to go to a dead church where they're preaching *"sermonettes"* for *"Christianettes"* that go home and smoke cigarettes while surfing the Internet. We need to be in a church where the truth is taught so we can grow. I mean, what would happen if you had a 36-year-old man that acted like a 5-year-old? That's not normal! Children should learn, grow, and mature. In the same way, the more you hear the Word, the more you enter into that place of deliverance – into that place of wholeness. There's a process of spiritual growth that takes place in your life.

> *Truth comes by layers.*
> *There are truths and there are greater truths.*

For example, servant-hood is a truth. We're servants of God. But friendship is a greater truth. Jesus said to His disciples, *"No longer do I call you servants, for a servant does not know what his master is doing; but I have called you friends, for all things that I heard from My Father I have made known to you."* ~ John 15 : 15 I'd rather be a friend of God than just be His servant. You may think that you already know God, but the more you grow, the more you discover new things about Him. You thought you were "Mr. Holy Man" or "Mrs. Perfect", and then you hear something from the Word, and you discover a new layer of truth. You are growing, and deliverance is coming into your life.

> *The deliverance you just received came when you comprehended "The Truth" in a certain area of your life. But the deliverance was already available.*

When Jesus died on the cross 2,000 years ago, you were delivered. Now you're getting acquainted with your deliverance. You just didn't realize it was available before. Scripture states, *"My people are destroyed because of the lack of knowledge."* ~ Hosea 4 : 6a There are truths and greater truths. You have been delivered. If you can grasp this truth, blinders and scales will fall off your spiritual eyes and you will begin to see more and more of God. You will enter into a greater reality of God.

God will bless us in proportion to our operating in truth. None of us possess all the truth at any given time, but if we walk in the truth that we know and in the light that we see, if we proceed faithfully to do what we know is right in the understanding that we possess, God will bless us proportionately.

> *You're not subject to tradition.*
> *You're not called to be under your circumstances.*
> *You're not called to be controlled by the world's system,*
> *but to live outside of it in the abundant life of Christ.*

When Christ preached the Gospel, abundant life was released and people were instantly set free from their bondages. The blind man began to see. The deaf man began to hear. The lame began to walk. They came out of bondage. They were delivered.

I like harvest, but I prefer inheritance.

> *Harvest is getting something that you*
> *have sown for. Inheritance is getting something*
> *that somebody else worked for.*

Our authority is based on what Jesus did for us through His work on the cross. We have been delivered. It is part of our inheritance. I know it's hard to believe this when you still see the old nature in you fighting the things of God, but that doesn't change anything. *The fact remains that you have been delivered.* You are not a sick man or woman trying to be healed. Technically – by righteous adjudication – you were healed 2000 years ago. *"By His stripes we are healed."* ~ Isaiah 53 : 5b No, you are not a sick person trying to be healed. You are a healed person whom the devil is trying to make sick. You are not a poor person trying to become rich. You are a rich person whom the devil is trying to make poor. Jesus took your poverty and gave you His riches. You need to begin to learn the truth about prosperity, to learn about sowing and reaping and paying your tithes. Then, you will begin to see the curse of poverty break off of your life. If you activate the principles of sowing and reaping and paying your tithes, God will rebuke the devourer, and before too long, you will come out from under the curse of poverty and be blessed.

"And I will rebuke the devourer for your sakes, so that he will not destroy the fruit of your ground, nor shall the vine fail to bear fruit for you in the field," says the Lord of hosts. "And all nations will call you blessed, for you will be a delightful land." Says the Lord of hosts.

~ Malachi 3 : 11 - 12

As I have said, truth comes in layers. We are going from glory to glory.

> *There is the milk of the Word, there is the bread of the Word, and there is the meat of the Word.*

The more you feed on the Word, the more you will grow and discover a greater reality of God. As you grow in the Word, the more you will be used by God, and you will feel able to operate in the supernatural.

What is Your Responsibility with the Authority You Have Been Given?

1. He gave you authority to maintain your deliverance.

Not only has Jesus delivered you, but He has also given you the power to maintain your deliverance.

Submit to God, resist the devil and he will flee from you.
~ James 4 : 7

Deliverance is maintained by resisting the enemy. The devil needs agreement in order for his will to be done in your life. If you yield to him, the will of the devil will be activated in your life. But if you yield to God, the will of God will be activated in your life.

> *Both the will of God and the will of the devil need your agreement to be activated in your life.*

How do you maintain your deliverance? …By resisting the devil and submitting to God. …By resisting the will of Satan and embracing the will of God. God has given you the authority to maintain your deliverance. Some people get healed, and then, lose their healing, because they are not maintaining their healing.

God gave us authority. Redemption pushes us back into a pre-Adamic fall adjudication. Adam was given authority to subdue the earth. The phrase, "subdue the earth," indicates that there will be resistance. The word, "subdue," is *kibosh*. My friend, you cannot stop a bird from flying above your head, but you can stop it from building a nest on your head! You may not be able to stop the evil thoughts that come into your mind, but you can cast them down. That's how you maintain your deliverance. In this way, God has given you the authority to maintain your deliverance. Refuse to agree with the feeling that says you're getting sick again. Refuse to agree with the feeling that says you're going to commit a certain sin again. Refuse to agree with it, and cast down those imaginations. Jesus delivered you. He gave you power to maintain your deliverance.

You are supposed to subdue, dominate, and cast down every imagination and every thought that exalts itself against the knowledge of God, and maintain your healing and deliverance Monday through Saturday.

Christianity is not a Sunday event. It is a lifestyle.

---

2. He gave you the authority to exercise your authority.

You are in a spiritual war. You've got to realize that the more you exercise your authority (with consistency), the more you will have victory.

> *In every move of God,*
> *there is a counter-move of the devil.*

You should not be struggling through the week, saying, "Oh, boy! I can't wait to get to church on Sunday where there are other Christians!" No. You should go to church to celebrate a lifestyle of domination. That is the lifestyle to which you are called. But... there will be resistance.

> When you come to church on Sunday,
> it should be a celebration of domination!

When dealing with the enemy in the area of prayer and deliverance, there are **3 Responses to Authority:**

• **Obedience**, or voluntary submission.

When you exercise authority against the enemy and he responds to you by obeying your command... that is voluntary submission.

• **Disobedience**, or rejection of authority.

Sometimes this is caused because the enemy has legal ground. A legal ground is established when a person has an unholy alliance with the enemy by practicing or doing things that have created strongholds. I will discuss this in more detail in another chapter.

- **Suppression**, or involuntary submission.

When God spoke to Adam and told him to subdue the earth, the Hebrew word He used was "kibosh". It means, "to come down hard." The Hebrew word chosen by God to give this instruction showed that there was going to be resistance. There is nothing to subdue if there is not a resistance.

> *Without resistance, there is no need to subdue anything.*

It is important that you know that your enemy will sometimes resist your authority. There are times in deliverance ministry when you exercise your authority and cast out devils, and the demons come out with no problem. Other demons challenge your authority. If you do not learn this, you might stop praying too soon. You might give up. There has to be a relentlessness on your part in exercising your authority against the things you are dealing with. The enemy will sometimes obey when you pray. Other times, he will reject your authority. That's when you need to move in what I call a *"kibosh anointing."* It is a different level of authority, it's a spiritual reinforcement.

Daniel experienced 21 days of resistance. Daniel was praying and fasting for 21 days. On the 21st day, he received his breakthrough. An angel appeared to him saying: *"Do not fear, Daniel, for from the first day that you set your heart to understand, and to humble yourself before your God, your words were heard; and I have come because of your words. But the prince of the kingdom of Persia withstood me twenty-one days; and behold, Michael, one of the chief princes, came to help me, for I had been left alone there with the kings of Persia."*
~ Daniel 10 : 12 – 13

From the time Daniel began to pray, heaven sent an angel with the answer, but there was a resistance of authority in the spiritual realm. There were spiritual interferences – demonic activities that resisted the authority of God. On the 21st day, God sent a kibosh anointing. He sent a stronger angel who came and fought against those demonic forces.

What would have happened if Daniel had stopped praying after 10 days? He probably would not have received his breakthrough, but as he continued to pray, reinforcement came. The enemy had no choice but to submit to the power of God. This is an example of suppression… involuntary submission.

How often do we stop fighting too early? How often do we give up before God is through? That's why we don't see miracles take place. We need to learn to pray and stand in faith until we see the breakthrough. We need to learn how to contend for our miracles if we want to be used by God.

> *You have to press with your prayers until you reach a kibosh anointing – an anointing of suppression where the enemy is forced to obey God… because God is speaking.*

Jesus said: "If you abide (continue) in My word, you are My disciples indeed."

~ John 8 : 31

There are times when we pray for healing, but don't see the healing. Yet, we should not stop praying; we should continue praying. There are times when we pray for deliverance, but the demons refuse to go. We pray for our cities to be changed, but there is resistance in the spiritual realm. That's why you have to continue in the Word. Continue to press in until the kibosh anointing comes... until heaven sends spiritual reinforcement and comes into the situation and deals with the enemy, the principality (or *force*), that seems to be resisting your authority. You have to stay with God until you reach that "place of kibosh" – when spiritual reinforcement arrives (like in the case of Daniel) and defeats the enemy.

When you travel above the speed limit and a police officer comes, he will pull you over. When an officer turns on his lights and his siren, cars start moving out of the way. That is what happens when you have authority. When you pray, demons move to the right and to the left, but sometimes they are resistant. They will not get out of the way.

Have you ever seen a police chase on TV? Sometimes people refuse to submit, but eventually, there is submission. The police department sends many, many police cars, officers and helicopters to suppress the rebellion. When they are caught, they are caught by suppression. More force is exercised to bring the fugitive into a place of submission. They don't submit voluntarily but they are forced into submission by the power of authority.

What would happen if a police officer gave you a ticket and you refused to pay it? Then, two years later, you get pulled over again, and there's a warrant out for your arrest. They would put you in those two wonderful bracelets! The first time, the police officer exercised authority, but you rejected it. Now, you will experience suppression. You will be forced to pay. You will submit even if it is not voluntary.

It's important to continue in the Word and prayer. I'm not going to say that every time you tell a demon to leave that he is going to go. The Bible says: *"Resist the devil and he will flee from you"*. ~ James 4 : 7b The instruction to resist indicates that there might be a struggle. You have to continue in the Word, and pray until you feel this "kibosh" kind of anointing – until you experience dominion. You may have been in a battle that has lasted months or even years. Perhaps you have been praying for your children to be saved. You may have been praying for a relative to change! Don't give up. Stay in the battle until the "kibosh anointing" comes.

When the influence of heaven comes into the scene, it does not matter where the demon is coming from. It is going to leave! Continue in His Word, in prayer and in worship. He has given you authority to exercise, but you have to continue in it.

He has given you authority to live a victorious life!

As a soldier in the army of God we need to walk in the supernatural if we want to be used by God.

Chapter 5

Walking in the Supernatural

Knowing how to operate in the supernatural does not guarantee that we will always have 100% success every time we do ministry. Not every person you pray for will be healed or saved. The man at the pool of Bethesda told Jesus that he had no one to put him into the pool. Someone else always jumped in before he could get into the water. *"Jesus said to him, 'Rise, take up your bed and walk.'"* ~ John 5 : 8 This was the only person Jesus healed there. A skeptical person might ask why Jesus didn't heal all the people who were there waiting for a chance to be healed. We don't really know why Jesus didn't heal them; perhaps it was because they were focusing on the water and the angels. The man who was healed was focused on Jesus. My point is: some people get healed… others do not. We do not always know the reason for it, but that does not mean you can dismiss the reality of the fact that God heals. Just as you can pray for someone to get saved, you can also pray for the sick to be healed.

The Bible says, *"And many lepers were in Israel in the time of Elisha the prophet, and none of them was cleansed except Naaman the Syrian."*

~ Luke 4 : 27

Think about that. What about the other lepers? We cannot explain such things. They are mysteries of God.

> *In heaven, God will reveal what on earth He chose to conceal.*

After He healed someone, Jesus said, *"Sin no more, lest a worse thing come upon you."* ~ John 5 : 14 What does that mean? It means that you can lose your healing. Some people will get healed and some people will get saved, but not all people will stay healed and saved. Some of the reasons why people don't receive miracles are doubt, unbelief, or sin in their lives.

Jesus instructed people to "go and sin no more" to prevent something worse from happening to them. Some people will get healed or saved, and then turn back to their old lifestyle of sin and lose what they have gained. Others will get healed and saved and stay healed and saved. You can find examples of both kinds of people.

The most important thing for you to understand is that:

> *It is your job to pray. It is God who heals.*

We have the power of the anointing. One of the definitions of "*anointed*" is set apart for a purpose. But you must know that,

> *Power without purpose will destroy you.*

So he came to a city of Samaria, which is called Sychar, near the plot of ground that Jacob gave to his son Joseph. Now Jacob's well was there. Jesus, therefore, being wearied from His journey, sat thus by the well. It was about the sixth hour. A woman of Samaria came to draw water. Jesus said to her, "Give me a drink." For His disciples had gone away into the city to buy food. Then the woman of Samaria said to Him, "How is it that You, being a Jew, ask a drink from me, a Samaritan woman?" For Jews have no dealings with the Samaritans. I want you to notice that the Jews had no dealings with the Samaritans. Jesus answered and said to her, "If you knew the gift of God, and who it is who says to you, 'Give Me a drink,' you would have asked Him and He would have given you living water." The woman said to him, "Sir you have nothing to draw with and the well is deep. Where then do you get that living water? Are you greater than our father Jacob, who gave us the well, and drank from it himself, as well as his son and his livestock?" Jesus answered and said to her, "Whoever drinks of this well will thirst again, but whoever drinks of the water that I shall give him will never thirst. But the water that I shall give him will become in him a fountain of water springing up into everlasting life." The woman said to him, "Sir, give me this water, that I may not thirst, nor come here to draw." Jesus said to her, "Go, call your husband, and come here." The woman answered and said, "I have no husband." Jesus said to her, "You have well said. 'I have no husband,' for you have had five husbands, and the one whom you now have is not your husband;

in that you spoke truly." The woman said to Him, "Sir, I perceive that you are a prophet."

The woman perceived that Jesus was a prophet, so she changed the topic of conversation away from her personal life to a religious debate. *"Our fathers worshiped on this mountain and you Jews say that in Jerusalem is the place where one ought to worship." Jesus said to her, "Woman, believe Me, the hour is coming when you will neither on this mountain, nor in Jerusalem, worship the Father. You worship what you do not know; we know what we worship, for salvation is of the Jews. But the hour is coming, and now is, when the true worshiper will worship the Father in spirit and truth; for the Father is seeking such to worship Him. God is Spirit, and those who worship Him must worship Him in spirit and truth." The woman said to him, "I know that Messiah is coming" (who is called Christ). "When He comes, He will tell us all things." Jesus said to her, "I who speak to you am He."*

~ John 4 : 5 - 26

This is a perfect example of evangelism. The Church is facing a territorial conflict of ideology, philosophy, and religion. If you haven't faced it already… you will. There are many voices of many religions that proclaim to be "the truth" and "the way". There are so many voices. When you begin to preach the Gospel to the unsaved, they are going to question why you think you have the right to say that Jesus is the only way.

That is, basically, what happened with this woman. When Jesus asked her for a drink, the woman was surprised because He was Jewish and she was Samaritan. There was so much prejudice between the two people groups that they didn't even talk to each other. Yet, Jesus crossed the boundary and shocked the woman. Jesus told her that He was the living water. He said that if she knew who was asking her for a drink of water, she would ask Him for living water. She wanted Jesus to show her the living water so she would not have to draw water anymore. She challenged Jesus in what he had to say. Then, she began a theological debate with Jesus saying, "You Jews say we should worship in Jerusalem while our fathers say we should worship on this mountain."

You need to understand that when you try to communicate the Gospel, people will challenge your theology. They will challenge what you believe. This woman challenged Jesus based on a ritual – a tradition. Jesus began to explain to her that the hour was coming when they would neither worship on the mountain nor in Jerusalem, because God is looking for worshippers who will worship Him in spirit and truth. But what really broke the argumentative mindset of the woman was not Jesus' theology. It was when Jesus stepped into the Spirit. He began to operate in the Word of Knowledge. He told her to go call her husband. She told Jesus that she had no husband. Jesus replied, "You have said right. You have had five husbands and the one you're now with is not your husband."

The woman who had been arguing against Jesus' theology suddenly became spiritual. She said, "Oh, I perceive that you are a prophet!" It was not the theology that brought the change in her mind. It was the power of the Holy Spirit. When Jesus gave her supernatural information, it collapsed her arguments.

My friend, if you want to be used by God and operate in the supernatural, you need more than just theology. You need more than just a degree. I agree that education is important, if you are going to be a preacher; you need to learn the Word of God. But you also need to have the supernatural dimension working with the Word. When people see the supernatural dimension operating in your ministry, God will show them that there's something more to it than just words.

> *It's natural to be religious; it's supernatural to be a Christian.*

You are "Under New Management" – Supernatural Management

The Bible says, *"For the kingdom of God is not in word but in power."*

~ I Corinthians 4 : 20

When you preach the Gospel, if you don't want people to think you are just preaching another religion, you must embrace the operation of the supernatural. It is necessary to allow the Gifts of the Spirit to flow in your ministry.

> *People don't care about the Jesus you talk about until they see the power of the Jesus you have.*

When they see the power that you have, they realize that this Gospel is supernatural and that God is real.

> *It is not just more preaching that is needed,*
> *but more gospel with power in the lives of Christians.*

We don't need to just produce Bible school students. The world does not need just another preacher to preach a new message. The Gospel is being preached in the pulpit, on television, and on the radio. That's not the issue. The Gospel is not always consistently being demonstrated with power. We must press into the realm of the Spirit. Yes, there will be opposition. People may criticize you over your healing ministry, but when people are healed, they will know that God is real. You have a greater impact with miracles than without them!

> *By nature most people are the same,*
> *but through the supernatural we are made different.*

We need the supernatural. We do not need just another preacher to simply repeat what the past has told us. We need something fresh – something new.

> *Learn from different voices,*
> *but learn to speak with your own voice.*

Be inspired by others, but establish your own identity. Find your mark in God and let Him release you into the dimension in which He wants you to function.

> *Don't be a carbon copy of someone else;*
> *make your own impression.*

A Miracle Answers the Question

What happened in Matthew chapter 11 : 3? John the Baptist was in prison, and his disciples went to see Jesus. They asked Jesus, *"Are you the Coming One, or do we look for another?"* John had sent them to ask Jesus this question. The secular world today is in a spiritual prison. People do not believe in God. The Bible says,

"But even if our gospel is veiled, it is veiled to those who are perishing, whose minds the god of this age has blinded, who do not believe, lest the light of the gospel of the glory of Christ, who is the image of God, should shine on them."

~ 2 Corinthians 4 : 3 – 4

Many people's eyes have been veiled by the god of this world. They are in a spiritual prison. People are imprisoned by philosophy, religion, agnosticism, and atheism. They are spiritually bound, and when you preach to them, they cannot even comprehend what you are talking about. They are asking questions like John the Baptist did. He sent his disciples to ask Jesus if He was the Messiah.

Now think about it. John had received a revelation at the Jordan River. He heard an audible voice that came from the heavens saying, *"This is my beloved son."* ~ Matthew 3 : 17 He heard a prophetic word from heaven. But sometimes, even though we have heard prophetic words, we need confirmation of those words to reassure us when things get tough. When we get that reassurance, we can stand on the word that we have received. John sent his disciples to ask Jesus because things were getting tough. He was in prison... about to be executed. He just wanted to make sure that everything was okay. He wanted to have a prophetic confirmation.

There is a prophetic parallel between this generation and this biblical story. This generation is in prison, too. The prison they are in is one of ideology – a prison of atheism, agnosticism, religion, and philosophy. Such things have imprisoned this generation into a mindset of blindness. This generation cannot see the truth of the Gospel, so they are asking questions: Are You the Messiah, or is there another one who is to come?

Jesus had an opportunity with this theological question. He could have gone back into expository or eschatological preaching – quoting the prophetic words that were given about Him hundreds of years earlier. There is nothing wrong with studying history, eschatology, and expository preaching. But, if this is all we are doing in church today – studying the Greek and the Hebrew to answer questions that nobody is asking – we will not be effective to reach our generation.

Some modern-day ministers are preaching about things that are irrelevant to the questions of the society. That's why so many people say, "I don't want to go to church to hear another theological debate or another sermon that will not change me. I do not want to hear another debate about the doctrines of various denominations. I do not want to hear that they are wrong over there, and we are right over here."

> *While the world is going to hell,*
> *we are answering questions that nobody is asking.*

No wonder some churches are not getting the maximum result! Many people feel like the church is irrelevant.

We recently did a tour in Europe. We went into the schools. The young people are into the hip-hop culture and do not want anything to do with churches. So, I took a hip-hop dance team, two rappers, and a drama team with me. When the students heard that a religious program was coming to town, they were excited for the chance to escape class – not because they were going to a religious meeting. They packed the gymnasium. The entire school was there.

When I went up on stage and introduced the team and then had one of the rappers begin a Christian rap song, their jaws just dropped. Their mindset began to change. Christian hip-hop and rap songs? This Christian thing is cool! Then the dance team performed. By the time it was time to preach, the students were ready to hear what I had to say. We went to schools in 14 cities, and saw over 600 students saved. After the meetings in the schools, we would invite the students to attend a youth rally outside of the schools. There, some received the Holy Spirit. For many of them, it was their first time in church.

Europe needs to have revival now. Only a small percentage of the population in Europe are born-again Christians. Something has to change. But, the Church in some places is resistant to change. While we were evangelizing to win these teens to Christ, some of the leaders in the Church came against us saying, "That Guy Peh has the music of the devil. Hip-hop, rap music, and dancing are from the devil." They told people not to come to my meetings. One of the leaders told me that some churches have been trying to reach the students of that nation for twenty years. They have not been successful. The difference is that we did not come with the language of tradition. We did not come with a religious debate. We spoke the language of the young people, and when I preached the Gospel, they gave their lives to Jesus. We need to stop having theological debates and demonstrate what the Gospel is all about, instead!

> *We don't need to just teach history in church, but His story.*

When John the Baptist's disciples asked Jesus if He was the Messiah or if someone else was coming, He did not enter into a theological debate. He said, "Okay, follow Me." He found a blind person, and healed him. He found a deaf person, and healed him. He found a lame person, and healed him, too. He found a man who was dead, and raised him back to life. Then, He turned around and said, *"Go and tell John the things which you hear and see. The blind see and the lame walk; the lepers are cleansed and the deaf hear; the dead are raised up and the poor have the gospel preached to them. And blessed is he who is not offended because of Me."*

~ Matthew 11 : 4 – 6

John was asking a theological question, but through His actions, Jesus was saying that the answer to that theological question is miracles. "The fact that the blind eyes see proves that I am the Messiah. The fact that the deaf hear proves that I am the Messiah. The fact that the lame walk proves that I am the Messiah. The fact that the dead are raised proves that I am the Messiah." Jesus was saying that these miracles testify that He is the Messiah.

> *The world has lost its faith because the church has lost its power.*

The answer to the many questions this generation is asking should be with "miracles and the demonstration of the supernatural." This will provoke this generation to believe and turn to God. This is the will of God for you, the believer. God wants to use you to reveal His glory – through your prayers and your preaching of the Gospel. Your confidence is in the fact that:

Jesus Christ is the same yesterday, today and forever.

~ Hebrews 13 : 8

> *The Gospel without miracles is not the full Gospel.*

The full Gospel must be preached with miracles. Whenever Jesus is preached, miracles will follow. Every miracle is a manifestation of the Messiah.

> *A miracle answers the questions in the minds of people.*

Some people will question you, but a miracle answers those questions. That is why you need to believe in miracles. Some people say, "Well, it is easy for you to say that. You already have a track record of people being healed in your ministry." But I did not start out with a worldwide, traveling ministry. I did not start a healing ministry by preaching to big crowds. Some of you have dreams that when you get started in ministry, you will immediately be invited to the greatest churches in the world. That is the wrong mentality.

> *The Kingdom of God is God's way of doing things.*
> *In His Kingdom we lead by serving, we live by dying,*
> *and we receive by giving.*

God is going to raise you up, but you have to start with some practical things. Then, He will progressively raise you up to the level where you need to be. People come to large meetings and they say, "Wow! One day I'm going to be an evangelist, an apostle, a prophet... I'm going to have meetings like that." They have no idea what it took for the preacher who is preaching at those meetings to get where he is. They think it was just something that happened overnight. Commitment is the key that unlocks doors to great opportunities.

> *If you wait until every hindrance is removed before serving*
> *the Lord, you will never attempt anything for Him.*

You see, my friend, you can't get anywhere unless you start. You must start where you are. God doesn't ask you to be the best, only do your best. Have the courage to let go of the things not worth sticking to. God will take you through a process... a journey of growth. From faith to faith. From glory to glory. Great things are little things done with a desire to please God. The best time to hold on is when you reach the place where the average person gives up. Don't be content by being average. Start where you are and run the race.

Pray for the sick until you see the sick healed.
Then, pray for the sick because you have seen the sick healed.

Cast out devils until you can cast out devils.
Then, cast out devils because you have cast them out.

Preach faith until you have faith.
Then preach faith because you have it!

Pray for the dead until you see them raised.
Then pray for the dead because you have seen them raised.

Start where you are right now.

Persistence will give you power to prevail over all problems.
- He who doesn't hope to win has already lost.
- A quitter never wins and a winner never quits.
- Trying times are no time to quit trying.

Raising the Dead

This is totally different than praying to the dead or worshipping the dead. Those things are forbidden by scripture.

There shall not be found among you anyone who... calls up the dead. For all who do these things are an abomination to the Lord, and because of these abominations the Lord your God drives them out from before you.

~ Deuteronomy 18 : 10 - 12

Don't be afraid to pray for the dead to be raised, the scripture commands us to do so.

Heal the sick, cleanse the lepers, raise the dead, cast out demons. Freely you have received, freely give.

~ Matthew 10 : 8

When I started my journey with God, this Bible verse always stirred my heart regarding the raising of the dead. A desire was born in me to see this happen, and I thank God that He gave me the opportunity to pray for several people that were medically proclaimed dead and (after prayer) see God raise them from the dead. I believe that God wants to perform such miracles through believers to reveal His glory, but we must follow the protocol of the Holy Spirit and use the wisdom of God.

Before you begin, always ask for permission from family members or whoever is in charge. Don't be foolish. Use the wisdom of God.

You must understand when dealing with a situation of life and death that there is a cycle of life and death. The Bible says, *"It is appointed for men to die once, but after this the judgment."* ~ Hebrews 9 : 27 Not every person who dies needs to be raised from the dead. Sometimes it is God's appointed time for a person to die. So, don't try to fight something that you are not called to fight and then get frustrated over it. There are certain reasons why some people are in the situation in which they find themselves. Sometimes God wants to display His power, and He will raise people from the dead.

Important Things Related to Praying for People to be Raised from the Dead

1. You need to know that it's God's will.

God will give you a witness in your spirit. In each situation, He will give you a witness regarding what He wants you to do. If the death is premature, He will let you know it in your spirit. Don't be like some Christians who are just power-seekers.

> *The beginning of wisdom is silence,*
> *the second step is listening.*

2. The power of God comes for a purpose.

A man called me one time who said he had heard that God had used me to raise the dead. He wanted to know what kind of technique I was using. I told him that there is no technique to raising the dead. He said that he had gone to a country in Africa and had asked them to take him to the mortuary. He said he had tried to pray for a couple of people, but they did not come back to life. So, he was kind of disappointed that he went all the way to Africa for this experience and nothing happened. That's the wrong spirit! The anointing is power. "Anointed" means, set apart for a purpose.

> *The power of God comes for a purpose.*
> *It's not just a toy that we can use.*

3. You cannot just turn the power on and off when you want to.

Even if you have the gifts of healing, they operate with the Holy Spirit. I don't try to make something happen in meetings. I preach and wait. I preach and look. I preach and am sensitive. I'm not in control of the meeting... the Holy Spirit is. I sometimes have a sense of what God wants to do in a meeting, but I'm there preaching and stopping and walking around and pausing... waiting for the Spirit to direct me. That is the way it happens, friends. God leads and we follow Him.

When you rest in Him, ministry is so much fun.

4. Relax, there is no pressure.

Relax, there is no pressure. Just be yourself. Shake off all the pressures that the religious world puts on you. Be genuine. Be who you are. When you are ministering, be the same person that you are outside the church. Be who you are. God will use your personality – your temperament. Don't apologize for your personality. Just learn how to manage it in such a way that you won't be offensive everywhere you go.

Some personalities can be offensive sometimes, because they are not afraid to say what they think. That can be dangerous. It is not always a wise thing to say what you think. Your mouth can get you in trouble at times.

> *You can grow in wisdom and maturity*
> *so you will not be offensive, yet still be yourself.*

God created you uniquely because He wanted you to be the way you are. Let Him use your personality.

5.   Pray in the name of Jesus as the *Spirit* leads you.

At the name of Jesus every knee should bow, of those in heaven, and those on earth, and those under the earth.
~ Philippians 2 : 10

6.   Ask God to breathe His life back into the body, and ask God to bring the soul back.

He cried out to the Lord and said, "O Lord my God, I pray, let this child's soul come back to him." Then the Lord heard the voice of Elijah; and the soul of the child came back to him, and he revived.
~ I Kings 17 : 21b - 22

Some people in the body of Christ who operate in power want you to believe that in order to operate at this level of power, you must be special or you must go through certain things. They want you to believe that they are special and that it is not for everybody to be used by God.

I, however, believe that every believer has a call to be used in the miraculous according to the Great Commission in Mark 16 : 15 – 18. It is in my heart to see the Lord raise up miracle-workers. Miracle-workers are desperately needed in the body of Christ. Every man, woman, and child needs to learn how to walk in healing, deliverance, and victory. When they do, they will be able to help, heal, and deliver others.

Origins of Sickness

One of the things that is important if you are going to be used by God to minister to the sick and flow in the supernatural, is the understanding of the origin of sickness. The understanding of the origins of sickness will help you apply your faith with knowledge and revelation in the place of prayer and ministry. To do so you can do what I call a *"Spiritual Diagnosis"*.

Spiritual Diagnosis

It's important to have a diagnosis if you're going to be ministering healing to a person. Allow the Holy Spirit to diagnose the situation.

In Mark 9 : 21, *Jesus asked his father, "How long has this been happening to him?"* "How long has the child been in this condition?" That's what I call a diagnosis. Try to understand why the person is in the situation that they are in. Not because you are trying to analyze everything, but when you understand the roots of the problem, it will help you to pray effectively so the person can be healed. That will save you a lot of trouble.

Roots of Sickness

✦ Unhealthy Diet and Lack of Exercise

Some sicknesses come to us as a lack of discipline in our diet and exercise.

Do you know that your body is the temple of the Holy Spirit who is in you, whom you have from God, and you are not your own? For you were bought at a price; therefore glorify God in your body and in your spirit, which are God's.
~ 1 Corinthians 6 : 19 - 20

We need to be good stewards of our body. Your body is your earthly suit. You only have one; glorify God with it by taking care of it.

✦ Viruses

Some sickness come because we might have been infected by a virus and much more. Not all sicknesses are spiritually related, but some are.

✛ Sin

Sometimes sickness can be sin related.

> *Sin is an ever-increasing desire with a never-ending satisfaction.*

Jesus told the men whom he healed at the pool of Bethesda, "Sin no more, lest a worse thing come upon you." ~ John 5 : 14b Sin can also be a hindrance (or a blockage) for someone to receive their miracle.

Behold, the Lord's hand is not shortened, that it cannot save; nor His ear heavy, that it cannot hear. But your iniquities have separated you from your God; and your sins have hidden His face from you, so that He will not hear.

~ Isaiah 59 : 1 – 2

Scripture says, "The prayer of faith will save the sick, and the Lord will raise him up." ~ James 5 : 15 But then it continues by saying, "*Confess your sin to one another and pray for one another that you might be healed.*" ~ James 5 : 16 Sometimes sickness comes because people are living in sin. As a matter of fact, Jesus once prayed for a man. He was healed and He said to him, "*Sin no more, lest a worse thing come upon you.*" ~ John 5 : 14b It is obvious that, sometimes, the origin of sickness is sin.

If my people who are called by My name will humble themselves, and pray and seek My face, and turn from their wicked ways, then I will hear from heaven, and will forgive their sin and heal their land.

~ 2 Chronicles 7 : 14

Sometimes you may fire a good shot, but you aim at the wrong target. If the person is sick because they are living in sin, the first thing necessary for them to be healed is not to be prayed for by the greatest evangelist in the world. The first thing they must do is confess their sin. They need to confess and repent, and then you can pray for them. You must understand that you cannot force the healing power of God into a person who is living in sin. They need to repent first.

3 Forms of Repentance

1) Great remorse – somebody's sorry because they are caught.

2) Awareness of the circumstances – a person realizes that they are caught in the circumstances.

3) Godly sorrow – the person realizes that Jesus died for their sins.

> *Late repentance is seldom true,*
> *but true repentance is never late.*

Christ offered comfort for the grieving and cleansing for the guilty. There are none so good that they can save themselves, and none so bad that God can't save them. Repentance means not only a heart broken for sin, but also from sin. Repentance is not only saying, "I am sorry for my sin." It is also saying, "I am through with my sin." To grieve over sin is one thing, to repent is another.

> *Mercy triumphs over judgment,*
> *but we must run to mercy to receive mercy.*

Jesus paid the debt for all our sins, because there is no other sacrifice in this world that could pay the debt for sin. Jesus totally washed away our sins.

Hebrews 10 : 4 teaches us that the blood of bulls and goats is powerless to take sin away. Some people may ask, "How could Jesus take our sins away?" Jesus could do it for two reasons. The first reason is that Jesus was infinitely valuable, and because of His infinite value, He could take the place of an infinite number of people on the cross. The second reason is that Jesus was infinitely righteous, and because He was infinitely righteous, He could take the punishment for an infinite number of sins.

> *He paid a debt He did not owe*
> *because we owed a debt we could not pay.*

Some people may say, "I am of this religion or that religion. I read my Bible and I go to church and I am a good person." Nothing is wrong with all of these things, but these things are not enough to get you to heaven. Knowing how to swim does not make you a fish, no matter how long you stay under water. Going to church and giving your money to the poor and being a good person does not make you a child of God. To be a fish you must be created by God as a fish, and to be a child of God, you must be born again. You must repent from your sins and accept Jesus Christ as your Lord and Savior.

> *The birth of Christ brought God to man,*
> *but it took the blood of Christ to bring man to God.*

Education can polish men but only the blood of Christ can cleanse them.

If someone is in rebellion against God, there is no preacher or no prayer warrior that is powerful enough to deliver that person. It is God who delivers, and He knows the depths of a person's heart. Each person holds the key for their deliverance in their own hands, and it is called "repentance".

If you need to repent now, just pray this prayer:

Heavenly Father,
I know that I have sinned against you and
that my sins separate me from you. I am truly sorry.
I now want to turn away from my sinful past
and turn to you for forgiveness.
Please forgive me, and help me avoid sinning again.
I believe that your Son, Jesus Christ, died for my sins,
that He was raised from the dead, is alive, and hears my prayer.
I invite Jesus to become my Savior and the Lord of my life -
to rule and reign in my heart from this day forward.
Please send your Holy Spirit to help me obey You
and to convict me when I sin.
My greatest purpose in life is to follow your example
and do Your will for the rest of my life.
In Jesus' name I pray. Amen

✦ Spirit of Infirmity

Some of the sick people that Jesus prayed for in the Bible were afflicted by a spirit of infirmity or a demonic power. The Bible is full of accounts in which Jesus ministers healing by casting out the evil spirit that was the cause of the sickness. It is important to have understanding in this area if we want to see God's power and healing released when a person is dealing with a sickness that is related to a demonic oppression. I want to walk you through biblical accounts that show us examples of how Jesus dealt with sickness and disease caused by demon spirits.

Deafness and Dumbness

Not all deafness or dumbness can be labeled under "demon power", but God's Word declares that there are specific cases caused by demons.

As they went out, behold, they brought to Him a man, mute and demon-possessed. And when the demon was cast out, the mute spoke. And the multitudes marveled, saying, "It was never seen like this in Israel!"

~ Matthew 9 : 32 - 33

When Jesus saw that the people came running together, He rebuked the unclean spirit, saying to it, "Deaf and dumb spirit, I command you, come out of him and enter him no more!"

~ Mark 9 : 25

Back Bowed

And behold, there was a woman who had a spirit of infirmity eighteen years, and was bent over and could in no way raise herself up. But when Jesus saw her, He called her to Him and said to her, "Woman, you are loosed from your infirmity." And He laid His hands on her, and immediately she was made straight, and glorified God. But the ruler of the synagogue answered with indignation, because Jesus had healed on the Sabbath; and he said to the crowd, "There are six days on which men ought to work; therefore come and be healed on them, and not on the Sabbath day." The Lord then answered him and said, "Hypocrite! Does not each one of you on the Sabbath loose his ox or donkey from the stall, and lead it away to water it? So ought not this woman, being a daughter of Abraham, whom Satan has bound – think of it – for eighteen years, be loosed from this bond on the Sabbath?"

~ Luke 13 : 11 - 16

Insanity, Lunacy, Epilepsy

Lord, have mercy on my son, for he is an epileptic and suffers severely; for he often falls into the fire and often into the water. And Jesus rebuked the demon, and it came out of him; and the child was cured from that very hour.

~ Matthew 17 : 15, 18

Wild Strength, Maniac

And when He had come out of the boat, immediately there met Him out of the tombs a man with an unclean spirit, who had his dwelling among the tombs; and no one could bind him, not even with chains, because he had often been bound with shackles and chains. And the chains had been pulled apart by him, and the shackles broken in pieces; neither could anyone tame him. And always, night and day, he was in the mountains and in the tombs, crying out and cutting himself with stones. When he saw Jesus from afar, he ran and worshipped Him. And he cried out with a loud voice and said, "What have I to do with You, Jesus, Son of the Most High God? I implore You by God that You do not torment me." For He said to him, "Come out of the man, unclean spirit!" Then He asked him, "What is your name?" and he answered, saying, "My name is Legion; for we are many." Also he begged Him earnestly that He would not send them out of the country. Now a large herd of swine was feeding there near the mountains. So all the demons begged Him saying, "Send us to the swine, that we may enter them." And at once Jesus gave them permission. Then the unclean spirits went out and entered the swine (there were about two thousand); and the herd ran violently down the steep place into the sea, and drowned in the sea. So those who fed the swine fled, and they told it in the city and in the country. And they went out to see what it was that had happened. Then they came to Jesus, and saw the one who had been demon-possessed and had the legion, sitting and clothed and in his right mind. And they were afraid.

~ Mark 5 : 2 – 15

Blindness

Then one was brought to Him who was demon-possessed, blind and mute; and He healed him, so that the blind and mute man both spoke and saw.

~ Matthew 12 : 22

Convulsions

Then one of the crowd answered and said, "Teacher, I brought You my son, who has a mute spirit and wherever it seizes him, it throws him down; he foams at the mouth, gnashes teeth and becomes rigid. So I spoke to Your disciples that they should cast it out, but they could not." He answered him and said, "O faithless generation, how long shall I be with you? How long shall I bear with you? Bring him to Me. Then they brought him to Him. And when he saw Him, immediately the spirit convulsed him, and he fell on the ground and wallowed, foaming at the mouth. So He asked his father, "How long has this been happening to him?" And he said, "from childhood and often he has thrown him both into the fire and into the water to destroy him. But if You can do anything, have compassion on us and help us." Jesus said to him, "If you can believe, all things are possible to him who believes." Immediately the father of the child cried out and said with tears, "Lord, I believe, help my unbelief!" When Jesus saw that the people came running together, He rebuked the unclean spirit, saying to it: "deaf and dumb spirit, I command you, come out of him and enter him no more!" Then the spirit cried out, convulsed him greatly and came out of him. And he became as one dead so that many said, "He is dead." But Jesus took him by the hand and lifted him up, and he arose." And when He had come into the house, His disciples asked Him privately, "Why could we not cast it out?" So He said to them, "This kind can come out by nothing but prayer and fasting."

~ Mark 9 : 17 – 29

Oppression
God anointed Jesus of Nazareth with the Holy Spirit and with power, who went about doing good and healing all who were oppressed by the devil, for God was with Him.

~ Acts 10 : 38

General Sickness
And Jesus went about all Galilee, teaching in their synagogues, preaching the gospel of the kingdom, and healing all kinds of sickness and all kinds of disease among the people. Then His fame went throughout all Syria; and they brought to Him all sick people who were afflicted with various diseases and torments, and those who were demon-possessed, epileptics, and paralytics; and He healed them.

~ Matthew 4 : 23 - 24

We see that in the ministry of Jesus, He took authority and rebuked demon spirits to bring healing to those that had a sickness that was caused by demons.

The question becomes, "Who can cast out the spirit of infirmity?" Believers!

The Lord Jesus Christ said, *"These signs will follow those who believe: In My name they will cast out demons and they will speak in new tongues."*

~ Mark 16 : 17

✦ Emotional Factors

How we *think* we feel has a definite affect on how we *actually* physically feel. If your mind tells you that you are tired, the body, the nerves accept the fact. Researchers found that some illnesses are psychosomatic; which means our thoughts make us physically sick. The research pointed out that negative thoughts of worry, fear and stress release chemicals which attack our cells from the inside out making us more susceptible to sickness. However, positive thoughts release other chemicals in our body which make us feel better and build our cells up from the inside out. (From the study, "Deadly Emotions" by Dr. Don Colbert)

For thousands of years, the Bible has said:

A merry (cheerful) heart does good, like medicine....

~ Proverbs 17 : 22a

Realms of Knowledge

To walk in the supernatural, we need to understand the different realms of knowledge.

But as it is written: *"Eye has not seen, nor ear heard, nor have entered into the heart of man, the things which God has prepared for those that who love Him." But God has revealed them to us through His Spirit. For the Spirit searches all things, yes, the deep things of God.*

~ 1 Corinthians 2 : 9 - 10

This Scripture describes **3 Realms of Knowledge:**

1. Perceptional Knowledge

"Eye has not seen, nor ear heard", refers to knowledge gained by perception – knowledge obtained through the senses. Everybody has this kind of knowledge. It is the type of knowledge upon which civil laws are based. Perceptual knowledge is common sense. It is natural knowledge.

2. Conceptual Knowledge

The second type of knowledge found in this passage is conceptual knowledge. This is referred to in the part of the passage that says, *"Nor has entered into the heart of man."* When the Bible talks about the heart, it is usually speaking about your soul. There are three parts to your soul: your mind, your will, and your emotions. Your mind consists of your mental disposition or your intellectual ability to process information. This scripture says,

"Nor has entered into the heart of man, the things which God has prepared for those that who love Him."

Most people live within these two levels of knowledge (knowledge by perception and knowledge by conception). That's why people worry about everything. That's why they are controlled by their circumstances.

3. Revelatory Knowledge

Through the third type of knowledge, God is saying to us that there is a certain power that, no matter how smart you are or whether you graduated from the greatest university in the world, there are certain things in the realm of the Spirit that you will never be able to tap into with your own natural, human ability. The Bible says, *but God has revealed them to us through His Spirit. For the Spirit searches all things, yes, the deep things of God.* This third level of knowledge is revelatory knowledge. As a minister of the Gospel – which every Christian is – whether or not you preach in front of the multitudes, you'll be powerfully used when you begin to operate in the realm of revelatory knowledge. You will face situations that, in the natural, you would never be able to understand, because in the natural, your life is governed by only two realms of knowledge, and therefore, you have limited information. Life on the earth is not only influenced by what you can see. There are also invisible forces in operation that can influence all aspects of a person's life.

A child of God is called to live in the supernatural, because we live in two worlds at the same time. We are seated with Christ in the heavenly places, but we are also living on the earth. We live and are connected to both the spiritual realm and the natural realm. There are invisible forces from the spiritual realm that influence the natural realm. That's why we need a spiritual perspective in life.

3 Kinds of Moves

Life here on earth is influenced by 3 kinds of moves:

- **Moves of God**
  Which is what God wants to do and what He is doing.

- **Moves of the Devil**
  Which is what the devil is trying to do to undermine the work of God.

- **Moves of the Church**
  Which is what people who believe in God are doing.

Spiritual warfare is about "the moves of God and the Church" verses "the moves of the devil and his demonic forces." Every time God moves, the devil will attempt to counter it. Every time there is a move of the devil, God will move. Spiritual warfare is about moves and counter-moves, attacks and counter-attacks.

You might say, "I am under attack. Something bad happened to my family." If you only operate in the two natural realms of knowledge, you have limited information, and Satan may have an upper hand in spiritual warfare concerning your life. That's why you need revelatory knowledge. The Bible says, *"but God has revealed them to us through His Spirit."* The Spirit mentioned here is the Spirit of God.

> *The Holy Spirit is the executor of the will of God on earth. He's the Agent of Power and the Helper in the life of the believer.*

The Holy Spirit will help you operate in the supernatural. He carries supernatural information about your past, your present, and your future.

Jesus said, *"Nevertheless I tell you the truth. It is to your advantage that I go away; for if I do not go away, the Helper will not come to you; but if I depart, I will send Him to you."*

~ John 16 : 7

But when the Helper comes, whom I shall send to you from the Father, the Spirit of truth who proceeds from the Father, He will testify of Me.

~ John 15 : 26

> *God is omnipresent – He is everywhere.*
> *He is omnipotent – He can do everything.*
> *He is omniscient – He knows everything.*

When you operate in revelatory knowledge, the Spirit gives you supernatural information about the situation with which you are dealing. That information will be a prophetic strategy to release the power of God into the situation. That's why you need to have the gifts of the Spirit in operation in your life. If you want to be used by God, or if you desire to be part of a church that believes in the supernatural and fullness of the Gospel, you must operate in the gifts of the spirit.

Spiritual Gifts

The gifts of the Spirit are very important. That's why the Apostle Paul expressed his concern about the spiritual gifts:

Now concerning spiritual gifts, brethren, I do not want you to be ignorant.

~ 1 Corinthians 12 : 1

We should not be ignorant about the spiritual gifts. One of the definitions of the word, "ignorant", is, *not to perceive or know; not to understand or comprehend.* It can also mean, being misinformed, which is how the Amplified Bible expresses it: *"Now about the spiritual gifts (the special endowments of supernatural energy), brethren, I do not want you to be misinformed."* Some people are misinformed because they are ignorant. If you want to be used by God, you cannot be ignorant about the spiritual gifts. *Study to shew thyself approved unto God, a workman that needeth not to be ashamed, rightly dividing the word of truth.*

~ 2 Timothy 2 : 15 KJV

I want to give you some practical insights regarding the gifts of the Spirit. In the Kingdom of God, there are nine levels of operation of power and they fall into 3 categories. These nine levels of operation are what we call the *gifts of the Spirit.*

There are diversities of gifts, but the same Spirit. There are differences of ministries, but the same Lord. And there are diversities of activities, but it is the same God who works all in all. But the manifestation of the Spirit is given to each one for the profit of all: for to one is given the word of wisdom through the Spirit, to another the word of knowledge through the same Spirit, to another faith by the same Spirit, to another gifts of healings by the same Spirit, to another the working of miracles, to another prophecy, to another discerning of spirits, to another different kinds of tongues, to another the interpretation of tongues.

~ I Corinthians 12 : 4 - 10

The gifts of the Holy Spirit are visible expressions of God that go beyond human reasoning and comprehension. They are given by God to be used to do ministry in the Body of Christ.

3 Categories of Gifts

1. The gifts that **see** something (revelatory gifts):
    Word of Knowledge
    Word of Wisdom
    Discernment of spirits

2. The gifts that **say** something (vocal gifts):
    Diverse tongues
    Interpretation of tongues
    Prophecy

3. The gifts that **do** something (power gifts):
    Healings
    Faith
    Working of miracles

9 Levels of Operation of Power

Let's take a closer look at the levels of operation of power.

1. <u>Word of Knowledge</u>

To better comprehend and to be balanced, we need to understand what the word of knowledge is not.

✓ **It is not natural knowledge.**

While natural knowledge is important, the word of knowledge is not natural knowledge. It is not psychology, mental reasoning, or schooling. People who do not even have the Holy Spirit can do all of these.

✓ **It is not divination.**

Divination and fortune-telling are supernatural and can even impress someone that is ignorant about the things of God. When we talk about the word of knowledge, it is not divination or fortune-telling. God's Word prohibits divination, fortune telling, astrology, spiritism, stargazing, witchcraft as being of the devil. (Isaiah 47 : 10 – 15, Deuteronomy 4 : 19, Jeremiah 27 : 9, Daniel 2 : 27)

There shall not be found among you anyone who makes his son or his daughter pass through the fire, or one who practices witchcraft, or a soothsayer, or one who interprets omens, or a sorcerer, or on who conjures spells, or a medium, or a spiritist, or one who calls up the dead. For all who do these things are an abomination to the Lord, and because of these abominations the Lord your God drives them out from before you. You shall be blameless before the Lord your God. For these nations which you will dispossess listened to soothsayers and diviners; but as for you, the Lord your God has not appointed such for you.

~ Deuteronomy 18 : 10 – 14

The devil counterfeits (imitates) God's gifts and would make divination and fortune-telling seem like the word of knowledge, but there is a difference. If a fortune-teller knows something supernaturally, you can be sure that it is not the supernatural Spirit of God that gives him or her that knowledge. The devil uses fortune-tellers to tell you something that will worry you and break-up your home, break your heart, break your finances, and mess up your future. But God – by the word of knowledge – is generally trying to build His people up in these areas. As a Christian, you should never go to a psychic, or someone that practices astrology, or consult your horoscope. The Bible speaks against such practices. If you have done it… repent. Ask God to cleanse you and break the power of the words spoken over you by the psychic. For more information about this, you can read my book, *Keys to Receiving Your Miracles*.

✓ It is not the gift of all knowledge.

This gift is not the gift of knowledge, but the gift of the *word* of knowledge given by the Holy Spirit. God does not give us all of His knowledge, but just a word (a portion or part).

For we know in part and we prophecy in part. But when that which is perfect has come, then that which is in part will be done away.

~ I Corinthians 13 : 9 - 10

✓ It is not the talent to make good guesses.

This gift is not about making good assumptions, guesses, judgments or having a good imagination. It is not about the working of the mind. People that do not know God can make good assumptions, good guesses, and good judgments. The word of knowledge is not just making a guess based upon outward appearance. Sometimes people judge others by what they see.

For the Lord does not see as man sees; for man looks at the outward appearance, but the Lord looks at the heart."

~ I Samuel 16 : 7b

✓ It is not simply knowledge about God.

This gift is not knowledge of God or of God's Word. Although these are good and necessary things, they come by learning, hearing, studying, and experience. For instance, Eli, the priest, had vast knowledge of God and His Word through experience; but the child, Samuel (who had neither), was given a Word directly from the throne of God by the Holy Spirit. Eli had come to the place where he had no open vision (1 Samuel 3 : 7, 11 - 14).

Just because you are not educated in the things of God doesn't mean that God cannot use you.

The Word of Knowledge Is:

Let us, first of all, break it down to its original Greek meaning:

• "Word": "logos" is the spoken word – not the written word.

• "Knowledge": "gnosis": meaning, *knowing or recognition; the knowledge or understanding of a thing; the insight which proves itself in the detailed understanding of the subject.*

> *Words of Knowledge are God-given disclosures.*

The word of knowledge is the revelation of facts (past, present, or future) which were not learned through the efforts of the natural mind. It is knowledge received from the Holy Spirit to enable us to more effectively minister to the needs of people, to know and understand situations, circumstances, and strategies of the enemy (the kingdom of darkness). The word of knowledge enables us to know how to speak in the above situations with a knowledge that can amaze, surprise, disarm, and open-up. It can bring answers, healing, and understanding. This gift can tell the whereabouts, conditions, nature, or thoughts of a person, animal, place, or thing – even when it is impossible to learn it in the natural.

> *A word of knowledge is a supernatural insight or understanding of circumstances, situations, problems, or facts by revelation that is without assistance of human resources – solely by Divine help.*

With the word of knowledge, God enables someone to look into the heart, mind, or nature of a man and to know his secrets and intentions. The gift of the word of knowledge is the revelation of the divine will and plan of God; it involves moral wisdom for right living and relationships. It has helped find lost articles, as in 2 Kings 6, and helped find lost souls, as in the book of Acts.

God speaks in diverse manners, such as a dream, a vision, or a knowing. It can come to you in the form of a mental picture, an impression, a definite conviction, a revelation, or sometimes even in an audible voice. God can also speak a word of knowledge through a scripture that is quickened to you. It is always given supernaturally, as is any other spiritual gift.

• Through the **Word of God**
This is the most clear and effective way of God's communication with his people. If you want to know how things work perfectly, you need to read the manual. The Bible is God's manual for His people. But, as in the case with other manuals, we often ignore the Bible. How often do we try everything else, but His words? It is important for us to look at the written word with the right perspective. The Word of God is more than just a history book, it is alive.

> *God's Word is like a highway sign.*
> *You don't have to pay any attention to it*
> *if you don't care what happens to you.*

All Scripture is given by inspiration of God, and is profitable for doctrine, for reproof, for correction, for instruction in righteousness.

~ 2 Timothy 3 : 16

> *The Bible is a telescope;*
> *it is not to look at, but to look through.*

• *Through* **the Inner, Still, Small Voice of the Holy Spirit**

God can speak to you through the still, small voice of the Holy Spirit. Here are some biblical examples:

And after the earthquake a fire, but the Lord was not in the fire; and after the fire a still small voice.

~ I Kings 19 : 12

Then the Spirit told me to go with them, doubting nothing. Moreover these six brethren accompanied me, and we entered the man's house.

~ Acts 11 : 12

As they ministered to the Lord and fasted, the Holy Spirit said, "Now separate to Me Barnabas and Saul for the work to which I have called them."

~ Acts 13 : 2

Now when they had gone through Phrygia and the region of Galatia, they were forbidden by the Holy Spirit to preach the word in Asia. After they had come to Mysia, they tried to go into Bithynia, but the Spirit did not permit them.

~ Acts 16 : 6 – 7

Your ears shall hear a word behind you, saying, "This is the way, walk in it," Whenever you turn to the right hand or whenever you turn to the left.

~ Isaiah 30 : 21

• Through **the Audible Voice of God**

God can speak to you with an audible voice – just as you can hear the voice of someone. Here is a biblical example:

Then he fell to the ground, and heard a voice saying to him, "Saul, Saul, why are you persecuting Me?" And he said, "Who are You, Lord?" Then the Lord said, "I am Jesus, whom you are persecuting. It is hard for you to kick against the goads."

~Acts 9 : 4 - 5

• Through **Dreams**

There are many instances in the Bible, when God clearly communicates through dreams.

But while he thought about these things, behold, an angel of the Lord appeared to him in a dream, saying, "Joseph, son of David, do not be afraid to take to you Mary your wife, for that which is conceived in her is of the Holy Spirit. And she will bring forth a Son, and you shall call His name Jesus, for He will save His people from their sins."

~ Matthew 1 : 20 - 21

- Through **Visions**

God speaks through visions. A vision is a mental picture given by God.

The next day, as they went on their journey and drew near the city, Peter went up on the housetop to pray, about the sixth hour. Then he became very hungry and wanted to eat; but while they made ready, he fell into a trance and saw heaven opened and an object like a great sheet bound at the four corners, descending to him and let down to the earth. In it were all kinds of four-footed animals of the earth, wild beasts, creeping things, and birds of the air. And a voice came to him, "Rise, Peter; kill and eat." But Peter said, "Not so, Lord! For I have never eaten anything common or unclean." And a voice spoke to him again the second time, "What God has cleansed you must not call common." This was done three times. And the object was taken up into heaven again.

~ Acts 10 : 9 – 18

- Through **Angels**

God can speak to us through angels. This is biblical, but sometimes there's a confusion brought on this subject by people who are practicing the worship of angels. We do not worship or command angels, but God can use angels to bring forth His message.

Now in the sixth month the angel Gabriel was sent by God to a city of Galilee named Nazareth, to a virgin betrothed to a man whose name was Joseph, of the house of David. The virgin's name was Mary. And having come in, the angel said to her, "Rejoice, highly favored one, the Lord is with you; blessed are you among women!" But when she saw him, she was troubled at his saying, and considered what manner of greeting this was. Then the angel said to her, "Do not be afraid, Mary, for you have found favor with God. And behold, you will conceive in your womb and bring forth a Son, and shall call His name Jesus. He will be great, and will be called the Son of the Highest; and the Lord God will give Him the throne of His father David. And He will reign over the house of Jacob forever, and of His kingdom there will be no end." Then Mary said to the angel, "How can this be, since I do not know a man?" And the angel answered and said to her, "The Holy Spirit will come upon you, and the power of the Highest will overshadow you; therefore, also, that Holy One who is to be born will be called the Son of God. Now indeed, Elizabeth your relative has also conceived a son in her old age; and this is now the sixth month for her who was called barren. For with God nothing will be impossible." Then Mary said, "Behold the maidservant of the Lord! Let it be to me according to your word." And the angel departed from her.

~ Luke 1: 26 - 38

• By **Inner Conviction and Peace**

It is similar to the inner, still, small voice of Holy Spirit. God can give you deep conviction and inner peace about something.

If you want to be used by God in the word of knowledge, you need to know that you are just the messenger. You are a go-between… an intermediary. You are passing on to others information from the Holy Spirit that He wants them to know at this time in their life. It is just like a postman: he's employed to deliver a message to pre-appointed people. His job is to take the message to the person whose name is on the envelope. It is not the postman's message; it comes from the sender. The postman doesn't have to know or understand the lifestyle of the person to whom the letter is addressed. His job is simply to deliver the message – whether he understands it or not. If the postman gets careless or steps outside his realm of authority, then there is every possibility that the message will be delayed or even delivered to the wrong person! That might bring confusion. Likewise, in the Holy Spirit ministry, our "employer" – the Holy Spirit – asks us to deliver a message to a certain person.

> *It is not "our" message and the message is not for us.*
> *We are simply the delivery person.*

When we do just as the Holy Spirit asks us – no more and no less – then, the message (the word of knowledge) will be delivered to the right person, in the right place, at the right time.

Remember, the Holy Spirit is the Spirit of truth. (John 14 : 15 - 17; John 15 : 26; John 16 : 13 - 15). It is when we try to interfere with that process that the Gifts of the Holy Spirit fall into discredit. Once that happens repeatedly, people will be turned off to the messenger, and not receive any words from them in their hearts – even if they appear to show otherwise at the time of reception or ministry. This example also applies to some of the other gifts.

There is only one Holy Spirit, but there are many different ways the word of knowledge can operate. God uses our personalities, and, as they are all different, there can be quite a variety of ways the gift can function. Don't be afraid of this variety.

Now there are distinctive varieties and distributions of endowments (extraordinary powers distinguishing certain Christians, due to the power of divine grace operating in their souls by the Holy Spirit) and they vary, but the (Holy) Spirit remains the same. And there are distinctive varieties of service and ministration, but it is the same Lord (Who is served). And there are distinctive varieties of operation — of working to accomplish things — but it is the same God Who inspires and energizes them all in all.

~ 1 Corinthians 12 : 4 – 6 AMP

A man came to the altar one day after a meeting and asked me if I could pray for him, he told me that he had financial problems. As I began to pray for him, I stopped. The Spirit of God showed me that he was not paying his tithes. So I asked him, "Do you pay your tithes?" He said, "No." I said, "That's your problem. If you take care of that, God will take care of the rest."

I was going through a prayer line when, suddenly, I stopped in front of a woman and I laid hands on her ears and commanded her ears to be healed in the Name of Jesus. She was instantly healed by the power of God after being deaf for 35 years. I did not know with my natural knowledge that this lady was deaf until I stopped in front of her and the Holy Spirit revealed her condition to me. He revealed it so that His name would be glorified.

Numerous examples of the Word of Knowledge can be found in the Bible. I am just relating a few here and I am giving you some of my personal experiences.

New Testament Examples:

✛ Saul's eyes were healed.

Paul was praying and needed a healing. God gave a word of knowledge to Ananias with specific information: the house where Saul was, the name of the street, and Saul's name. As a result Saul received his breakthrough.

Now there was a certain disciple at Damascus named Ananias; and to him the Lord said in a vision, "Ananias." And he said, "Here I am, Lord." So the Lord said to him, "Arise and go to the street called Straight, and inquire at the house of Judas for one called Saul of Tarsus, for behold, he is praying. And in a vision he has seen a man named Ananias coming in and putting his hand on him, so that he might receive his sight." Then Ananias answered, "Lord, I have heard from many about this man, how much harm he has done to Your saints in Jerusalem. And here he has authority from the chief priests to bind all who call on Your name." But the Lord said to him, "Go, for he is a chosen vessel of Mine to bear My name before Gentiles, kings, and the children of Israel. For I will show him how many things he must suffer for My name's sake." And Ananias went his way and entered the house; and laying his hands on him he said, "Brother Saul, the Lord Jesus, who appeared to you on the road as you came, has sent me that you may receive your sight and be filled with the Holy Spirit." Immediately there fell from his eyes something like scales, and he received his sight at once; and he arose and was baptized. So when he had received food, he was strengthened. Then Saul spent some days with the disciples at Damascus.

~ Acts 9 : 10 – 19

This becomes a point of encouragement to all of us: that we can have faith in God in difficult times. We can pray and God can give instructions to Christians that are sensitive to the Holy Spirit with your name, your address, your condition, and your need. This is what happened with Saul and Ananias. There is a lesson to be learned by all of us: that God can use us to be an answer to other people's prayers. Therefore, be sensitive to the Holy Spirit. You may be that person that God wants to use to impact another person's life.

✦ Paul received a warning to get out of Jerusalem quickly.

Paul was given a warning through a word of knowledge.

Now it happened, when I returned to Jerusalem and was praying in the temple, that I was in a trance and saw Him saying to me, "Make haste and get out of Jerusalem quickly, for they will not receive your testimony concerning Me". So I said, "Lord, they know that in every synagogue I imprisoned and beat those who believe on You. And when the blood of Your martyr Stephen was shed, I also was standing by consenting to his death, and guarding the clothes of those who were killing him." Then He said to me, "Depart, for I will send you far from here to the Gentiles."

~ Acts 22 : 17 – 21

This is a perfect example of how the life of a Christian can be preserved through a word of knowledge. I remember recently when I felt impressed to cancel a gathering that we were supposed to have in Manila in the Philippines. We had planned the meeting a year earlier, and it was supposed to take place in two months. We usually never cancel a prior commitment. My wife asked me why we should cancel it when we would already be in the region. There was no logical explanation for why I decided not to do the meetings, except that I received this information in my spirit. But, two months later, we understood why. At the time we would have been in Manila, the entire city flooded because of a heavy rain, and there would have been no possibility to conduct the meetings. This is how the word of knowledge can help us in our daily life.

✟ Cornelius received instructions to find Simon Peter.

An angel gave Cornelius a word of knowledge on how he would find Peter. It is possible to have angelical visitations for God's purpose in your life or in His Kingdom.

There was a certain man in Caesarea called Cornelius, a centurion of what was called the Italian Regiment, a devout man and one who feared God with all his household, who gave alms generously to the people, and prayed to God always. About the ninth hour of the day he saw clearly in a vision an angel of God coming in and saying to him, "Cornelius!" And when he observed him, he was afraid, and said, "What is it, lord?" So he said to him, "Your prayers and your alms have come up for a memorial before God. Now send men to Joppa, and send for Simon whose surname is Peter. He is lodging with Simon, a tanner, whose house is by the sea. He will tell you what you must do." And when the angel who spoke to him had departed, Cornelius called two of his household servants and a devout soldier from among those who waited on him continually. So when he had explained all these things to them, he sent them to Joppa.

~ Acts 10 : 1 – 8

We can learn from Cornelius. The scripture clearly says that Cornelius was a devout man: he feared God (with his entire household), he generously gave alms to people, and he prayed to God always. This is a great example for those that want to be used by God. His devotion to God positioned him to experience the supernatural. Cornelius' devotion in the privacy of his home created a memorial before God.

✦ Jesus spoke to the woman at the well.

In John 4 : 15 – 19, we read about Jesus ministering to the Samaritan woman and bringing great change into her life through a word of knowledge.

Jesus said to her, "Go, call your husband, and come here." The woman answered and said, "I have no husband." Jesus said to her, "You have well said. 'I have no husband,' for you have had five husbands, and the one whom you now have is not your husband; in that you spoke truly." The woman said to Him, "Sir, I perceive (see) that you are a prophet (public expounder)."

The impact of this word was a transformed life on the woman's part, and many of the Samaritans became believers. Revival came to their village!

While I was preaching one day, I was quickened in my Spirit to stop and minister to a man. I said to him, "Every time you try to take a step forward, you take three steps backward. You have been having problems in your marriage, and you are far from God." I said to his wife beside him, "You have been praying for him for a long time and have cried many times at night, but, today is your day of breakthrough because God is turning his life around." At the end of the service they told me that the woman was a Christian, but her husband was not. He had given her many problems for many years. That day, he was at church for the first time, and gave his life to Jesus after the word of knowledge came. God revealed the family's problems to him, and showed the man that He was real. This was a breakthrough for their family and for his salvation. It brought real change in their marriage, family, and spiritual life.

✦ Peter received a revelation that helped him break his prejudice against the Gentiles.

Peter's perspective was changed through a word of knowledge that came through a visitation. Because of his revelation, the Gospel was able to reach the Gentiles.

The next day, as they went on their journey and drew near the city, Peter went up on the housetop to pray, about the sixth hour. Then he became very hungry and wanted to eat; but while they made ready, he fell into a trance and saw heaven opened and an object like a great sheet bound at the four corners, descending to him and let down to the earth. In it were all kinds of four-footed animals of the earth, wild beasts, creeping things, and birds of the air. And a voice came to him, "Rise, Peter; kill and eat." But Peter said, "Not so, Lord! For I have never eaten anything common or unclean." And a voice spoke to him again the second time, "What God has cleansed you must not call common." This was done three times. And the object was taken up into heaven again.

~ Acts 10 : 9 – 17

And when Peter came up to Jerusalem, those of the circumcision contended with him, saying, "You went in to uncircumcised men and ate with them!" But Peter explained it to them in order from the beginning, saying: "I was in the city of Joppa praying; and in a trance I saw a vision, an object descending like a great sheet, let down from heaven by four corners; and it came to me. When I observed it intently and considered, I saw four-footed animals of the earth, wild beasts, creeping things, and birds of the air. And I heard a voice saying to me, 'Rise, Peter; kill and eat.' But I said, 'Not so, Lord! For nothing common or unclean has at any time entered my mouth.' But the voice answered me again from heaven, 'What God has cleansed you must not call common.' Now this was done three times, and all were drawn up again into heaven. At that very moment, three men stood before the house where I was, having been sent to me from Caesarea. Then the Spirit told me to go with them, doubting nothing. Moreover these six brethren accompanied me, and we entered the man's house. And he told us how he had seen an angel standing in his house, who said to him, 'Send men to Joppa, and call for Simon whose surname is Peter, who will tell you words by which you and all your household will be saved.' And as I began to speak, the Holy Spirit fell upon them, as upon us at the beginning. Then I remembered the word of the Lord, how He said, 'John indeed baptized with water, but you shall be baptized with the Holy Spirit.' If therefore God gave them the same gift as He gave us when we believed on the Lord Jesus Christ, who was I that I could withstand God?" When they heard these things they became silent; and they glorified God, saying, "Then God has also granted to the Gentiles repentance to life." Now those who were scattered after the persecution that arose over Stephen traveled as far as Phoenicia, Cyprus, and Antioch, preaching the word to no one but the Jews only.

~ Acts 11 : 2 – 19

Sometimes we don't feel skilled or adequate to minister to certain groups of people, but the word of knowledge can give us revelation, strategies, and insight that will help us go beyond the obstacles so that we can reach every appointed person.

✦ Three men were looking for Peter.

Peter was wondering about the vision that he had received, but the word of knowledge brought confirmation to Peter.

Now while Peter wondered within himself what this vision which he had seen meant, behold, the men who had been sent from Cornelius had made inquiry for Simon's house, and stood before the gate. And they called and asked whether Simon, whose surname was Peter, was lodging there. While Peter thought about the vision, the Spirit said to him, "Behold, three men are seeking you. Arise therefore, go down and go with them, doubting nothing; for I have sent them." Then Peter went down to the men who had been sent to him from Cornelius, and said, "Yes, I am he whom you seek. For what reason have you come?"

~ Acts 10 : 17 - 21

The word of knowledge can bring confirmation to us. Many times we wonder about things that we may receive in the Spirit through visions, dreams, or words that we received ourselves or from others. We shouldn't be moved only by what we see or by our emotions, but we should allow the Spirit of God to lead us in everything we do for God. Peter received a confirmation from God.

It is important to receive confirmation after initiation.

✦ The prophets at Antioch heard God's instructions.

God used the word of knowledge to help the church leadership in Antioch to know that Barnabas and Paul were to be separated (set apart) for the work of God.

Now in the church that was at Antioch there were certain prophets and teachers: Barnabas, Simeon who was called Niger, Lucius of Cyrene, Manaen who had been brought up with Herod the tetrarch, and Saul. As they ministered to the Lord and fasted, the Holy Spirit said, "Now separate to Me Barnabas and Saul for the work to which I have called them." Then, having fasted and prayed, and laid hands on them, they sent them away. So, being sent out by the Holy Spirit, they went down to Seleucia, and from there they sailed to Cyprus.

~ Acts 13 : 1 – 4

The word of knowledge can be used in the appointing of leaders in ministry or in the market place. The word of knowledge can help us know who to work with, and who not to work with. The apostle Paul didn't have the best resume or biography. Someone looking in the natural may have said, "He's an ex-murderer; we can't have him as a leader in the church." Sometimes we look at natural things to make our choices, but the word of knowledge can help us choose whom we can work with. Even though the person God has revealed to you may not look qualified, you will be amazed by what God does through them.

✦ Philip was told to jump on the Ethiopian's chariot.

Philip received a word from an angel to go to a specific road and minister to an Ethiopian eunuch.

Now an angel of the Lord spoke to Philip, saying, "Arise and go toward the south along the road which goes down from Jerusalem to Gaza." This is desert. So he arose and went. And behold, a man of Ethiopia, a eunuch of great authority under Candace the queen of the Ethiopians, who had charge of all her treasury, and had come to Jerusalem to worship, was returning. And sitting in his chariot, he was reading Isaiah the prophet. Then the Spirit said to Philip, "Go near and overtake this chariot." So Philip ran to him, and heard him reading the prophet Isaiah, and said, "Do you understand what you are reading?" And he said, "How can I, unless someone guides me?" And he asked Philip to come up and sit with him. The place in the Scripture which he read was this: "He was led as a sheep to the slaughter; And as a lamb before its shearer is silent, So He opened not His mouth. In His humiliation His justice was taken away, and who will declare His generation? For His life is taken from the earth." So the eunuch answered Philip and said, "I ask you, of whom does the prophet say this, of himself or of some other man?" Then Philip opened his mouth, and beginning at this Scripture, preached Jesus to him. Now as they went down the road, they came to some water. And the eunuch said, "See, here is water. What hinders me from being baptized?" Then Philip said, "If you believe with all your heart, you may." And he answered and said, "I believe that Jesus Christ is the Son of God." So he commanded the chariot to stand still. And both Philip and the eunuch went down into the water, and he baptized him. Now when they came up out of the water, the Spirit of the Lord caught Philip away, so that the eunuch saw him no more; and he went on his way rejoicing. But Philip was found at Azotus. And passing through, he reached in all the cities till he came to Caesarea.

~ Acts 8 : 26 – 40

This is a good example of prophetic evangelism. Some people get saved through church meetings or crusades, but that's not always the case. God wants to use you in prophetic evangelism just as he did with Philip. He wants you to use the word of knowledge on the street, at your job, in your school, in your family, with your friends, or any other place.

For many years I used to go do evangelism in New Orleans during Mardi Gras. This was a very dark place and many times the people who went there to party would try to disturb our street ministry. On one occasion, I was trying to witness to a group of five people when, suddenly, a man tried to split the group and he started to shout, "We are all Christians. Go home. Stop messing up our party." He said this repeatedly, when suddenly, the Holy Spirit spoke to me about his life. So, I asked him a question, "If you are a Christian as you said, 'We are all Christians,' why do you beat up your wife, and why did you punch her yesterday?" The man stopped suddenly, and looked at me and said, "I punched her, and I beat her up sometimes because she messes with me." I said, "This is not what the Bible says we should do. You have no reason to be here in the street. You should be home with your family." He said to me, "You are right. I am going home." He took his party necklaces off, threw them on the ground, and went home. This is a perfect example of how the word of knowledge can be used in prophetic evangelism.

✦ **Peter exposed the sin of Ananias and Sapphira.**

Peter knew by a word of knowledge that Ananias and Sapphira were lying.

But a certain man named Ananias, with Sapphira his wife, sold a possession. And he kept back part of the proceeds, his wife also being aware of it, and brought a certain part and laid it at the apostles' feet. But Peter said, "Ananias, why has Satan filled your heart to lie to the Holy Spirit and keep back part of the price of the land for yourself? While it remained, was it not your own? And after it was sold, was it not in your own control? Why have you conceived this thing in your heart? You have not lied to men but to God." Then Ananias, hearing these words, fell down and breathed his last. So great fear came upon all those who heard these things. And the young men arose and wrapped him up, carried him out, and buried him. Now it was about three hours later when his wife came in, not knowing what had happened. And Peter answered her, "Tell me whether you sold the land for so much?" She said, "Yes, for so much." Then Peter said to her, "How is it that you have agreed together to test the Spirit of the Lord? Look, the feet of those who have buried your husband are at the door, and they will carry you out." Then immediately she fell down at his feet and breathed her last. And the young men came in and found her dead, and carrying her out, buried her by her husband. So great fear came upon all the church and upon all who heard these things.

~ Acts 5 : 1 – 11

This is a perfect example of how God can enable someone to look into the heart or mind of a man or woman, and to know his or her secrets and intentions. This is very important for those in leadership. The word of knowledge will help you lead effectively.

Old Testament Examples:

We can see the word of knowledge operating through some men of God in the Old Testament.

✦ Elijah received a command from God to present himself to King Ahab.

And it came to pass after many days that the word of the Lord came to Elijah, in the third year, saying, "Go, present yourself to Ahab, and I will send rain on the earth." So Elijah went to present himself to Ahab; and there was a severe famine in Samaria.

~ 1 Kings 18 : 1 – 2

✦ Elijah anointed Elisha as his successor.

Then the Lord said to him: "Go, return on your way to the Wilderness of Damascus; and when you arrive, anoint Hazael as king over Syria. Also you shall anoint Jehu the son of Nimshi as king over Israel. And Elisha the son of Shaphat of Abel Meholah you shall anoint as prophet in your place."

~ 1 Kings 19 : 15 - 16

✦ Elisha knew about the corruption of his servant Gehazi.

But Gehazi, the servant of Elisha the man of God, said, "Look, my master has spared Naaman this Syrian, while not receiving from his hands what he brought; but as the Lord lives, I will run after him and take something from him." So Gehazi pursued Naaman. When Naaman saw him running after him, he got down from the chariot to meet him, and said, "Is all well?" And he said, "All is well. My master has sent me, saying, 'Indeed, just now two young men of the sons of the prophets have come to me from the mountains of Ephraim.

Please give them a talent of silver and two changes of garments.'" So Naaman said, "Please, take two talents." And he urged him, and bound two talents of silver in two bags, with two changes of garments, and handed them to two of his servants; and they carried them on ahead of him. When he came to the citadel, he took them from their hand, and stored them away in the house; then he let the men go, and they departed. Now he went in and stood before his master. Elisha said to him, "Where did you go, Gehazi?" And he said, "Your servant did not go anywhere." Then he said to him, "Did not my heart go with you when the man turned back from his chariot to meet you? Is it time to receive money and to receive clothing, olive groves and vineyards, sheep and oxen, male and female servants? Therefore the leprosy of Naaman shall cling to you and your descendants forever." And he went out from his presence leprous, as white as snow.

~ 2 Kings 5 : 20 – 27

✦ Samuel speaks of finding Saul's donkeys and the call of God on Saul.

Now the Lord had told Samuel in his ear the day before Saul came, saying, "Tomorrow about this time I will send you a man from the land of Benjamin, and you shall anoint him commander over My people Israel, that he may save My people from the hand of the Philistines; for I have looked upon My people, because their cry has come to Me." So when Samuel saw Saul, the Lord said to him, "There he is, the man of whom I spoke to you. This one shall reign over My people." Then Saul drew near to Samuel in the gate, and said, "Please tell me, where is the seer's house?" Samuel answered Saul and said, "I am the seer. Go up before me to the high place, for you shall eat with me today; and tomorrow I will let you go and will tell you all that is in your heart. But as for your donkeys that were lost three days ago, do not be anxious about them, for they have been found. And on whom is all the desire of Israel? Is it not on you and on all your father's house?" And Saul answered and said, "Am I not a Benjamite, of the smallest of the tribes of Israel, and my family the least of all the families of the tribe of Benjamin? Why then do you speak like this to me?" Now Samuel took Saul and his servant and brought them into the hall, and had them sit in the place of honor among those who were invited; there were about thirty persons. And Samuel said to the cook, "Bring the portion which I gave you, of which I said to you, 'Set it apart.'" So the cook took up the thigh with its upper part and set it before Saul. And Samuel said, "Here it is, what was kept back. It was set apart for you. Eat; for until this time it has been kept for you, since I said I invited the people." So Saul ate with Samuel that day. When they had come down from the high place into the city, Samuel spoke with Saul on the top of the house. They arose early; and it was about the dawning of the day that Samuel called to Saul on the top of the house, saying, "Get up, that I may send you on your way." And Saul arose, and both of them went outside, he and Samuel. As they were going down to the outskirts of the city, Samuel said to Saul, "Tell the servant to go on ahead of us." And he went on. "But you stand here awhile, that I may announce to you the word of God."

~ I Samuel 9 : 15 – 27

When we give a word of knowledge to others, sometimes there is in operation (at that one delivery) more than just the word of knowledge. Another of the nine gifts can be in operation as well.

The gifts of the word of wisdom and the word of knowledge function together; knowledge is raw material and wisdom builds on it.

For example, there can be:

- **The word of knowledge** – the information or ministry to pass on.
- **The word of wisdom** – knowing the time and place to give a word of knowledge.
- **The gift of discerning of spirits** – depending on the message and circumstances, discerning of spirits helps you to know the spirit of the person to whom you are to minister.
- **The gift of prophecy** – some words of knowledge come out to congregations in prophecy.
- **The gift of faith** – it takes this gift to make known spiritual or supernaturally-gained knowledge about others.
- **The gift of healing** – where a word of knowledge involves the physical condition of a person.
- **The working of miracles** – where there is a miraculous confirmation, straight-away, of the word of knowledge given.

2. Word of Wisdom

Wisdom is applying knowledge with skill.

To understand what the word of wisdom is, we need to understand what it is not.

✓ **It is not spiritual insight.**

This gift is not the ability to give spiritual insight. One may be mature in the Lord's Word and have many years of experience in rightly dividing the Word of truth, and yet, not have this supernatural spiritual gift. There is a vast difference between spiritual fruit and spiritual gifts. The fruit of the Spirit is something one must work at and be dedicated to obtaining. The gifts of the Spirit are manifested as the Spirit wills.

But the manifestation of the Spirit is given to each one for the profit of all.

~ 1 Corinthians 12 : 7

✓ It is not learned by the natural mind.

The word of wisdom is not learned by the natural mind. It cannot be acquired by education, training, methods, or natural wisdom in any sense. Man, in his natural state, does not have supernatural wisdom. He may have natural logic, but logic and natural wisdom err in that they always put the individual first. Supernatural wisdom comes only from God through Jesus Christ, who "became for us wisdom from God." Only those plugged into God can receive supernatural wisdom.

> *You can buy education, but the gift of wisdom is a gift from God.*

A man without the Spirit may use methods which prove, many times, both helpful and harmful. What works beautifully in one situation may not work at all in another... especially when it comes to churches. Many pastors and church workers have problems that no one but God can help them with. No man knows the solution. The question is, then, "Why not go to God?" Conferences and seminars are fun to go to, but they are not to be confused with the spiritual gift of the word of wisdom.

✓ **It is not just wisdom.**

This gift is not just wisdom which every Christian gains from studying God's Word. Solomon had wisdom from God; but only once or twice did he receive a word of wisdom or a special revelation for a special problem. A young convert may have the revelation gift of the word of wisdom and have very little biblical wisdom because of a lack of spiritual maturity.

✓ **It is not psychology.**

The supernatural gift of the word of wisdom is not something one learns in a classroom studying the natural tendencies of mankind. It is not a science of the mind. It is not any earthly wisdom. It is supernaturally given.

✓ **It is not all of God's wisdom.**

This gift is the gift of the word of wisdom; it is not the gift of wisdom. God speaks to us giving us a word or a portion of His wisdom. He doesn't give us the whole storehouse of His wisdom.

✓ **It is not just a guess or a new idea.**

This gift is not just a guess or a new idea which accidentally pops into one's head. The same experience happens to lost people who do not have the Holy Spirit.

✓ **It is not just for preachers and church leaders.**

This gift is not just for those who are preachers and church leaders or special workers in the church. It is a gift for all who have received the Holy Spirit and who are faced with a problem beyond their own understanding. It is for all who want to be used by God.

The Word of Wisdom Is:

Let us, first of all, break it down to its original Greek meaning:

• "Word": "logos" is the spoken word — not the written word.

• "Wisdom": "sophia" or "sofia": meaning, *cleverness; skill; a right application of knowledge; the result of an ability to think and act utilizing knowledge, experience, understanding, common sense, and insight.*

Wisdom is knowledge rightly applied.

> *The spiritual gift of the word of wisdom is the supernatural ability to apply knowledge already possessed.*

It is God showing the "what, why, where, when, and how" of a problem. It is the supernatural solution to trouble. It carries the mark of the wisdom of God.

> *God's wisdom beats all other wisdom known to man.*

The word of wisdom is needed in our lives to enable us to share the other gifts of the spirit correctly. For example, it is one thing to receive a word of prophecy, knowledge, faith, healing, etc., but it is entirely another thing to deliver that gift in such a way as to allow it to have its fullest impact. Many people receive information and gifts in the Holy Spirit, but do not always know how to deliver it... nor to whom.

> *If we do not minister in God's wisdom, we can make mistakes, cause disrespect for the gifts,*
> *be insensitive to the person or people we are delivering the information to, and even cause offense.*

The gift may be right, but the manner of delivering it may be wrong. The word of wisdom helps us to deliver it in the right way - the right application of knowledge. It may come by visions, dreams, a revelation, a still small voice, or an audible voice. God speaks in many ways and there are diversities of operation.

There are diversities of activities, but it is the same God who works all in all.

~ I Corinthians 12 : 6

The gift of the word of wisdom is also the revealing of the future prophetically. It is speaking hidden truths of what is not known. Furthermore, this gift involves having a sense of divine direction – being led by the Holy Spirit to act appropriately in a given set of circumstances, and rightly applying knowledge. The gift of the word of wisdom enables one to express the Holy Spirit's revelation, knowledge or answers to either an individual, to a group of people, or to a church.

It is very important that we apply things rightly. In the biblical account of the wise and foolish men who built their houses - one on a rock, the other on the sand - the wise man rightly applied the word of Jesus. The foolish man heard exactly the same words from the mouth of the same Jesus, but did not apply them correctly. As a result... he came to ruin.

Therefore whoever hears these sayings of Mine, and does them, I will liken him to a wise man who built his house on the rock: and the rain descended, the floods came, and the winds blew and beat on that house; and it did not fall, for it was founded on the rock. But everyone who hears these sayings of Mine, and does not do them, will be like a foolish man who built his house on the sand: and the rain descended, the floods came, and the winds blew and beat on that house; and it fell. And great was its fall.

~ Matthew 7 : 24 - 27

The word of wisdom comes from the Holy Spirit. Let's make sure we are listening and acting accordingly.

Numerous examples of the word of wisdom can be found in the Bible. I am just relating a few here.

New Testament Examples:

✦ A cripple man healed.

Paul prayed for a cripple man after observing him and seeing that he had faith to be healed.

And they were preaching the gospel there. And in Lystra a certain man without strength in his feet was sitting, a cripple from his mother's womb, who had never walked. This man heard Paul speaking. Paul, observing him intently and seeing that he had faith to be healed, said with a loud voice, "Stand up straight on your feet!" And he leaped and walked.

~ Acts 14 : 7 - 10

This is a good example of spiritual knowledge, skillfully and rightly applied. The crippled man's faith rose as Paul preached. Paul perceived in the spirit what was happening and, through the word of wisdom, knew the right moment to pray for the man, so that he could release his faith to be healed, and he was healed.

✦ Dealing with the spirit of divination in a young woman.

Paul and several disciples were followed by a certain girl possessed by a spirit of divination.

Now it happened, as we went to prayer, that a certain slave girl possessed with a spirit of divination met us, who brought her masters much profit by fortune-telling. This girl followed Paul and us, and cried out, saying, "These men are the servants of the Most High God, who proclaim to us the way of salvation." And this she did for many days. But Paul, greatly annoyed, turned and said to the spirit, "I command you in the name of Jesus Christ to come out of her." And he came out that very hour.

~ Acts 16 : 16 – 18

Paul did not rush immediately to deliver the girl. He waited many days before confronting the spirit of divination in her. That was wisdom. This example does not mean that a similar case would necessarily be handled the same way. We may need to act today, tomorrow, next week, next month, or next year. Let wisdom prevail. Wisdom gets the timing right.

✦ Peter in dealing with Ananias and Sapphira.

A word of wisdom was given to Peter in his dealing with the lies of Ananias and Sapphira.

But a certain man named Ananias, with Sapphira his wife, sold a possession. And he kept back part of the proceeds, his wife also being aware of it, and brought a certain part and laid it at the apostles' feet. But Peter said, "Ananias, why has Satan filled your heart to lie to the Holy Spirit and keep back part of the price of the land for yourself? While it remained, was it not your own? And after it was sold, was it not in your own control? Why have you conceived this thing in your heart? You have not lied to men but to God." Then Ananias, hearing these words, fell down and breathed his last. So great fear came upon all those who heard these things. And the young men arose and wrapped him up, carried him out, and buried him. Now it was about three hours later when his wife came in, not knowing what had happened. And Peter answered her, "Tell me whether you sold the land for so much?" She said, "Yes, for so much." Then Peter said to her, "How is it that you have agreed together to test the Spirit of the Lord? Look, the feet of those who have buried your husband are at the door, and they will carry you out." Then immediately she fell down at his feet and breathed her last. And the young men came in and found her dead, and carrying her out, buried her by her husband. So great fear came upon all the church and upon all who heard these things. And through the hands of the apostles many signs and wonders were done among the people. And they were all with one accord in Solomon's Porch. Yet none of the rest dared join them, but the people esteemed them highly. And believers were increasingly added to the Lord, multitudes of both men and women, so that they brought the sick out into the streets and laid them on beds and couches, that at least the shadow of Peter passing by might fall on some of them. Also a multitude gathered from the surrounding cities to Jerusalem, bringing sick people and those who were tormented by unclean spirits, and they were all healed.

~ Acts 5 : 1 – 16

Peter used the word of wisdom to make sure that both Ananias and Sapphira exposed their own evil doings and, so, suffered the consequences of their own actions. He did not accuse Sapphira on the confession of her husband alone, but wisely heard from her as well.

Old Testament Examples:

The word of wisdom operated through some men of God in the Old Testament.

✦ Solomon used Godly wisdom to settle a dispute between two women.

And all Israel heard of the judgment which the king had rendered; and they feared the king, for they saw that the wisdom of God was in him to administer justice.

~ I Kings 3 : 28

A good Old Testament example is that of Solomon passing judgment on the women who were arguing over their two children. One child was dead and one was alive. Both women were claiming that the remaining live child was theirs and the dead child was the other's. Solomon called for a sword to divide the remaining live child in two, so the women could each have half! When Solomon made that decision known, the true mother of the living child cried out to give her child to the other woman in order to save its life. Solomon then knew who the real mother was. This judgment from Solomon caused all of Israel to see that the wisdom of God was in him to do judgment.

✦ Elisha received a wise strategy through the word of wisdom in times of war.

"But now bring me a musician." Then it happened, when the musician played, that the hand of the Lord came upon him. And he said, "Thus says the Lord: 'Make this valley full of ditches.'"

~ 2 Kings 3 : 15 - 16

Three kings told Elisha that the Moabites were coming to capture them. At first, Elisha did not know what to do. He called for a minstrel and listened and praised the Lord. Then a gift of the word of wisdom was given to him, and Elisha told them to make the valley full of ditches. The Moabites were defeated and three kingdoms were saved.

One of the things that you will need is the word of wisdom if you want to be used by God, to fulfill God's purposes, and to lead others into all that God has for them. Let's allow the person of the Holy Spirit to share His wisdom, revelation, knowledge, and understanding with us in ways that will tremendously bless ourselves and those we meet.

While ministering at a church service, I received a word of knowledge concerning someone that had planned to kill somebody after the service. The moment I gave the word in front of the church, I also received a word of wisdom to tell that person to come and talk to me discretely after the service was dismissed. At the end of the service, a man approached me saying that he had decided to kill his girlfriend after the service, and told God if he didn't stop him during the service that he was going to do it. He hugged me and began to cry. It was the supernatural solution for that problem at that moment. A life was saved by the word of knowledge, but I believe the man came forward at the end because of the word of wisdom. There was no embarrassment for him. The word of wisdom helped me deliver the message wisely. What if I had told him to come to the front during my message when I received the word of knowledge? It could have created gossip, and perhaps the man wouldn't have come forward and this could have created confusion in the meeting.

The gift of the word of wisdom works interactively with the other two revelation gifts: knowledge and discernment.

3. Discernment of Spirits

To understand what discernment of spirits is, we need to understand what it is not.

✓ **It is not suspicion.**
The gift of discerning of spirits is not simply being suspicious of others. A person who has never had the Holy Spirit can be suspicious of everyone, and often they are.

> *Suspicion is like a pair of sunglasses,*
> *it makes all the world look dark.*

✓ **It is not the gift of criticism.**
This gift is not discerning of faults, but of spirits. It's the influence of the devil which causes people to accuse one another. The devil is called the accuser of the brethren.

Then I heard a loud voice saying in heaven, "Now salvation, and strength, and the kingdom of our God, and the power of His Christ have come, for the accuser of our brethren, who accused them before our God day and night, has been cast down."

~ Revelation 12 : 10

> *People always emphasize the negative;*
> *no one puts up a sign: Beware Nice Dog.*

If you take pleasure in criticism, it's time to hold your tongue.

Judge not, that you be not judged. For with what judgment you judge, you will be judged; and with the measure you use, it will be measured back to you. And why do you look at the speck in your brother's eye, but do not consider the plank in your own eye? Or how can you say to your brother, "Let me remove the speck from your eye"; and look, a plank is in your own eye? Hypocrite! First remove the plank from your own eye, and then you will see clearly to remove the speck from your brother's eye. Do not give what is holy to the dogs; nor cast your pearls before swine, lest they trample them under their feet, and turn and tear you in pieces.

~ Matthew 7 : 1 - 6

One of the hardest things to take is one of the easiest things to give: criticism. Many of the suspicions we have of others are formed from the knowledge we have of ourselves. Our own faults are sometimes the ones we condemn most quickly in others. Most of the time people criticize in order to forget their own weakness. Never accuse others to excuse yourself.

> *You cannot whitewash yourself by blackening others.*

Sometimes to speak ill of others is a dishonest way of praising ourselves.

> *As long as you belittle, you will be little.*

✓ It is not the gift of discernment.

This gift is not simply the ability to discern things; it is the gift of discerning of spirits. Most anyone can discern different colors, shapes, and sizes of things, but it takes a supernatural gift from God to discern spirits.

✓ It is not spiritism.

This gift is not to be confused with spiritism, which is condemned in the scriptures. The spirits of our dead relatives are not floating around in our houses or in the air outside. They are either with Jesus, or else they have gone to hell. As spiritism and demon-possessed people increase in number, we need the gift of discerning of spirits more and more.

There shall not be found among you anyone who... conjures spells, or a medium, or a spiritist, or one who calls up the dead. For all who do these things are an abomination to the Lord, and because of these abominations the Lord your God drives them out from before you.

~ Deuteronomy 18 : 10a, 11 - 12

And when they say to you, "Seek those who are mediums and wizards, who whisper and mutter," should not a people seek their God? Should they seek the dead on behalf of the living? To the law and to the testimony! If they do not speak according to this word, it is because there is no light in them.

~ Isaiah 8 : 19 - 20

Discernment of Spirits Is:

Let us, first of all, break it down to its original Greek meaning:

• "Discerning": "diakrisis": meaning, a thorough judging; a distinguishing; discerning clearly; discriminating, recognizing, or perceiving clearly the differences.

> *Discerning of spirits is God's Spirit informing a spirit-filled Christian, which type of spirit is being manifested.*
> *It is a supernatural look into the spiritual world.*

Discerning of spirits is the supernatural ability given by the Holy Spirit to perceive the source of a spiritual manifestation and determine whether it is of God, of the devil (Acts 16 : 16 - 18), of man (Acts 8 : 18 - 23), or of the world. This gift discerns both good and bad spirits. It gives the Christian insight into the supernatural world. It is to enable the person to know the motivation behind a situation or person.

Discerning of spirits must be done by the power of the Holy Spirit; He bears witness with our spirit when something is or is not of God. The gift of discerning of spirits is the supernatural power to detect the realm of the spirits and their activities. It implies the power of spiritual insight - the supernatural revelation of plans and purposes of the enemy and his forces. This gift can show the kinds of spirits which are working in people today — such as unclean spirits, deaf and dumb spirits, demonic spirits, oppressing spirits, or even the Holy Spirit.

This gift is a requirement for all who are used of God in the deliverance ministry. Without it, those who seek to minister deliverance are simply left guessing at whether or not a demonic spirit is actually present, and if so, what type of demonic spirit it is. This gift is also a requirement of all those who operate in the prophetic ministry. Without it, they would not be able to sit by and judge the prophesies of others as they are called to do in ~ I Corinthians 14 : 29 which says, *"Let two or three prophets speak, and let the others judge."*

This gift is given to keep the church safe from demonic presence and practices. It is a gift which protects and guards your Christian life.

How to Test a Spirit

You can discern or test whether or not a spirit is of God the following three ways:

1.   Observing what a person does. Jesus explained that false prophets are known by their fruit - by their conduct and actions.

Beware of false prophets, who come to you in sheep's clothing, but inwardly they are ravenous wolves. You will know them by their fruits. Do men gather grapes from thorn bushes or figs from thistles? Even so, every good tree bears good fruit, but a bad tree bears bad fruit. A good tree cannot bear bad fruit, nor can a bad tree bear good fruit. Every tree that does not bear good fruit is cut down and thrown into the fire. Therefore by their fruits you will know them.

~ Matthew 7 : 15 - 20

2.   Observing whether or not a person exalts Jesus Christ as the Son of God and as Lord and Savior.

Therefore I make known to you that no one speaking by the Spirit of God calls Jesus accursed, and no one can say that Jesus is Lord except by the Holy Spirit.

~ I Corinthians 12 : 3

3.   By listening to what a person says. Does their confession line up with the truth of God's Word?

Beloved, do not believe every spirit, but test the spirits, whether they are of God; because many false prophets have gone out into the world. By this you know the Spirit of God: Every spirit that confesses that Jesus Christ has come in the flesh is of God, and every spirit that does not confess that Jesus Christ has come in the flesh is not of God. And this is the spirit of the Antichrist, which you have heard was coming, and is now already in the world.

~ I John 4 : 1 - 3

I remember preaching in Africa, and in the middle of my message, I sensed a spirit of witchcraft in the meeting. I received in my spirit that there were witchdoctors in the meeting. I said, "There are people practicing witchcraft here; God wants to set you free from it." Nobody came forward. Then I shared a story of how a witchdoctor, who was controlling an entire region, had died in one of my meetings after we prayed for somebody in that same meeting whom he had cursed. Immediately, three women got up and were getting ready to walk away from the meeting. The Lord told me that these were the witches who had come to disturb the meeting. I said to them, "You don't have to leave the meeting if you are a witchdoctor." They kept walking. Then I said, "If you die in this meeting, I will pray for you and God will raise you from the dead." Then they turned around and came back to their seats. When I gave an altar call for salvation, they were among the first to get saved. When we prayed for them, they manifested demons and a great deliverance took place. Our God is an awesome God! The witchdoctors got saved and delivered. This is what can happen when you allow God to use you. You will know through discernment what spirit is in operation at your job, in your house, in your family, in the market place, in your ministry, and at your church.

Numerous examples of discernment of spirits can be found in the Bible. Just a few will be related here.

New Testament Examples:

✦ Paul and the slave girl.

Paul discerned the evil spirit behind the slave girl's praise.

Now it happened, as we went to prayer, that a certain slave girl possessed with a spirit of divination met us, who brought her masters much profit by fortune-telling. This girl followed Paul and us, and cried out, saying, "These men are the servants of the Most High God, who proclaim to us the way of salvation." And this she did for many days. But Paul, greatly annoyed, turned and said to the spirit, "I command you in the name of Jesus Christ to come out of her." And he came out that very hour.

~ Acts 16 : 16 – 18

Just because somebody says nice things about you or flatters you, it doesn't mean that the person is sent by God. A certain slave girl, possessed with a spirit of divination, followed Paul and Silas around saying, over-and-over, that they were servants of the most High God. Instead of making her one of the favorite members of the church, Paul cast the demon out of her. Paul had a gift of discerning of spirits from the Holy Spirit to know that she had a demon, and he cast it out of her.

> *Not everything that sounds good comes from God.*

Flattering words can be a mask that hides the reality of what is truly in the heart of somebody.

> *Flattery corrupts both the receiver and the giver.*
> *He that rewards flattery, begs it.*

Let's watch out for flatterers. Don't allow yourself to be deceived by flattering words. Don't believe your own press, because it can corrupt you. Don't surround yourself with people that flatter you, but with people that will tell you the truth.

✦ Dealing with a sorcerer.

Paul, being filled with the Holy Spirit, knew who the sorcerer was. Bar-Jesus sought to turn away Sergius Paulus from the faith. But, Paul first discerned that this evil spirit was there before he spoke.

Now when they had gone through the island to Paphos, they found a certain sorcerer, a false prophet, a Jew whose name was Bar-Jesus, who was with the proconsul, Sergius Paulus, an intelligent man. This man called for Barnabas and Saul and sought to hear the word of God. But Elymas the sorcerer (for so his name is translated) withstood them, seeking the turn the proconsul away from the faith. Then Saul, who also is called Paul, filled with the Holy Spirit, looked intently at him and said, "O full of all deceit and all fraud, you son of the devil, you enemy of all righteousness, will you not cease perverting the straight ways of the Lord?"

~ Acts 13 : 6 – 10

Sometimes we don't understand why people don't receive the Word when we try to minister to them. In this story, we can see how an evil spirit can hinder people from receiving the Word of God. Sometimes it is not the person, but the spirit behind them, that doesn't want them to receive the Word of God. That's why we need discernment when we evangelize or minister to people.

✦ Peter and Simon the sorcerer.

Peter discerned the condition of Simon. Philip had let a man be baptized without discerning the evil spirit that was still in the man. But when Peter started to pray for him, he discerned it and said, "For I perceive that thou art in the gall of bitterness and the bond of iniquity." Simon had believed with his mind and was baptized and converted by Philip, but his heart was not right with God.

Now when the apostles who were at Jerusalem heard that Samaria had received the word of God, they sent Peter and John to them, who, when they had come down, prayed for them that they might receive the Holy Spirit. For as yet He had fallen upon none of them. They had only been baptized in the name of the Lord Jesus. Then they laid hands on them, and they received the Holy Spirit. And when Simon saw that through the laying on of the apostles' hands the Holy Spirit was given, he offered them money, saying, "Give me this power also, that anyone on whom I lay hands may receive the Holy Spirit." But Peter said to him, "Your money perish with you, because you thought that the gift of God could be purchased with money! You have neither part nor portion in this matter, for your heart is not right in the sight of God. Repent therefore of this your wickedness, and pray God if perhaps the thought of your heart may be forgiven you. For I see that you are poisoned by bitterness and bound by iniquity." Then Simon answered and said, "Pray to the Lord for me, that none of the things which you have spoken may come upon me."

~ Acts 8 : 14 - 24

If the gift of discerning of spirits would be more in operation in our churches, there would be less people with perverse spirits and hearts full of wickedness in the church. The operation of discerning of spirits will help them change their hearts as well as their minds.

4.   <u>Diverse Tongues</u>

To understand what the gift of diverse tongues is, we need to understand what it is not.

✓   **It is not the ability to learn foreign languages.**

Some have claimed that the gift of tongues is nothing more than the ability to learn foreign languages. They have claimed that this is an ability which God sometimes gives those who are preparing themselves to go into a foreign country to preach the gospel so they can communicate with those to whom they are going to witness. However, this idea does not line up with the Word of God where Paul plainly states that he doesn't know what he is saying when he speaks in tongues.

For if I pray in a tongue, my spirit prays, but my understanding is unfruitful. (my mind is helping nobody; I don't know what I am saying; my mind is blank).

~ I Corinthians 14 : 14

Paul says his spirit (the inner man) knows, but Paul's mind does not understand it. This plainly rules out the ability to learn a foreign language, because a person who speaks in a foreign language is both able to speak it and understand it.

✓   **It is not something which has passed away.**

Another common argument which is used against the gift of tongues is the idea that this gift has ceased or has been done away with. This faulty idea comes from a misinterpretation of I Corinthians 13 : 8 - 10. It is claimed that this passage of scripture teaches that the gift of tongues ceased when the canon of scripture was completed and that the gift of tongues is no longer in existence. This is based on the idea that "that which is perfect" (of verse 10) is a reference to the canon of scripture. I firmly agree that the scripture is perfect, but I disagree that the perfect thing mentioned here is the scripture. If we allow scripture to interpret scripture, we have an interpretation of Paul's meaning back in 1 Corinthians 1 : 7, where Paul prays under the inspiration of the Holy Spirit that the church would not lose any spiritual gifts until the perfect Lord Jesus returns.

So that you come short in no gift, eagerly waiting for the revelation of our Lord Jesus Christ.

~ 1 Corinthians 1 : 7

Thus, the gift of tongues will definitely be a part of the church and its ministry until the coming of the Lord.

✓ It is not just putting away a filthy mouth.

Some have claimed that the gift of tongues is just a reference to the sanctifying of the tongue of born-again believers. This faulty idea quickly falls apart when one looks at the gift of tongues on the day of Pentecost in Acts 2. It plainly states that those from foreign countries were amazed to hear them speak in their own foreign tongues. Why would anyone be "amazed" or "marvel" at someone speaking without cursing?

And there were dwelling in Jerusalem Jews, devout men, from every nation under heaven. And when this sound occurred, the multitude came together, and were confused, because everyone heard them speak in his own language. Then they were all amazed and marveled, saying to one another, "Look, are not all these who speak Galileans? And how is it that we hear, each in our own language in which we were born?"

~ Acts 2 : 5 - 8

✓ **It is not a sign of immaturity.**

Some have claimed that the gift of tongues is a childish thing which was meant only for the most immature Christians. They have claimed that the more mature Christians go on to better things and eventually cast off the gift of tongues. If this was the case, the Apostle Paul (a mature Christian and apostle) would not have claimed that he spoke in tongues more than all of the immature believers at Corinth. Paul makes this statement:

"I thank my God I speak with tongues more than you all."

~ I Corinthians 14 : 18

✓ **It is not a false gift.**

Some have told me that the gift of tongues is a false gift, and that those who think they are speaking in tongues are actually just fooling themselves. However, our Father in Heaven has promised us in His Word that we would receive the Holy Spirit when we ask for Him, and that our Father would not give us a serpent, a scorpion, or anything false.

If a son asks for bread from any father among you, will he give him a stone? Or if he asks for a fish, will he give him a serpent instead of a fish? Or if he asks for an egg, will he offer him a scorpion? If you then, being evil, know how to give good gifts to your children, how much more will your heavenly Father give the Holy Spirit to those who ask Him!"

~ Luke 11 : 11 - 13

✓ **It is not something to be forbidden in church.**

Do not forbid to speak with tongues.

~ I Corinthians 14 : 39

✓ **It is not of the devil.**
And they were all filled with the Holy Spirit and began to speak with other tongues, as the Spirit gave them utterance.

~ Acts 2 : 4

✓ **It is not a sign of emotionalism.**
Some people say that tongues is a sign of emotionalism to which I have answered with:

And these signs will follow those who believe: In My name they will cast out demons; they will speak with new tongues.

~ Mark 16 : 17

✓ **It is not magnifying self.**
You do not magnify yourself when you speak in tongue. You magnify God, but you edify yourself when you speak in tongues.

For they heard them speak with tongues and magnify God.

~ Acts 10 : 46

He who speaks in a tongue edifies himself.

~ I Corinthians 14 : 4

"Edify" is the Greek word, *oikodomeo,* and it literally means, *to house-build; to strengthen; to restore.*

But you, beloved, building yourselves up on your most holy faith, praying in the Holy Spirit.
~ Jude 20

The Gift of Diverse Tongues Is:

The gift of tongues is a supernatural utterance in a language or languages (earthly or heavenly) which the one doing the speaking does not understand. It is a vocal miracle. It is a miracle of speech.

> *The gift of tongues is the supernatural ability to speak to others and/or to God in a language or utterance never learned by the speaker.*

It is a supernatural utterance in languages not known to the speaker. These languages may be existent in the world, revived from some past culture, or "unknown" in the sense that they are a means of communication inspired by the Holy Spirit. The spiritual gift involves the ability to speak in foreign language(s) not previously studied by uttering sounds which those without the gift of interpretation could not understand.

The gift of tongues may be used:
- To witness. (Acts 2)
- To pray. (1 Corinthians 14 : 2)
- To sing. (1 Corinthians 14 : 15)
- To give thanks. (1 Corinthians 14 : 16 - 17)
- To praise the Lord. (Acts 10 : 46)

The gift of tongues is a sign to the unbelieving Jew who has read or heard the Old Testament prophecies concerning this gift.

Compare 1 Corinthians 14 : 21 - 22 with Isaiah 28 : 11:

In the law it is written: "With men of other tongues and other lips I will speak to this people; and yet, for all that, they will not hear Me," says the Lord. Therefore tongues are for a sign, not to those who believe but to unbelievers; but prophesying is not for unbelievers but for those who believe.

~ 1 Corinthians 14 : 21 - 22

For with stammering lips and another tongue He will speak to this people.

~ Isaiah 28 : 11

Through this gift, the Holy Spirit may pray through a believer and make intercession according to the will of God – causing everything to work together for good.

Likewise the Spirit also helps in our weaknesses. For we do not know what we should pray for as we ought, but the Spirit Himself makes intercession for us with groanings which cannot be uttered. Now He who searches the hearts knows what the mind of the Spirit is, because He makes intercession for the saints according to the will of God. And we know that all things work together for good to those who love God, to those who are the called according to His purpose.

~ Romans 8 : 26 - 28

*The gift of tongues is a free-will gift.
God doesn't force anyone to speak in tongues.
This gift is received by faith and stirred up
by an act of the will.*

- A person can **neglect** a spiritual gift.

Do not neglect the gift that is in you, which was given to you by prophecy with the laying on of the hands of the eldership.

~ 1 Timothy 4 : 14

- A person can **stir up** a spiritual gift.

Therefore I remind you to stir up the gift of God which is in you through the laying on of my hands.

~ 2 Timothy 1 : 6

- The spirits of the prophets **are subject** to the prophets.

And the spirits of the prophets are subject to the prophets.

~ 1 Corinthians 14 : 32

It is obvious from these passages that God does not force a person to use a spiritual gift. God doesn't just take over a person's spirit (inner man) and control that individual's body and mind. This is also why we are encouraged to **desire spiritual gifts.**

We are to desire this gift and seek it.

~ 1 Corinthians 14 : 1

God will not force the gift of tongues on us. On the other hand, God does not tease His people. He doesn't tell us to desire something, and then, refuse to give us what He has told us to desire.

> *The gift of tongues is a product of both God and man.*

Every believer has a part to play in speaking in tongues; for the Spirit gives you utterance, and you do the talking. You will be doing the talking in the flesh. After all, God said He would pour out His Spirit on all flesh. Everyone who has ever spoken in tongues was in the flesh. However, he or she was inspired by the Spirit when they spoke.

At Pentecost the church received the gift to communicate the gospel in foreign languages (Acts 2). God gave His Spirit to all of His people to empower them to witness and prophesy. In Corinth, some members of the church uttered sounds which the rest of the congregation did not understand (1 Corinthians 12 - 14). This led to controversy and division. Paul tried to unite the church, assuring the church that there are different gifts but only one Spirit (1 Corinthians 12 : 4 - 11).

■ **An unknown tongue speaks unto God.**

For he who speaks in a tongue does not speak to men but to God, for no one understands him; however, in the spirit he speaks mysteries.

~ 1 Corinthians 14 : 2

This Type of Tongue:

- Edifies You

He who speaks in a tongue edifies himself.

~ 1 Corinthians 14 : 4

But you, beloved, building yourselves up on your most holy faith, praying in the Holy Spirit.

~ Jude 20

- Assists You in Prayer

Likewise the Spirit also helps in our weaknesses. For we do not know what we should pray for as we ought, but the Spirit Himself makes intercession for us with groanings which cannot be uttered. Now He who searches the hearts knows what the mind of the Spirit is, because He makes intercession for the saints according to the will of God.

~ Romans 8 : 26 – 27

- Refreshes Your Soul

For with stammering lips and another tongue He will speak to this people, To whom He said, "This is the rest with which you may cause the weary to rest," and, "This is the refreshing"; yet they would not hear.

~ Isaiah 28 : 11 - 12

- Gives Victory Over the Devil

Praying always with all prayer and supplication in the Spirit, being watchful to this end with all perseverance and supplication for all the saints.

~ Ephesians 6 : 18

- Helps You Worship in the Spirit

For if I pray in a tongue, my spirit prays, but my understanding is unfruitful. What is the conclusion then? I will pray with the spirit, and I will also pray with the understanding. I will sing with the spirit, and I will also sing with the understanding.

~ 1 Corinthians 14 : 14 – 15

- Aids You in Intercession

Likewise the Spirit also helps in our weaknesses. For we do not know what we should pray for as we ought, but the Spirit Himself makes intercession for us with groanings which cannot be uttered. Now He who searches the hearts knows what the mind of the Spirit is, because He makes intercession for the saints according to the will of God.

~ Romans 8 : 26

■ A known tongue is a sign to unbelievers.

And when this sound occurred, the multitude came together, and were confused, because everyone heard them speak in his own language.

~ Acts 2 : 6

■ A tongue is understood through interpretation and edifies the church.

Even so you, since you are zealous for spiritual gifts, let it be for the edification of the church that you seek to excel. Therefore let him who speaks in a tongue pray that he may interpret.

~ 1 Corinthians 14 : 12 - 13

I was preaching in Germany. Before the meeting, we were in a prayer meeting with the church leaders. The pastor asked everyone to pray for the meeting and to pray for me. The associate pastor was at my right side. I heard him pray in English, "Lord I ask you to bless Guy, use him for your glory. Confirm your Word with miracles. Touch and bless the people in this meeting today." This was normal to me. That night after dinner, the pastor's wife told me that the associate pastor was going to America. So I asked him, "Which part of the USA are you going to visit on this trip?" He didn't answer and started to speak German with the pastor's wife. She said to me, "He doesn't understand or speak English." I protested and said, "But I heard him pray for me in English just before the service this morning." She said, "Yes, I understand. He doesn't speak or understand English, but his prayer language is sometimes in English. When he prays in tongues, he sometimes speaks English." If I had heard this story from someone else, it would have challenged my thinking, but I experienced it myself, so I know it's the truth.

I was preaching in a meeting in Finland. Suddenly, during the altar call for salvation, I felt inspired to speak a tongue I had never spoken before. While I was speaking in that tongue, a man rushed to the altar and started to cry. He gave his life to Jesus.

At the end of the meeting, he came to me and asked me, "Do you speak this African dialect?" I said, "No." He told me that during the altar call I was speaking the dialect of his village in Africa, and I was saying, "Come to me now, come to me!" He was so touched; he realized that God was real. Later, the pastor told me that he was the son of a diplomat of an African country. He didn't believe in God because his family went through so many sufferings and injustice. He had a lot of wounds. They witnessed to him for over a year, but his heart was hardened. It was a miracle and a breakthrough that he gave his heart to Jesus.

There are five passages in the book of Acts which record how people received the Holy Spirit. They are Acts 2 : 1 – 4; Acts 8 : 14 – 18; Acts 9 : 17; Acts 10 : 44 – 46; and Acts 19 : 1 - 7.

Three times out of these five, it states that the people spoke with tongues when they received the Holy Spirit, and the other two infer that they did. The three obvious passages are: Acts 2 : 1 – 4; Acts 10 : 44 – 46; and Acts 19 : 1 – 7.

New Testament Examples:

✦ The Day of Pentecost.

When the Day of Pentecost had fully come, they were all with one accord in one place. And suddenly there came a sound from heaven, as of a rushing mighty wind, and it filled the whole house where they were sitting. Then there appeared to them divided tongues, as of fire, and one sat upon each of them. And they were all filled with the Holy Spirit and began to speak with other tongues, as the Spirit gave them utterance.

~ Acts 2 : 1 - 4

✦ Cornelius' house.

While Peter was still speaking these words, the Holy Spirit fell upon all those who heard the word. And those of the circumcision who believed were astonished, as many as came with Peter, because the gift of the Holy Spirit had been poured out on the Gentiles also. For they heard them speak with tongues and magnify God.

~ Acts 10 : 44 - 46

✦ Disciples of John the Baptist.

And it happened, while Apollos was at Corinth, that Paul, having passed through the upper regions, came to Ephesus. And finding some disciples he said to them, "Did you receive the Holy Spirit when you believed?" So they said to him, "We have not so much as heard whether there is a Holy Spirit." And he said to them, "Into what then were you baptized?" So they said, "Into John's baptism." Then Paul said, "John indeed baptized with a baptism of repentance, saying to the people that they should believe on Him who would come after him, that is, on Christ Jesus." When they heard this, they were baptized in the name of the Lord Jesus. And when Paul had laid hands on them, the Holy Spirit came upon them, and they spoke with tongues and prophesied. Now the men were about twelve in all.

~ Acts 19 : 1 - 7

✦ The Samaritans.

We know that the Samaritans spoke with tongues, because the early church fathers said that they did, and because it is implied in the fact that Simon observed something when they received the Holy Spirit. There had to be some kind of sign (or evidence) that registered with Simon's physical senses for him to know that the Samaritans had received the Holy Ghost.

Now when the apostles who were at Jerusalem heard that Samaria had received the word of God, they sent Peter and John to them, who, when they had come down, prayed for them that they might receive the Holy Spirit. For as yet He had fallen upon none of them. They had only been baptized in the name of the Lord Jesus. Then they laid hands on them, and they received the Holy Spirit. And when Simon saw that through the laying on of the apostles' hands the Holy Spirit was given, he offered them money.

~ Acts 8 : 14 - 18

✦ Ananias laying hands on Saul.

And Ananias went his way and entered the house; and laying his hands on him he said, "Brother Saul, the Lord Jesus, who appeared to you on the road as you came, has sent me that you may receive your sight and be filled with the Holy Spirit."

~ Acts 9 : 17

Paul himself said,
"I thank my God I speak with tongues more than you all."

~ 1 Corinthians 14 : 18

We know that Paul didn't receive the gift of tongues before he received the Holy Spirit, so it is logical to believe that he received the Holy Spirit the same way that everybody else did: with the evidence of speaking in other tongues. I've often been asked, "Do you believe a person can be baptized in the Holy Spirit and **not** ever speak in tongues?" Let's look closely at one of the passages mentioned above. In Acts 8 : 18, it says that Simon **saw** that through the laying on of the apostle's hands the Holy Ghost was given.

And when Simon saw that through the laying on of the apostles' hands the Holy Spirit was given.

~ Acts 8 : 18a

We know that a person cannot see the Holy Ghost with his physical eyes because the Holy Ghost is a Spirit. Therefore, there had to be some physical sign or evidence that registered with Simon's physical senses for him to know that the Samaritans had received the Holy Ghost. What was this sign that Simon saw?

* It wasn't just joy. The Samaritans already had joy.
And there was great joy in that city.

~ Acts 8 : 8

* It wasn't deliverance or that devils were cast out, because the devils had already been cast out.

For unclean spirits, crying with a loud voice, came out of many who were possessed.

~ Acts 8 : 7a

* It wasn't healing, because this had already occurred.
Many who were paralyzed and lame were healed.

~ Acts 8 : 7b

And the multitudes with one accord heeded the things spoken by Philip, hearing and seeing the miracles which he did.

~ Acts 8 : 6

* It wasn't salvation and water baptism, because they had already been saved and then water baptized.

But when they believed Philip as he preached the things concerning the kingdom of God and the name of Jesus Christ, both men and women were baptized.

~ Acts 8 : 12

What was this sign or physical evidence that registered with Simon's physical senses for him to know that the Samaritans had received the Holy Spirit? It is logical to assume that it is the same evidence that was registered elsewhere. It was the same evidence that convinced the six Jewish brothers who went with Peter to Cornelius' house.

For they heard them speak with tongues and magnify God.

~ Acts 10 : 46

To answer the question, "Is it necessary to speak in tongues?" Let me put it this way. If you want a New Testament experience, and want to make sure you have the same Holy Ghost that the apostles and the early church had, then you want to speak in tongues.

People sometimes question the fact that people speak in tongues together in a cooperate meeting. I think that it is not out-of-order to do so, because in the passage below, all twelve men spoke in tongues together.

When they heard this, they were baptized in the name of the Lord Jesus. And when Paul had laid hands on them, the Holy Spirit came upon them, and they spoke with tongues and prophesied. Now the men were about twelve in all.

~ Acts 19 : 5 – 7

5. Interpretation of Tongues

To understand what interpretation of tongues is, we need to understand what it is not.

✓ It is not simply imagination.

It cannot be the imagination of the mind, because it works through the spirit of man, and not his mind. Mental ability is no more used in interpretation of tongues than medical science was used when Paul said, "Stand upright on your feet," and the man leaped and walked.

✓ It is not the ability to translate languages.

Interpretation of tongues cannot be a translation of languages. A person without the Spirit of God can have the natural talent of translating languages.

✓ It is not translation, but it is interpretation.

Because interpretation is not a word-for-word translation, it may be given in first, second, or third person. It is not always in the first person. For instance, one person may bring the interpretation like this: "Behold, I am coming soon; be ye ready." The next one may say, "The Lord says He is coming soon, and He says for you to be ready." Still another may bring the same message in other words, such as, "The Lord is coming very soon; be ye ready." This gift does not always quote the exact words as translators do, for interpretation is not translation. It tells the meaning of a message as one may tell the meaning of a dream, symbol, parable, sign, or an action.

Two preachers bringing the same message from God do not use the same words. I may understand one better because he is from the same part of the country as I am. One interpreter may speak such large words that the message would have to be interpreted again to someone in the audience who did not have a large vocabulary. Daniel's interpretation of the heavenly language written on the wall (Daniel 5) consisted of many times the number of words on the wall. One interpretation may consist of just one-half as many words as another, because one congregation may be better educated than another.

To understand what interpretation of tongues is, we need to understand what it is *not.*

✓ It is not repetition of scripture.

This gift is not repetition of scripture, but can be sometimes.

✓ It is not simply the gift of interpretation.

This gift is not the gift of interpretation, but interpretation of tongues. It is not, and cannot, be used if there has been no supernatural tongues spoken. It is not interpretation of people, thoughts, hard sayings, actions, dreams, or anything in the natural. It is interpretation of supernatural tongues. It cannot be learned at school, but can be given by the Spirit in a moment of time to any Spirit-filled person.

Interpretation of Tongues Is:

Let us, first of all, break it down to its original Greek meaning:

• "Interpretation" : "harmeneia" : meaning, *explanation or full interpretation.*

It is the ability through the inspiration of the Holy Spirit to bring understandable meaning to an inspired public message in tongues. It is a vocal miracle.

> *The Spiritual gift of the interpretation of tongues is the supernatural manifestation of the Spirit of God using one's vocal organs, giving utterance in one's own language, telling the meaning of the words which have been spoken with tongues.*

Paul says that the gift of interpretation of tongues helps us to understand the message spoken in tongues.

That is the conclusion then? I will pray with the spirit, and I will also pray with the understanding. I will sing with the spirit, and I will also sing with the understanding. Otherwise, if you bless with the spirit, how will he who occupies the place of the uninformed say "Amen" at your giving of thanks, since he does not understand what you say?

~ I Corinthians 14 : 15 - 16

Paul also says that interpretation of tongues is good as prophecy.

I wish you all spoke with tongues, but even more that you prophesied; for he who prophesies is greater than he who speaks with tongues, unless indeed he interprets, that the church may receive edification.

~ I Corinthians 14 : 5

There are many places in the Bible where it states, "the Holy Ghost said" or "hear what the Spirit saith unto the churches." It is not known in every case whether it was interpretation or prophecy, but some things we do know are:

• The gift of interpretation of tongues was set in the Church. (I Corinthians 12)

- This gift is necessary. (1 Corinthians 12 : 22)
- This gift was never taken out of the Church.
- This gift was used all down through Church history.
- Paul taught the members of the church at Corinth to use this gift. (1 Corinthians 14)

6. <u>Prophecy</u>

To understand what prophecy is, we need to understand what it is *not*.

✓ **It is not fortune-telling.**

People sometimes think that "prophecy" means, "to predict (foretell) what will happen in the future."

One of the accusations which the Lord brought against the evil King Mannaseh was that he used fortune-tellers. The Bible says concerning Mannaseh:

He practiced black magic and used fortune-telling and patronized mediums and wizards. So the Lord was very angry....

~ 2 Kings 21 : 6 (TLB)

Then there were false prophets or supposed fortune-tellers in Jeremiah's day. God said concerning them:

For thus says the Lord of hosts, the God of Israel: Do not let your prophets and your diviners who are in your midst deceive you, nor listen to your dreams which you cause to be dreamed. For they prophesy falsely to you in My name; I have not sent them, says the Lord.

~ Jeremiah 29 : 8 – 9

✓ Is not the ability to preach.

The words "preach" and "prophesy" come from two entirely different Greek words. To "preach" means, to proclaim; to announce; to cry; to tell.

And He said to them, "Go into all the world and preach the gospel to every creature.

~ Mark 16 : 15

Note that He didn't say to "prophesy" the Gospel. Many politicians, lawyers, and teachers have oratorical ability even though they have never received the Holy Spirit. There is nothing supernatural about oratorical ability.

Prophecy is not simple oratorical ability.

The word, "prophecy", means, *to bubble up; to flow forth; or to cause to drop like rain.*

> *Teaching and preaching are preplanned,*
> *but prophecy is not.*

Prophecy is a supernatural gift, whereas, oratorical ability is a natural gift at best.

> *Oratorical ability can come through*
> *education and training, but prophecy*
> *only comes through the Holy Ghost.*

✓ **It is not the ability to quote scripture.**

Scripture quotes may be a part of prophecy, but the gift of prophecy should not be confused with the natural ability some people have to remember and quote scripture. Even the devil can quote scriptures.

✓ **It is not to be despised.**

Do not despise prophecies.

~ I Thessalonians 5 : 20

It's to be desired.

Pursue love, and desire spiritual gifts, but especially that you may prophesy.

~ I Corinthians 14 : 1

Prophecy Is:

Let us, first of all, break it down to its original Greek meaning:

• "Prophecy": "propheteia": meaning, *to speak for another; speaking on behalf of God.*

It means, *to be the spokesman for someone else. Literally, it means, to speak for God or to be His mouthpiece.*

The Hebrew word for "prophecy" means, *to flow forth or to spring forth.* It also carries the thought of bubbling forth like a fountain, or to tumble forth.

Prophecy is a vocal miracle of speech in one's own language. It is speaking under the inspiration of God for edification, exhortation, and comfort.

> *Prophecy is divinely inspired and is an anointed utterance;*
> *a supernatural proclamation in a known language.*

It is the manifestation of the Spirit of God – not of intellect – and it may be possessed and operated by all who are filled with the Holy Spirit.

For you can all prophesy one by one, that all may learn and all may be encouraged.

~ I Corinthians 14 : 31

Intellect, faith, and will are operative in this gift, but its exercise is not intellectually based. It is calling forth words from the Spirit of God.

Prophecy is for women as well as men, according to the scriptures. It is for all spirit-filled believers.

I will pour out My Spirit on all flesh; your sons and your daughters shall prophesy.

~ Joel 2 : 28

The gift of prophecy operates when:

• There is high worship.

After that you shall come to the hill of God where the Philistine garrison is. And it will happen, when you have come there to the city that you will meet a group of prophets coming down from the high place with a stringed instrument, a tambourine, a flute, and a harp before them; and they will be prophesying. Then the Spirit of the Lord will come upon you, and you will prophesy with them and be turned into another man.

~ I Samuel 10 : 5 – 6

• Other prophets are present.

So it was, when he had turned his back to go from Samuel that God gave him another heart; and all those signs came to pass that day. When they came there to the hill, there was a group of prophets to meet him; then the Spirit of God came upon him, and he prophesied among them.

~ I Samuel 10 :9 - 10

• Hands are laid on you by ministers.

And it happened, while Apollos was at Corinth, that Paul, having passed through the upper regions, came to Ephesus. And finding some disciples he said to them, "Did you receive the Holy Spirit when you believed?" So they said to him, "We have not so much as heard whether there is a Holy Spirit." And he said to them, "Into what then were you baptized?" So they said, "Into John's baptism." Then Paul said, "John indeed baptized with a baptism of repentance, saying to the people that they should believe on Him who would come after him, that is, on Christ Jesus." When they heard this, they were baptized in the name of the Lord Jesus. And when Paul had laid hands on them, the Holy Spirit came upon them, and they spoke with tongues and prophesied.

~ Acts 19 : 1 - 6

The Office of the Prophet

The gift of prophecy (I Corinthians 12) and the office of the prophet (Ephesians 4 : 11) are not the same thing.

There is a ministry of the prophet, but not everyone is a prophet.

I love basketball. In a basketball game, there are always fans with the team's jersey and cap in the stands. A fan can wear a jersey and a cap, but that does not mean that he is a professional athlete playing basketball. You may prophesy, but operating in the simple gift of prophecy does not qualify you to stand in the office of a prophet, much like wearing a basketball hat and jersey does not qualify you to play basketball for a professional team… you must be gifted. To stand in the office of a prophet, one must have a consistent manifestation of the revelation gifts (word of knowledge, word of wisdom, and discerning of spirits) and prophecy.

And He Himself gave some to be apostles, some prophets, some evangelists, and some pastors and teachers.

~ Ephesians 4 : 11

Prophecy is not the interpretation of tongues.

I wish you all spoke with tongues, but even more that you prophesied; for he who prophesies is greater than he who speaks with tongues, unless indeed he interprets, that the church may receive edification.

~ 1 Corinthians 14 : 5

> *Tongues are inspired utterances in an "unknown" tongue. Prophecy is inspired utterance in a "known" tongue.*

Both are inspired utterances. The interpretation of tongues is inspired utterance telling that which was spoken in tongues. The difference between interpretation and prophecy is that interpretation is dependent upon tongues, whereas prophecy is not.

Ways to Judge Prophecy

Prophecies have to be judged.
Let two or three prophets speak, and let the others judge.

~ 1 Corinthians 14 : 29

• By their fruits you shall know them.

You will know them by their fruits. Do men gather grapes from thorn bushes or figs from thistles? Even so, every good tree bears good fruit, but a bad tree bears bad fruit. A good tree cannot bear bad fruit, nor can a bad tree bear good fruit. Therefore by their fruits you will know them.

~ Matthew 7 : 16 - 18, 20

One of the ways we know a true prophet is by his or her fruits. Today in the Body of Christ, often, people's gift takes them places where their character cannot keep them. Sometimes we make the mistake of emphasizing the gift more than the character. God will give you the gift, but character is developed through personal discipline. If you want to be used by God, make sure that you produce the right and good fruits.

- The prophecy should glorify Christ.

He will glorify Me, for He will take of what is Mine and declare it to you.
~ John 16 : 14

Beloved, do not believe every spirit, but test the spirits, whether they are of God; because many false prophets have gone out into the world. By this you know the Spirit of God: Every spirit that confesses that Jesus Christ has come in the flesh is of God.
~ 1 John 4 : 1 – 2

The difference between a ministry that is authentic and anointed by God, and one that is not, is that the authentic ministry will always point you to Jesus and give the glory to God. A ministry that operates in the prophetic but points to man or elevates and worships man's accomplishments is not of God - even though the prophetic may be in operation. God said He will share His glory with no one.

> *If you want to be used by God, make sure that you know that the power of God flows through you, but does not come from you.*

- The prophecy should agree with the scriptures.

To the law and to the testimony! If they do not speak according to this word, it is because there is no light in them.
~ Isaiah 8 : 20

For You have magnified Your word above all Your name.
~ Psalm 138 : 2b

God will never speak outside the realm of His Word, principally speaking. If the prophecy is leading you to violate the principles of God's Word, it is not from God. That's why we need to know God's Word; to be able to judge prophecy.

• The prophecy should be fulfilled.

When a prophet speaks in the name of the Lord, if the thing does not happen or come to pass, that is the thing which the Lord has not spoken; the prophet has spoken it presumptuously; you shall not be afraid of him.

~ Deuteronomy 18 : 22

I have met so many people – even church leaders – that built their lives and expectations around a prophetic word that somebody gave them that never came to pass. They are frustrated and not satisfied with what they are doing for God because of the prophecy. Sometimes we need to realize that if a prophetic word did not come to pass, it was maybe not from God. Other times, the fulfillment of a prophecy requires that we align ourselves, through prayer and decisions that we make, to facilitate the fulfillment of the Word. Some prophecies are not of God, even though they may come to pass. The benchmark remains, that all prophecies should exalt the Lord Jesus.

• It is important that prophecy is not disjointed or confused. True prophecy is line upon line and precept upon precept.

But the word of the Lord was to them, " Precept upon precept, precept upon precept, line upon line, line upon line, here a little, there a little", that they might go and fall backward, and be broken and snared and caught.

~ Isaiah 28 : 13

It is important that whenever a prophetic word is given that the people receiving the prophetic word understand what is spoken to them. God is not the author of confusion. If the Word is given from the Lord, the Word itself has to be clear, not confusing. Sometimes people who give prophetic words are not clear, and this may sometimes create more confusion in the people that are recipients of the word.

• The prophecy should produce liberty, not bondage.

For you did not receive the spirit of bondage again to fear, but you received the Spirit of adoption by whom we cry out, "Abba, Father."

~ Romans 8 : 15

The prophetic ministry should produce freedom and liberty, not fear and bondage. Some prophetic ministries today use their gift to manipulate and control the people around them through fear tactics, and they also use their gift to tie people to them. This is an indication that something is wrong. If you want to be used by God, don't use your gift to manipulate people and don't be mentored or attached to someone that uses their gift to control and manipulate people.

• All believers have an unction (anointing) within them that tells them when something is wrong. Prophecies should witness with our spirit.

But you have an anointing from the Holy One, and you know all things. But the anointing which you have received from Him abides in you, and you do not need that anyone teach you; but as the same anointing teaches you concerning all things, and is true, and is not a lie, and just as it has taught you, you will abide in Him.

~ I John 2 : 20, 27

- It can bring life.

The hand of the Lord came upon me and brought me out in the Spirit of the Lord, and set me down in the midst of the valley; and it was full of bones. Then He caused me to pass by them all around, and behold, here were very many in the open valley; and indeed they were very dry. And He said to me, "Son of man, can these bones live?" So I answered, "O Lord God, You know." Again He said to me, "Prophesy to these bones, and say to them, 'O dry bones, hear the word of the Lord!'"

~ Ezekiel 37 : 1 – 4

Prophecy brought life to the valley of dry bones. Your tongue lives in proximity to your spirit, and your words have creative potential. When you speak out of prophetic word, the life of God can be released through you.

- It can give spiritual vision.

Where there is no revelation (prophetic vision), the people cast off restraint (perish); but happy is he who keeps the law.

~ Proverbs 29 : 18

> *Prophetic insight is the spiritual ability to see the purpose of God in any given context.*

Through the prophetic you can receive a spiritual vision by an insight given to you by the Holy Spirit. Prophetic insight operates as the Spirit leads.

- It can edify, exhort, and comfort.

But he who prophesies speaks edification and exhortation and comfort to men.

~ 1 Corinthians 14 : 3

- It can bring revival and restoration.

But this is what was spoken by the prophet Joel: "And it shall come to pass in the last days," says God, "that I will pour out of My Spirit on all flesh; your sons and your daughters shall prophesy, your young men shall see visions, your old men shall dream dreams. And on My menservants and on My maidservants I will pour out My Spirit in those days; and they shall prophesy."

~ Acts 2 : 16 - 18

- It can guide you to your right position in Christ.

Now in the church that was at Antioch there were certain prophets and teachers: Barnabas, Simeon who was called Niger, Lucius of Cyrene, Manaen who had been brought up with Herod the tetrarch, and Saul. As they ministered to the Lord and fasted, the Holy Spirit said, "Now separate to Me Barnabas and Saul for the work to which I have called them." Then, having fasted and prayed, and laid hands on them, they sent them away.

~ Acts 13 : 1 - 3

As children of God, we are primarily led by the Spirit, not by prophecy, but prophecy can be used by God to direct you where you need to go.

Those who are led by the Spirit of God are sons of God.

~ Romans 8 : 14 (NIV)

Numerous examples of prophecy can be found in the Bible. Just a few will be related here.

New Testament Examples:

This is not an exhaustive list of New Testament examples of prophecy. I am merely pointing out a few which show the prevalence of this gift in the New Testament church.

✠ Believers prophesied.

Then Paul said, "John indeed baptized with a baptism of repentance, saying to the people that they should believe on Him who would come after him, that is, on Christ Jesus." When they heard this, they were baptized in the name of the Lord Jesus. And when Paul had laid hands on them, the Holy Spirit came upon them, and they spoke with tongues and prophesied.

~ Acts 19 : 4 – 6

✠ Philip's daughters prophesied.

On the next day we who were Paul's companions departed and came to Caesarea, and entered the house of Philip the evangelist, who was one of the seven, and stayed with him. Now this man had four virgin daughters who prophesied.

~ Acts 21 : 8 - 9

Old Testament Examples:

Prophecy operated through some men and women of God in the Old Testament.

✦ **Eldad and Medad were prophesying in the camp.**

Then the Lord came down in the cloud, and spoke to him, and took of the Spirit that was upon him, and placed the same upon the seventy elders; and it happened, when the Spirit rested upon them, that they prophesied, although they never did so again. But two men had remained in the camp: the name of one was Eldad, and the name of the other Medad. And the Spirit rested upon them. Now they were among those listed, but who had not gone out to the tabernacle; yet they prophesied in the camp. And a young man ran and told Moses, and said, "Eldad and Medad are prophesying in the camp." So Joshua the son of Nun, Moses' assistant, one of his choice men, answered and said, "Moses my lord, forbid them!" Then Moses said to him, "Are you zealous for my sake? Oh, that all the Lord's people were prophets and that the Lord would put His Spirit upon them!" And Moses returned to the camp, he and the elders of Israel.

~ Numbers 11 : 25 – 29

✦ **Saul prophesied.**

So it was, when he had turned his back to go from Samuel that God gave him another heart; and all those signs came to pass that day. When they came there to the hill, there was a group of prophets to meet him; then the Spirit of God came upon him, and he prophesied among them. And it happened, when all who knew him formerly saw that he indeed prophesied among the prophets, that the people said to one another, "What is this that has come upon the son of Kish? Is Saul also among the prophets?"

~ 1 Samuel 10 : 9 - 11

There were numerous prophets in the Old Testament. There were so many, that there is not room enough here to list all of them and their deeds. Elijah and Elisha were powerful prophets of God who did mighty exploits for Him. Isaiah, Jeremiah, Ezekiel, and Daniel were all prophets of God who wrote the books which bear their names. Then, there were also 12 Minor Prophets whose writings make up the last 12 books of the Old Testament, from Hosea to Malachi.

7. <u>Healing</u>

To understand what healing is, we need to understand what it is *not*.

✓ **It is not simply medical science.**

I believe in medical science, and I encourage sick people to visit a medical doctor. However, this gift cannot simply be medical science, because any sinner can learn medical science without the leading or the anointing of the Holy Spirit. Furthermore, there is sometimes a supernatural element at the root of some diseases which cannot be dealt with by medical science. Such disease cannot be cured by any natural knowledge, natural treatment, or other method of natural man.

✓ **It is not Christian science.**

This gift is not, so called, Christian Science. Christian Science is a misnomer. It is neither Christian nor scientific. It is similar to a guinea pig which is neither a guinea nor a pig. It is similar to Grape Nuts breakfast cereal which is neither grapes nor nuts. Christian Science is not Christian because it denies the deity of Christ, denies the fact of sin, and denies the blood atonement of Christ. Christian Science is not scientific because it employs a system of mind-cure, in which a happy frame of mind is supposed to cure sickness. There is no doubt that worry, fear, hatred, and other negative emotions can cause physical problems, and may prevent a person from the natural recovery from an illness. Many times, removing these negative emotions can have a healing effect on a person if the illness is psychosomatic. However, this method does not work on real sickness and disease. It is not the gift of healing.

✓ It is not spiritism.

The gift of healing is not spiritism, which sometimes seems to cure sick people. When spiritism is used, the trouble only moves around the body – leaving the patient possessed with many other troubles than at the beginning. Spiritism often brings a patient to an early death. Spiritism is of the devil and, according to John 10 : 10, the devil's motives are to steal, kill, and destroy.

The thief does not come except to steal, and to kill, and to destroy. I have come that they may have life, and that they may have it more abundantly.
~ John 10 : 10

The devil may give one the feeling or the idea of being healed, but it is only temporary, and it opens the door to something worse. Satan does not come to cast out himself.

If Satan casts out Satan, he is divided against himself. How then will his kingdom stand?
~ Matthew 12 : 26

✓ It is not extreme unction.

Some churches practice a sacrament known as "extreme unction" in which a priest visits the sick just before death and anoints the dying with oil. This sacrament is never given to bring healing, but to prepare the sick for death. The pretense for this "unction" of dying men is supposedly taken from James 5 : 14 - 15, but when this passage is quoted, it becomes obvious that the sacrament of "extreme unction" does not find its roots in the scriptures.

Is anyone among you sick? Let him call for the elders of the church, and let them pray over him, anointing him with oil in the name of the Lord. And the prayer of faith will save the sick, and the Lord will raise him up. And if he has committed sins, he will be forgiven.

~ James 5 : 14 - 15

It is evident that this prayer and anointing were intended for the recovery of the sick, because it is written in the Word that the Lord will raise him up, and not merely as a preparation for death. The "extreme unction" is not intended for healing or recovery, but for preparation of death when all hope of recovery is supposedly gone, and death is seen as imminent. The gift of healing is not extreme unction.

Healing Is:

Let us, first of all, break it down to its original Greek meaning:

• "Working": "energema": meaning, *an energy, in working; to be in work; to be effective; active; operative; to energize or to be energized.*

• "Miracles": "dunamis": meaning, *act of power; special miraculous power (usually by implication… a miracle itself); capability, power to do anything; power – might in action; a work with reference to the power required for its performance.*

The spiritual gift of healing is the supernatural manifestation of the Spirit of God that miraculously brings healing and deliverance from disease and infirmities whether functional, organic, or nervous. It is the power of God that destroys the work of the devil in the human body.

> *The spiritual gift of healing is a remarkable or surprising event that happens by the direct intervention of God, not following the general known laws of nature.*

Healing Techniques of Jesus' Ministry

If we want to be used by God, Jesus is our model. Let's look at the different ways he ministered healing. I call them the **Healing Techniques of Jesus' Ministry.**

- **Technique 1: He healed them with a word.**

He cast out the spirits with a word, and healed all who were sick,

~ Matthew 8 : 16b

The centurion answered and said, "Lord, I am not worthy that You should come under my roof. But only speak a word, and my servant will be healed."

~ Matthew 8 : 8

If you want to be used by God in the area of healing, you have to believe that God can heal people through His Word. God's Word is God's power. The Scripture says:

"He sent His word and healed them."

~ Psalm 107 : 20a

This Book of the Law shall not depart from your mouth, but you shall meditate in it day and night, that you may observe to do according to all that is written in it. For then you will make your way prosperous, and then you will have good success.

~ Joshua 1 : 8

Blessed is the man who walks not in the counsel of the ungodly, nor stands in the path of sinners, nor sits in the seat of the scornful; but his delight is in the law of the Lord, and in His law he meditates day and night. He shall be like a tree planted by the rivers of water, that brings forth its fruit in its season.

~ Psalm 1 : 1 – 3a

So then faith comes by hearing, and hearing by the word of God.

~ Romans 10 : 17

> *God's Word is His power, and God's power is His truth.*
> *The truth that you know shall set you free.*

God's Word has enough power to change your life, but you must have faith in His Word. One Word from God can change your entire life!

> *We can use His Word to receive healing, and we can use His Word to minister healing to other people.*

• **Technique 2: He healed them by His touch.**

So He touched her hand, and the fever left her. And she arose and served them.
~ Matthew 8 : 15

But when the crowd was put outside, He went in and took her by the hand, and the girl arose.
~ Matthew 9 : 25

Then He touched their eyes, saying, "According to your faith let it be to you."
~ Matthew 9 : 29

We must have faith in His touch. One touch from God can wipe away all your problems. One touch from God can wipe away all your sickness. One touch from Jesus can turn your marriage around. One touch from God can change the lives of your children. One touch from God can change your city. People who have faith believe that they can be changed by the touch of God.

> *The touch of God can come through the touch of men.*

They will lay hands on the sick, and they will recover.
~ Mark 16 : 18b

And they went out and preached everywhere, the Lord working with them and confirming the word through the accompanying signs.
~ Mark 16 : 20

- ## **Technique 3: He healed them by their touch.**

You can touch God with your faith. The Bible says in Mark 5 : 24 – 35, that the woman with the issue of blood said to herself, "If only I can touch His garment, I shall be made well." When she touched Him, Jesus turned around and asked the disciples, "Who touched Me?" The disciples said, "You have people pushing You from all directions, and You are asking who touched You?" Jesus knew a lot of people were pushing Him, but it was not the hundreds of people He was noticing. It was a special touch... the touch of faith. There was something about the touch of the woman with the issue of blood. It was full of faith, and He felt virtue leave Him. He felt life leave Him to meet her need.

> *The anointing is tangible, capable of being touched, and it is perceptible, capable of being seen.*

Something happened when this woman touched Jesus. Everybody was touching Him, but nothing happened to them. But, when she touched Jesus, something happened both to her and to Jesus. The life of God came out of Jesus and went into her, and the sickness came out of her body through the touch of faith.

- ## **Technique 4: He healed them using a medium.**

When He had said these things, He spat on the ground and made clay with the saliva; and He anointed the eyes of the blind man with the clay.

~ John 9 : 6

The implication here is not that we should go around using mud to pray for the sick. The principle here is obedience to the Holy Spirit.

> *He might ask you to do something ridiculous,*
> *but sometimes God's miraculous starts in the ridiculous.*

The Purpose of the Gift of Healing

- To prove the resurrection of Jesus Christ. ~ Acts 3 : 15 - 16, ~ Hebrews 13 : 8
- To prove His power to forgive sins. ~ Mark 2 : 10
- To build faith and save souls. ~ John 6 : 2
- To confirm the Word of God. ~ Mark 16 : 17 - 20
- To bring glory to God. ~ Mark 2 : 12

We have experienced the healing power of God in our ministry as we travel around the world preaching the gospel of power.

Sometimes healing can be instant through the laying on of hands. I remember ministering at a church just before taking a trip overseas. On my way out of the church, a man approached me asking for prayer for healing. He was diagnosed with a brain tumor; they had taken a scan, and the pictures showed that he had a tumor in his brain. My wife and I were in a hurry, so we briefly laid hands on him and commanded the tumor to disappear in Jesus' name; then ran to the airport. A month later we received a report by email from the man saying that he went back to the doctors, they did another scan, and the tumor could not be found. He was completely healed by the power of God.

Sometimes God heals people where they are. I remember preaching in South America at a large gathering with over a 100,000 people. In these types of meetings we cannot lay hands on people, so we pray from the platform and God performs so many miracles. Like the teenage boy whose back was bowed; he had not been able to walk straight for many years. The power of God touched him in the back of the stadium, and he could walk straight when he walked across the platform.

In the same meeting, a woman that was deaf received her hearing back. Another woman received her sight back. God never ceases to amaze me that even though we never laid hands on any of the persons above, they were supernaturally touched and healed by the power of God. Some people think that they always have to have a preacher lay his hands on them to receive their healing. While I believe in the laying on of hands, sometimes God can heal you where you are, when you put your faith in Him. People really need to understand this dynamic.

Healing is sometimes a process, and there is no distance in the realm of the Spirit. A young adult approached me after one of the meetings in the USA. I knew her family well. She told me that she had HIV, and asked if I could help her. Her world had just collapsed, and she was so desperate, and didn't know what to do. She told me not to tell her family. I promised to keep her secret. We exchanged phone numbers after I prayed for her. She would often call me and I would give her Bible verses on healing and told her she should turn away from her sins and live a consecrated life before God. She agreed. After a few months, she called me one day and told me that she was ready to receive her healing. I prayed with her over the phone. She went to see her doctor the next day, and her blood result said HIV negative. She called me with the exciting news that she was completely healed. We can see here that healing is sometimes a process. A person must feed themselves with the Word and turn away from their wicked ways.

You can read more testimonies of healing at www.guypeh.com. Numerous examples of healings can be found in the Bible. Just a few will be related here.

New Testament Examples:

✦ Healing of the father of Publius.

In that region there was an estate of the leading citizen of the island, whose name was Publius, who received us and entertained us courteously for three days. And it happened that the father of Publius lay sick of a fever and dysentery. Paul went in to him and prayed, and he laid his hands on him and healed him. So when this was done, the rest of those on the island who had diseases also came and were healed.

~ Acts 28 : 7 - 9

This verse gives the account of Paul, on the island of Melitus, laying his hands on Publius' father who was very sick with a fever and a bloody flux, and he was healed. This caused the people to bring many others for healing. Notice that it was a spiritual gift and not Luke's medicine kit that healed the people on this island.

✦ Lame man healed.

Now Peter and John went up together to the temple at the hour of prayer, the ninth hour. And a certain man lame from his mother's womb was carried, whom they laid daily at the gate of the temple which is called Beautiful, to ask alms from those who entered the temple; who, seeing Peter and John about to go into the temple, asked for alms. And fixing his eyes on him, with John, Peter said, "Look at us." So he gave them his attention, expecting to receive something from them. Then Peter said, "Silver and gold I do not have, but what I do have I give you: In the name of Jesus Christ of Nazareth, rise up and walk." And he took him by the right hand and lifted him up, and immediately his feet and ankle bones received strength. So he, leaping up, stood and walked and entered the temple with them walking, leaping, and praising God. And all the people saw him walking and praising God. Then they knew that it was he who sat begging alms at the Beautiful Gate of the temple; and they were filled with wonder and amazement at what had happened to him.

~ Acts 3 : 1 - 10

Peter is taking a lame man by the hand and leading him to be healed in the name of Jesus. It was Luke, the physician, who stated the man's condition both before and after the healing. He gave all praise and glory to God for this marvelous work.

✦ Aeneas, a paralyzed man, was healed.

Now it came to pass, as Peter went through all parts of the country that he also came down to the saints who dwelt in Lydda. There he found a certain man named Aeneas, who had been bedridden eight years and was paralyzed. And Peter said to him, "Aeneas, Jesus the Christ heals you. Arise and make your bed." Then he arose immediately. So all who dwelt at Lydda and Sharon saw him and turned to the Lord.

~ Acts 9 : 32 - 35

Peter is speaking here to a man who had been bedfast for 8 years and saying, "Aeneas, Jesus the Christ heals you. Arise and take thy bed." This caused the people of two cities to turn to the Lord. The healing power of God can cause people to turn to God. Healing is a tool that can help confirm the truth of the gospel to people.

✢ Many were healed through Philip.

And the multitudes with one accord heeded the things spoken by Philip, hearing and seeing the miracles which he did. For unclean spirits, crying with a loud voice, came out of many who were possessed; and many who were paralyzed and lame were healed.

~ Acts 8 : 6 - 7

A deacon, named Philip, was ministering in the early church. He was not an apostle or a prophet; he was just a deacon, a servant of God. The lame and those who were sick with palsy were healed under his ministry.

Old Testament Examples:

✢ Elisha.

The prophet Elisha told Naaman that he had to wash himself 7 times in the Jordan River to receive his healing. When Naaman complied, the Lord healed him.

Then Naaman went with his horses and chariot, and he stood at the door of Elisha's house. And Elisha sent a messenger to him, saying, "Go and wash in the Jordan seven times, and your flesh shall be restored to you, and you shall be clean." But Naaman became furious, and went away and said, "Indeed, I said to myself, 'He will surely come out to me, and stand and call on the name of the Lord his God, and wave his hand over the place, and heal the leprosy.' Are not the Abanah and the Pharpar, the rivers of Damascus, better than all the waters of Israel? Could I not wash in them and be clean?" So he turned and went away in a rage. And his servants came near and spoke to him, and said, "My father, if the prophet had told you to do something great, would you not have done it? How much more then, when he says to you, 'Wash, and be clean'?" So he went down and dipped seven times in the Jordan, according to the saying of the man of God; and his flesh was restored like the flesh of a little child, and he was clean.

~ 2 Kings 5 : 9 – 14

Some miracles are connected to obedience to unusual requests. Even Mary told the servants at the feast in John 2, "Whatever He tells you to do, just do it."

His mother said to the servants, "Whatever He says to you, do it."

~ John 2 : 5

✦ Isaiah.

In those days Hezekiah was sick and near death. And Isaiah the prophet, the son of Amoz, went to him and said to him, "Thus says the Lord: 'Set your house in order, for you shall die and not live.'" Then Hezekiah turned his face toward the wall, and prayed to the Lord, and said, "Remember now, O Lord, I pray, how I have walked before You in truth and with a loyal heart, and have done what is good in Your sight."

And Hezekiah wept bitterly. And the word of the Lord came to Isaiah, saying, "Go and tell Hezekiah, 'Thus says the Lord, the God of David your father: "I have heard your prayer, I have seen your tears; surely I will add to your days fifteen years. I will deliver you and this city from the hand of the king of Assyria, and I will defend this city."'

~ Isaiah 38 : 1 - 6

Hezekiah turned his face to the wall and besought God alone, for healing. The Lord sent Isaiah the prophet with a healing balm which God used to heal Hezekiah and add 15 more years to his life.

There are other accounts of healing in the life of Moses, Elijah, Elisha, and others in the Old Testament.

8.   Faith

To understand what faith is, we need to understand what it is *not*.

✓   **It is not simply confidence.**
It is not natural courage or confidence. It is not ambition or natural business ability. These are very important and they keep people going, but they should not be confused with the gift of faith. Even those who deny the Spirit of God may possess courage and confidence. There are many things that a person can do in the natural to build one's confidence, but the gift of faith is not built up by natural means. It is a manifestation of the Spirit of God.

But the manifestation of the Spirit is given to each one for the profit of all.

~ I Corinthians 12 : 7

✓ **It is not saving faith.**

It is not saving faith, which every Christian must have in order to truly be a Christian. The gift of faith is a supernatural manifestation of the Holy Spirit to help someone who is already a Christian.

✓ **It is not simply hoping something will happen.**

The gift of faith is not simply trying to have faith. It doesn't come from gesturing, screaming, yelling, jumping, or supposing. It is not guess-work, predicting, or positive confession. Simply hoping something will happen may keep a person working towards a goal, but it is not a manifestation of the Spirit of God. A person doesn't necessarily need the Holy Spirit to hope something good will happen.

✓ **It is not one's theology.**

It is not a doctrine, a theory, a dogma, a theological principle, a disciplined prayer life, a conviction, a creed, or any man-made policy. It is a supernatural manifestation of the Holy Spirit.

Faith Is:

Let us, first of all, break it down to its original Greek meaning:

• "Faith": *"pistis": meaning, faith; faithfulness; steadfastness; firm persuasion; the conviction which is based upon hearing, not upon sight or knowledge; a firmly-relying confidence in what we hear from God in His Word.*

The gift of faith is the mysterious surge of confidence which sometimes arises within a person when faced with a specific situation or need.

> *The Spiritual gift of faith is the supernatural manifestation of the Spirit of God that miraculously drops the assurance of the answer to one's prayers into his heart, even before he sees it come to pass with his natural eyes.*

It is believing you have it when you pray.

Therefore I say to you, whatever things you ask when you pray, believe that you receive them, and you will have them.

~ Mark 11 : 24

> *Faith is knowing the roots are cursed before you see the tree die. It ceases to be faith the minute you see it come to pass.*

Numerous examples of the gift of faith can be found in the Bible. Just a few will be related here.

New Testament Example:

✦ Jesus in the storm.
On the same day, when evening had come, He said to them, "Let us cross over to the other side."

~ Mark 4 : 35

By the gift of faith, Jesus rested his head on the pillow during the storm. He already had the assurance that they were going over to the other side.

Faith is an act, faith without works is dead.

> *Real faith is trust. You will walk out on it.*

Old Testament Examples:

✟ Abraham's faith for a son.

It was the gift of faith that caused Abraham to claim that God had given him a son even before he saw any natural evidence. He understood that God calls those things which do not exist as though they did.

(As it is written, "I have made you a father of many nations") In the presence of Him whom he believed - God, who gives life to the dead and calls those things which do not exist as though they did.

~ Romans 4 : 17

✟ The walls of Jericho.

But it came to pass on the seventh day that they rose early, about the dawning of the day, and marched around the city seven times in the same manner. On that day only they marched around the city seven times. And the seventh time it happened, when the priests blew the trumpets that Joshua said to the people: "Shout, for the Lord has given you the city!" So the people shouted when the priests blew the trumpets. And it happened when the people heard the sound of the trumpet, and the people shouted with a great shout, that the wall fell down flat.

~ Joshua 6 : 15 – 16, 20a

Through the gift of faith, the children of Israel marched around the city of Jericho claiming that God had given them the city (past tense) before the walls ever fell.

✦ Elijah and the rain.

And Elijah the Tishbite, of the inhabitants of Gilead, said to Ahab, "As the Lord God of Israel lives, before whom I stand, there shall not be dew nor rain these years, except at my word."

~ I Kings 17 : I

Elijah had the assurance that there would be no rain for three-and-a-half years. By the gift of faith, Elijah had assurance that it would rain when he asked for rain, even though he couldn't see the rain.

Then Elijah said to Ahab, "Go up, eat and drink; for there is the sound of abundance of rain." So Ahab went up to eat and drink. And Elijah went up to the top of Carmel; then he bowed down on the ground, and put his face between his knees, and said to his servant, "Go up now, look toward the sea." So he went up and looked, and said, "There is nothing." And seven times he said, "Go again." Then it came to pass the seventh time, that he said, "There is a cloud, as small as a man's hand, rising out of the sea!" So he said, "Go up, say to Ahab, 'Prepare your chariot, and go down before the rain stops you.'"

~ I Kings 18 : 41 - 44

✦ Faith that the famine would end.

Then Elisha said, "Hear the word of the Lord. Thus says the Lord: 'Tomorrow about this time a seah of fine flour shall be sold for a shekel, and two seahs of barley for a shekel, at the gate of Samaria.'"

~ 2 Kings 7 : I

By the gift of faith, Elisha had the assurance that the victory would be won in the camp the day before the natural eyes saw it come to pass. No wonder he could tell the man so. He had already won the victory for them! He had it in his soul!

9. Working of Miracles

To understand what the working of miracles is, we need to understand what it is *not*.

✓ **It is not so-called miracles of science.**

The gift of the working of miracles is not what some call miracles of science. Natural science is not a supernatural miracle. It is a natural man using natural intellect to deal with natural laws. Natural wisdom is foolishness when compared to God's wisdom.

Some preachers stand in their pulpit attempting to explain:

To another the working of miracles, to another prophecy, to another discerning of spirits, to another different kinds of tongues, to another the interpretation of tongues.

~ I Corinthians 12 : 10

These preachers refer to the "marvelous miracle age" in which we are now living. But, the modern medical science and technological age are produced by natural brains, and it has nothing to do with the manifestation of the Spirit of God which is known as the working of miracles.

✓ **It is not simply a wonder of nature.**

This gift must not be reduced to a surprise or wonder. Many people look at the wonders of nature and say, "Oh that is a miracle". Some who are unlearned in the things of God attempt to reduce the working of miracles to a time in the distant past when God created this magnificent world in which we live. However, the working of miracles is a manifestation of the Spirit of God in our day.

So that you come short in no gift, eagerly waiting for the revelation of our Lord Jesus Christ.
~ I Corinthians 1 : 7

The apostle Paul prays here under the inspiration of the Holy Spirit, that the church would not lose any spiritual gifts until the Lord Jesus returns. Thus, the gift of working of miracles has not been relegated to the distant past. It is a current gift which will remain in operation at least until Jesus returns.

✓ **It is not simply a surprise.**

Often, when modern church buildings, college buildings, hospital buildings, school buildings, etc., are completed, someone will say, "It's a miracle of God". However, a building in and of itself is not a miracle. The size and shear beauty of it may be surprising, along with the fact that it was ever completed. It may be surprising that it turned out decent and usable. But, such things can also be produced by natural sinners who fight against God's miracle working power.

✓ **It is not modern surgical skills.**

This gift cannot be our modern surgical skills – though such skills are very valuable. Our modern surgeons can take man apart, but they cannot put him together again. They sew him together with surgical sutures, but they must wait for the wound to heal. There is nothing supernatural about that. Doctors who do not even know God can possess modern surgical skills.

The Working of Miracles Is:

Let us, first of all, break it down to its original Greek meaning:

• "Working" : "energema" : meaning, *an energy; to be in work; to be effective; active; operative; to energize or to be energized.*

• "Miracles" : "dunamis" : meaning, *act of power; special miraculous power (usually by implication a miracle itself); capability; power to do anything; power – might in action; a work with reference to the power required for its performance.*

> *The Spiritual gift of the working of miracles is a supernatural manifestation of the Spirit of God doing a supernatural act that none of the other eight spiritual gifts do.*

It is a remarkable or surprising event that happens by the direct intervention of God – not following the general known laws of nature.

And these signs will follow those who believe: In My name they will cast out demons; they will speak with new tongues; they will take up serpents; and if they drink anything deadly, it will by no means hurt them; they will lay hands on the sick, and they will recover." So then, after the Lord had spoken to them, He was received up into heaven, and sat down at the right hand of God. And they went out and preached everywhere, the Lord working with them and confirming the word through the accompanying signs.

~ Mark 16 : 17 – 20

The working of miracles is always supernatural and contrary to nature. It is used to confirm the Word of God preached by God's servants. God works miracles to build faith in His Word.

But the witness which I have is greater than that of John; for the works which the Father has given Me to accomplish, the very works that I do, bear witness of Me, that the Father has sent Me.

~ John 5 : 36 (NASV)

Jesus answered them, "I told you, and you do not believe. The works that I do in My Father's name, they bear witness of Me."

~ John 10 : 25

The absence of miracles will often cause people to doubt God's Word. For instance, when God called Gideon, Gideon asked God, "If I am a mighty man of valor, where are all the miracles?" This was why Moses asked God to be with him to perform miracles. This is why Elisha asked, "Where is the Lord God of Elijah?" This is why God told Joshua, "As I was with Moses, so I will be with thee." This is why we are required to do the same things Jesus did, and take up the work where He left off.

Most assuredly, I say to you, he who believes in Me, the works that I do he will do also; and greater works than these he will do, because I go to My Father.

~ John 14 : 12

Jesus answered them, "I told you, and you do not believe. The works that I do in My Father's name, they bear witness of Me."

~ John 10 : 25

Miracles accomplish God's divine will. Miracles are performed to deliver people in danger, to perform judgments upon those who interfere with His work, to calm storms, to cast out devils, to bind up broken hearts, to deliver the captives, and to deliver people from natural stubbornness and rebellion so they may receive the Holy Ghost. Miracles cause people to be saved. Denying miracles does not!

Numerous examples of working of miracles can be found in the Bible. Just a few will be related here.

New Testament Examples:

✦ Jesus turned the water into wine.

Through the gift of working of miracles, Jesus turned water into wine.

Jesus said to them, "Fill the water pots with water." And they filled them up to the brim. And He said to them, "Draw some out now, and take it to the master of the feast." And they took it. When the master of the feast had tasted the water that was made wine, and did not know where it came from (but the servants who had drawn the water knew), the master of the feast called the bridegroom. And he said to him, "Every man at the beginning sets out the good wine, and when the guests have well drunk, then the inferior. You have kept the good wine until now!"

~ John 2 : 7 - 10

✦ Lazarus' resurrection.

Through this gift, Jesus commanded Lazarus to come forth from the dead after he had already been embalmed.

Now when He had said these things, He cried with a loud voice, "Lazarus, come forth!" And he who had died came out bound hand and foot with grave clothes, and his face was wrapped with a cloth. Jesus said to them, "Loose him, and let him go."

~ John 11 : 43 - 44

✦ Multiplication of fish and bread.

Through a miracle, Jesus fed 5,000 with five loaves and two fish.

And when He had taken the five loaves and the two fish, He looked up to heaven, blessed and broke the loaves, and gave them to His disciples to set before them; and the two fish He divided among them all. So they all ate and were filled. And they took up twelve baskets full of fragments and of the fish. Now those who had eaten the loaves were about five thousand men.

~ Mark 6 : 41 - 44

✦ The leper made whole.

Nine lepers were healed; but one of them was made whole as he later worshipped Jesus. The nine that were healed did not have their missing limbs restored. The man who returned found that he had a whole nose, a whole ear, a whole hand, etc. It was more than just a healing... it was a miracle!

And Jesus answering said, "Were there not ten cleansed? But where are the nine? There are not found that returned to give glory to God, save this stranger." And he said unto him, "Arise, go thy way: thy faith hath made thee whole."

~ Luke 17 : 17 – 19 (KJV)

✦ Woman raised from the dead.

When Peter went into a room and found the people weeping over a corpse, he first knelt and prayed. Then he arose, and commanded the woman to arise. She was restored to life. This miracle resulted in many turning to God.

Then Peter arose and went with them. When he had come, they brought him to the upper room. And all the widows stood by him weeping, showing the tunics and garments which Dorcas had made while she was with them. But Peter put them all out, and knelt down and prayed. And turning to the body he said, "Tabitha, arise." And she opened her eyes, and when she saw Peter she sat up. Then he gave her his hand and lifted her up; and when he had called the saints and widows, he presented her alive. And it became known throughout all Joppa, and many believed on the Lord. So it was that he stayed many days in Joppa with Simon, a tanner.

~ Acts 9 : 39 - 43

✦ A young man raised from the dead.

Through the gift of the working of miracles, Paul raised a man back to life after the man fell out of a window and was killed.

But we sailed away from Philippi after the Days of Unleavened Bread, and in five days joined them at Troas, where we stayed seven days. Now on the first day of the week, when the disciples came together to break bread, Paul, ready to depart the next day, spoke to them and continued his message until midnight. There were many lamps in the upper room where they[a] were gathered together. And in a window sat a certain young man named Eutychus, who was sinking into a deep sleep. He was overcome by sleep; and as Paul continued speaking, he fell down from the third story and was taken up dead. But Paul went down, fell on him, and embracing him said, "Do not trouble yourselves, for his life is in him." Now when he had come up, had broken bread and eaten, and talked a long while, even till daybreak, he departed. And they brought the young man in alive, and they were not a little comforted.

~ Acts 20 : 6 - 12

✦ Special miracles.

God worked special, unusual miracles through handkerchiefs and aprons.

Now God worked unusual miracles by the hands of Paul, so that even handkerchiefs or aprons were brought from his body to the sick, and the diseases left them and the evil spirits went out of them.

~ Acts 19 : 11 - 12

✦ The sorcerer became blind.

Through this gift, Paul struck a man blind.

"And now, indeed, the hand of the Lord is upon you, and you shall be blind, not seeing the sun for a time." And immediately a dark mist fell on him, and he went around seeking someone to lead him by the hand.

~ Acts 13 : 11

We can also see the operation of this through two deacons, Philip and Stephen. They had signs and wonders follow their ministry confirming the Word of God which they preached (Acts 6 - 8). Through Ananias, who held no known office in the church, he laid hands on Paul, and Paul was healed and received the Holy Spirit.

Most of these are instances where God trusted men with miracles.

> *The Bible is a book of miracles, and God is a God of miracles.*

Old Testament Examples:

✦ The dead raised.
God raised the dead through the prayers of Elijah.

And he stretched himself out on the child three times, and cried out to the Lord and said, "O Lord my God, I pray, let this child's soul come back to him."

~ I Kings 17 : 21

✦ Elijah had power over rain.
And Elijah the Tishbite, of the inhabitants of Gilead, said to Ahab, "As the Lord God of Israel lives, before whom I stand, there shall not be dew nor rain these years, except at my word."

~ I Kings 17 : 1

Then Elijah said to Ahab, "Go up, eat and drink; for there is the sound of abundance of rain." So Ahab went up to eat and drink. And Elijah went up to the top of Carmel; then he bowed down on the ground, and put his face between his knees, and said to his servant, "Go up now, look toward the sea." So he went up and looked, and said, "There is nothing." And seven times he said, "Go again." Then it came to pass the seventh time, that he said, "There is a cloud, as small as a man's hand, rising out of the sea!" So he said, "Go up, say to Ahab, 'Prepare your chariot, and go down before the rain stops you.'"

~ I Kings 18 : 41 - 44

✛ Children who mocked Elisha were eaten by bears.

Then he went up from there to Bethel; and as he was going up the road, some youths came from the city and mocked him, and said to him, "Go up, you baldhead! Go up, you baldhead!" So he turned around and looked at them, and pronounced a curse on them in the name of the Lord. And two female bears came out of the woods and mauled forty-two of the youths.

~ 2 Kings 2 : 23 - 24

✛ Men who came to arrest Elijah were killed by the fire.

And he said, "It is Elijah the Tishbite." Then the king sent to him a captain of fifty with his fifty men. So he went up to him; and there he was, sitting on the top of a hill. And he spoke to him: "Man of God, the king has said, 'Come down!'" So Elijah answered and said to the captain of fifty, "If I am a man of God, then let fire come down from heaven and consume you and your fifty men." And fire came down from heaven and consumed him and his fifty. Then he sent to him another captain of fifty with his fifty men. And he answered and said to him: "Man of God, thus has the king said, 'Come down quickly!'" So Elijah answered and said to them, "If I am a man of God, let fire come down from heaven and consume you and your fifty men." And the fire of God came down from heaven and consumed him and his fifty.

~ 2 Kings I : 8b - 12

✦ Gehazi gets Naaman's leprosy.

Now he went in and stood before his master. Elisha said to him, "Where did you go, Gehazi?" And he said, "Your servant did not go anywhere." Then he said to him, "Did not my heart go with you when the man turned back from his chariot to meet you? Is it time to receive money and to receive clothing, olive groves and vineyards, sheep and oxen, male and female servants? Therefore the leprosy of Naaman shall cling to you and your descendants forever." And he went out from his presence leprous, as white as snow.

~ 2 Kings 5 : 25 - 27

✦ The 10 plagues in Egypt were unusual miracles.

Plague 1   :   Water changing to blood. (Exodus 7 : 20)

Plague 2   :   Frogs. (Exodus 8 : 6)

Plague 3   :   Lice. (Exodus 8 : 17)

Plague 4   :   Flies. (Exodus 8 : 24)

Plague 5   :   Livestock diseased. (Exodus 9 : 6)

Plague 6   :   Boils. (Exodus 9 : 10)

Plague 7   :   Hail. (Exodus 9 : 23)

Plague 8   :   Locusts. (Exodus 10 : 13)

Plague 9   :   Darkness. (Exodus 10 : 22)

Plague 10 :   Death of firstborn. (Exodus 12 : 29)

✦ The sun stood still when Joshua prayed.

Then Joshua spoke to the Lord in the day when the Lord delivered up the Amorites before the children of Israel, and he said in the sight of Israel: "Sun, stand still over Gibeon; and Moon, in the Valley of Aijalon." So the sun stood still, and the moon stopped, till the people had revenge upon their enemies. Is this not written in the Book of

Jasher? So the sun stood still in the midst of heaven, and did not hasten to go down for about a whole day. And there has been no day like that, before it or after it, that the Lord heeded the voice of a man; for the Lord fought for Israel.

~ Joshua 10 : 12 - 14

✦ God took the burn out of the fire for the 3 Hebrew children in the fiery furnace.

Then Nebuchadnezzar was full of fury, and the expression on his face changed toward Shadrach, Meshach, and Abed-Nego. He spoke and commanded that they heat the furnace seven times more than it was usually heated. And he commanded certain mighty men of valor who were in his army to bind Shadrach, Meshach, and Abed-Nego, and cast them into the burning fiery furnace. Then these men were bound in their coats, their trousers, their turbans, and their other garments, and were cast into the midst of the burning fiery furnace. Therefore, because the king's command was urgent, and the furnace exceedingly hot, the flame of the fire killed those men who took up Shadrach, Meshach, and Abed-Nego. And these three men, Shadrach, Meshach, and Abed-Nego, fell down bound into the midst of the burning fiery furnace. Then King Nebuchadnezzar was astonished; and he rose in haste and spoke, saying to his counselors, "Did we not cast three men bound into the midst of the fire?" They answered and said to the king, "True, O king." "Look!" he answered, "I see four men loose, walking in the midst of the fire; and they are not hurt, and the form of the fourth is like the Son of God." Then Nebuchadnezzar went near the mouth of the burning fiery furnace and spoke, saying, "Shadrach, Meshach, and Abed-Nego, servants of the Most High God, come out, and come here." Then Shadrach, Meshach, and Abed-Nego came from the midst of the fire.

~ Daniel 3 : 19 - 26

✦ God's hand was over the children of Israel.

And I have led you forty years in the wilderness. Your clothes have not worn out on you, and your sandals have not worn out on your feet.

~ Deuteronomy 29 : 5

He also brought them out with silver and gold, and there was none feeble among His tribes.
~ Psalm 105 : 37

Fruits of the Spirit

*Well-balanced Christians not only know their faith...
they show it.*

It is one thing to have revelation from the Holy Spirit for someone else (gifts); it is entirely another thing to be able to administer or deliver that revelation according to the fruit of the Holy Spirit. When we can have the two working together, we shall see and experience a much greater impact of the Kingdom of God in our midst than ever before. Gifts can be instant, developing fruit takes time. The exercising of the Spiritual Gifts should be a growing and maturing ministry that sees us becoming more effective and accurate as we allow the fruits of the Spirit to come forth within us.

For the gifts to be developed in us in a God-glorifying way, we need to also demonstrate a consistency in displaying the fruit.

> *You can fake the gift of the Spirit,*
> *but you cannot fake the fruits of the Spirit.*

But the fruit of the Spirit is love, joy, peace, longsuffering, kindness, goodness, faithfulness, gentleness, self-control. Against such there is no law. And those who are Christ's have crucified the flesh with its passions and desires. If we live in the Spirit, let us also walk in the Spirit. Let us not become conceited, provoking one another, envying one another.
>   ~ Galatians 5 : 22 - 26

> *Christians should out-live, out-love and out-laugh anyone else.*

Love is the Christian's ID card. It is easy to love sometimes. It is easy to be joyful sometimes. But, we need to demonstrate an ongoing consistency in these fruits. It is obvious that life is not simply love, joy, and peace. Other fruits speak strongly of the need for endurance (when things are going against us), for self-control (when we feel like giving in to temptations), and for faithfulness (when it seems others are not remaining faithful).

> *When we yield ourselves to the Spirit's control,*
> *we do not lose our self-control.*

The gifts display the revelation and power of God that is available to bless and edify others. The fruit will bring the cross of Jesus Christ to bear in our lives, for it will cause us to deny ourselves, as well as guard ourselves against those who would want to manipulate us to live differently.

> *Let your testimony be written in large enough letters*
> *that the world can always read it.*
> *Your life needs to help paint your neighbor's picture of God.*

God has not called us to prove the gospel, He has called us to practice it.

> *God wants spiritual fruits, not religious nuts.*

Good Advice When You Operate in the Gifts of the Spirit:

> *Advice is like snow, the softer it falls, the deeper it goes.*

✦ Have a **strong desire** to release the gifts of the Holy Spirit. No one will flow in the gifts if there is no desire to do so. God responds to desire.

Delight yourself also in the Lord, and He shall give you the desires of your heart.
                                                                    ~ Psalm 37 : 4

You open Your hand and satisfy the desire of every living thing. The Lord is righteous in all His ways, gracious in all His works. The Lord is near to all who call upon Him, to all who call upon Him in truth. He will fulfill the desire of those who fear Him.; He also will hear their cry and save them. The Lord preserves all who love Him, but all the wicked He will destroy. My mouth shall speak the praise of the Lord, and all flesh shall bless His holy name forever and ever.

                                                          ~ Psalm 145 : 16 – 19a

You have given him his heart's desire, and have not withheld the request of his lips.

~ Psalm 21 : 2

The desire of the righteous will be granted.

~ Proverbs 10 : 24b

Paul desired to impart spiritual gifts into the saints: *"For I long* (desire earnestly) *to see you, that I may impart* (give a share of) *to you some spiritual* ˙(belonging to the Spirit, determined by, influenced by, or proceeding from it) *gift, so that you may be established* (set fast, fixed firmly)."

~ Romans 1 : 11

The Apostle also exhorted us to: *"Earnestly (serious in mind or intention; demanding serious attention) desire (be zealous for, covet) the best gifts."*

~ 1 Corinthians 12 : 31a

> *Desire creates the power.*
> *Desire is the starting point of all achievement.*

Pursue love, and desire spiritual gifts.

~ 1 Corinthians 14 : 1a

Cultivate your desire to flow in spiritual gifts. Pray for God to stir your spirit over these matters. Don't be afraid to ask! It is always good to learn from others. When someone is functioning in a lovely way in the gifts, don't be afraid to approach them to learn more.

✛ Be **sensitive to God.** That means building a personal relationship with Jesus and the Holy Spirit in prayer, and the studying of the Word of God. It is through taking time to be with God that we learn to recognize His voice, and when He is speaking to us. If we do not know His voice, we will never be able to respond to Him or exercise the gifts. Seek God's face, not just His hands.

> *To walk with God we must make it*
> *a practice to talk to God.*

When you relate to God as a person, you develop a personal relationship with Him.

✛ Know the **right time** to deliver that certain information God wants to make known through you.

> *The right thing at the wrong time is the wrong thing,*
> *but the right thing at the right time is the right thing.*

> *Well – timed silence has more eloquence than speech.*

The gifts of the Holy Spirit are usually for exercising in a public manner. Therefore, we need to cultivate a sensitive spirit towards God and also towards the meeting or environment we are in. God is not a God of disorder or chaos, and if we are sensitive to Him, He will show us how to operate in the gifts in a way that is beautiful.

> *Sensitivity will also help give us the right timing and the right way to go about things.*

✦ Know **how to minister** that "word" in an edifying way.

> *Often the ministering of the gift is spoiled and discredited by the mannerism of the delivery rather than the accuracy of what is being said or done.*

A lot of people mean well, but their meanness is greater than their wellness.

> *Knowing what to say is not enough; we must know how to say it.*

Gentle words fall lightly, but they have great weight. Some oil of kindness will save a lot of friction. Kind words do not wear out the tongue. Cultivating kindness is a most important part of your life.

> *The kindly words that fall today*
> *may bear its fruit tomorrow.*

Sometimes it is not what you say that counts, but how you say it.

> *Prepare and prevent instead of repair and repent.*

If you must criticize, try criticizing the fault instead of the person. The hardest criticism, if cushioned with kindness and enthusiasm, becomes bearable and helpful.

✦ Be willing and prepared to accept any **fine-tuning, teaching** and **correction** from those over us in the Lord.

Rebuke a wise man, and he will love you. Give instruction to a wise man and he will be still wiser; teach a just man, and he will increase in learning.
~ Proverbs 9 : 8b - 9

> *The largest room... is room for improvement.*

Take firm hold of instruction, do not let go; keep her, for she is your life.
~ Proverbs 4 : 13

> *When you're all wrong*
> *and willing to admit it, you're all right.*

He who disdains (ignores, refuses) instruction (discipline) despises his own soul (himself), but he who heeds rebuke (correction) gets understanding.

~ Proverbs 15 : 32

> *Don't despise correction or criticism. If it is untrue,*
> *disregard it; if it is unfair, don't let it irritate you;*
> *if it is ignorant, smile; if it is justified, learn from it.*

Fools despise wisdom and instruction.

~ Proverbs 1 : 7b

✦ **Take responsibility** for what effects the word of knowledge has after you have "delivered" or "spoken" it.

> *Take responsibility,*
> *the more you are willing to accept responsibility*
> *for your actions, the more credibility you will have.*

Having to suffer the consequences of our acts tends to develop responsibility. If God writes opportunity on one side of the door, he writes responsibility on the other. Are you willing to risk your reputation to fill your responsibility?

On the other hand, it is better to prepare and prevent than to repair and repent. Never accuse others to excuse yourself.

> *Blaming your faults on your nature*
> *does not change the nature of your faults.*

Gain **knowledge from God.**

> *He is wise that takes God for a teacher.*

The answer to ignorance is knowledge. Become informed about what the Word of God has to say. I Corinthians chapters 12 to 14 and Romans 12 are important portions of scripture to know well. Knowledge is power only when it is turned on. Like power, it must be hitched to something effective. The highest knowledge is the knowledge of God.

> *The most important thing about knowledge is to have an appetite for it.*

 Gain **knowledge from people.**

Wise people store up knowledge.

~ Proverbs 10 : 14a

> *He who will not learn from anyone but himself has a fool for a teacher.*

It is not good for a soul to be without knowledge.

~ Proverbs 19 : 2a

Have a teachable spirit. In matters of the gifts of the Holy Spirit, there are many things to learn. If we do not have a humble, teachable spirit, then we may finish up in real trouble.

> *As long as you're green, you're growing.*
> *As soon as you're ripe, you start to rot.*

But the excellence (advantage, profit) of knowledge (knowing, understanding, intelligence, skill) is that wisdom gives life to those who have it.

~ Ecclesiastes 7 : 12b

I thank God for those who have spoken into my life – both to give correction and encouragement. The result of that is that I have grown in confidence and faith to exercise the gifts of the Holy Spirit as I recognize His promptings. Some marvelous things have happened over the years! If we are not teachable and we begin to develop "gifts" through a wrong understanding or in error, we will certainly self-destruct further down the road. The tragedy is that many lives can also be ruined in the process as well. If you want to be used by God, don't be too proud to receive loving instruction!

> *Christianity is a movement, not a condition;*
> *a journey, not a harbor.*

He shall die for lack (without) of instruction (receiving correction, discipline, listening to the truth), and in the greatness of his folly (abounding of his perversity) he shall go astray (stagger to ruin).

~ Proverbs 5 : 23

> *Leadership and learning are indispensable to each other.*

He who ceases to learn cannot adequately teach.

> *Others' experience is yesterday's answer to today's problem.*

✦ **Observe other people** who flow in the gifts of the Holy Spirit.

> *The best education is caught, not taught.*

Imitate (follow, pattern after) me, just as I also imitate (follow, pattern after) Christ.

~ I Corinthians 11 : 1

Learn from the mistakes of others. You'll never live long enough to make them all yourself. Learn from their good points and also their not so good points.

> ### Eat the meat, spit out the bones.

Recognize that the human part of us can make mistakes, even in the Holy Spirit ministry!

✦ Have the **right motivation.** Make sure that your motivation is always to serve God and lift up His people.

For the ways of man are before the eyes of the Lord, and He ponders (surveys, takes account, considers, examines) all his paths.

~ Proverbs 5 : 21

Always remember that the Gifts of the Holy Spirit are to edify, exhort and comfort people.

He who prophecies speaks edification (strengthening, building up) and exhortation (encouragement) and comfort to men.

~ I Corinthians 14 : 1 - 3

✦ To minister effectively in the gifts, one needs to **love people** and have good relationships with people.

> ### God's Word tells us of His love;
> ### our words should tell others about our love
> ### because of His love.

In 1 Corinthians 13, we are told that it is possible to develop great gifts of God in our lives, yet still not love! We can separate our gifts, develop them to a tremendous degree, and still be impersonal and unloving towards people. The Bible says if we do that, then we are nothing! We have missed God somewhere – even though we can use His gifts. That is a great tragedy and, far too often, is the testimony of too many Christians over the years.

> *It is love for God and people that teaches us the most about the exercising of spiritual gifts.*

If you want to be a ministering vessel, you need to know something about love and compassion. You are dealing with eternal souls, and the result of our operation in the gifts can mean release or ruin for many years to come.

> *No one is too big to be kind and courteous; a great man shows his greatness by the way he treats little men.*

It is not by chance that 1 Corinthians 13 is placed where it is – right in the middle of chapters 12 and 14 which teach us about spiritual gifts.

> *A broken heart can be mended into a more beautiful pattern if the stitches are made with kindness and love.*

Some people think that in order to walk in the supernatural, you have to be super-spiritual, weird or spooky. They think that you have to live in your own world, talking to nobody, isolating yourself in the name of spirituality. That's not what God has called us to be.

✦   When we flow in the gifts of the spirit, we cannot demand that the people accept what we say. They have a free will.

✦   **A right relationship** in a **doctrinally-sound, spirit-filled** church is very important if you want to be used by God. The importance of being established into the life of a church cannot be overemphasized.

> *A Christian outside a church is like an athlete without a team.*
> *A Christian without a church is like a bee without a hive.*

If we want to be effective in the gifts of the Spirit, we must have roots growing in a church home where our gifts can be exercised, developed, and proven that they are, indeed, the Holy Spirit and not some human ego trip. It is vital that our gifts can be judged by the body of Christ.

Let two or three prophets speak, and let the others judge.

~ I Corinthians 14 : 29

Do not quench the Spirit, do not despise prophecies. Test all things; hold fast what is good. Abstain from every form of evil.

~ I Thessalonians 5 : 19 - 22

✦ Be obedient!

> *Obedience sheds light on the hidden things of God.*

Your obedience to God today determines what you'll be for God tomorrow. A small step of obedience is a giant step to blessings.

> *Obeying God is the best prescription for spiritual health.*

Now it shall come to pass, if you diligently obey the voice of the Lord your God, to observe carefully all His commandments which I command you today, that the Lord your God will set you high above all nations of the earth.
                                                      ~ Deuteronomy 28 : 1 - 3

> *The cost of obedience*
> *is nothing compared to the cost of disobedience.*

True obedience is true freedom.

For your obedience has become known to all. Therefore I am glad on your behalf; but I want you to be wise in what is good, and simple concerning evil.
                                                      ~ Romans 16 : 19

There is no shame in taking orders from those who, themselves, have learned to obey. Unwavering obedience to the true principles we learn will assure our spiritual survival. Why do you obey? Out of fear, or out of love? Some men obey from fear; good men obey from love.

Give God the glory!

> *We are mirrors to reflect the glory of God; a mirror never calls attention to itself unless there are flaws in it.*

I am the Lord, that is My name; and My glory I will not give to another, nor my praise to carved images.

~ Isaiah 42 : 8

> *If you want your influence to last, put Christ first.*

If anyone speaks, let him speak as the oracles of God. If anyone ministers, let him do it as with the ability which God supplies, that in all things God may be glorified through Jesus Christ, to whom belong the glory and the dominion forever and ever. Amen.

~ I Peter 4 : 11

> *Christ is not valued at all unless He is valued above all.*

The Christian's greatest joy is found in letting God fully possess everything that is His. Putting God first brings satisfaction that lasts.

 ## 3 Kinds of Revelation.

If you want to be used by God, you need to understand that there are different kinds of revelation. Not everything that you receive when you are praying necessarily comes from God. There are three kinds of revelation.

In Matthew 16 : 13 – 19 and 23, Jesus calls Peter by three different names. He calls him *"Simon"*, He calls him *"Peter"*, and He calls him "Satan".

Jesus had asked the disciples, *"Who do men say that I, the Son of Man, am?"* They answered, *"Some say John the Baptist, some Elijah, and others Jeremiah or one of the prophets."* But Peter said, *"You are the Christ, the Son of the living God."* Jesus said, *"Blessed are you, Simon Bar-Jonah, for flesh and blood has not revealed this to you, but My Father who is in heaven."* In other words, it was by revelation that Simon knew that Jesus was the Christ. At that point, Jesus changed Simon's name. *"And I also say to you that you are Peter, and on this rock (this revelation that you have received which came from above, this revelation, that I am the Christ), I will build My church and the gates shall not prevail against it. And I will give you the keys of the kingdom of heaven."*

Simon walked in flesh-and-blood revelation. Jesus made that clear when he said, *"Blessed are you, Simon Bar-Jonah, for flesh and blood has not revealed this to you."*

Later, Peter tried to stop Jesus from going to Jerusalem. At that point, Jesus called him "Satan". Jesus said, *"Get behind Me, Satan!"*

> ## 3 Kinds of Revelation:
> *As Simon, he walked in flesh-and-blood revelation,*
> *as Peter, he walked in Holy Spirit-inspired revelation,*
> *as Satan, he walked in demonic-inspired revelation.*

Just because a man was right yesterday, does not mean that he will be right today. Here's the chief of the apostolic team. At one point, he was in the flesh. At one point, he was in the Spirit. At another point, the devil was speaking through him. That's why, as a believer, you need to have discernment. Otherwise, some prophet coming around saying this or that might be able to deceive you. You need discernment to understand what is of God and what is not.

> *Your revelation reflects your name.*
> *Your revelation is your spiritual identity.*

When the disciple's name was "Simon", he walked in flesh and blood revelation. When his name was called "Peter", it was because he walked in Holy Spirit-inspired revelation. And, when Jesus called him "Satan", it was because he was walking in demonic-inspired revelation. Your revelation is your name. You are what you believe. That's why your identity must be in Christ. Christ in you is the hope of glory.

✦ Put your **mind** on the **things from above.**

Look at that verse again. After Jesus said, *"Get behind me, Satan,"* ~ Matthew 16 : 23 He rebuked Satan that was trying to sneak through. Then He said, *"Peter, you are an offense to Me, for you are not mindful of the things of God, but the things of men."* Peter had placed his mind on the things of men. That means that his mind was not on the things of God.

> *You walk in the spirit
> by keeping your mind on the things from above.*

This will help you in your walk with God. The Bible says:

Finally, brethren, whatever things are true, whatever things are noble, whatever things are just, whatever things are lovely, whatever things are in good report, if there is any virtue and if there is anything praiseworthy- meditate on these things.

~ Philippians 4 : 8

> *Walking in the Spirit is being in tune with God.*

You can be in tune with God no matter what you are doing. You can be in the Spirit as you are reading a book or having a conversation with someone. Most of the time, when somebody is sharing a problem with me at the altar or when I am praying with someone (even while they are still speaking), I put my mind on the things from above. I'm in the Spirit to see what God will tell me. Often when people tell you about a problem, they don't tell you the whole story. They only tell you what they want you to know so you will be compassionate, take their side, and help them immediately. They leave out the other part of the story. So, when people tell you their stories, always listen to the Spirit of God – by putting your mind on the things from above. Just ask the Father to show you the truth. God will begin to give you the information you need to minister effectively.

How does that information come to you? Sometimes it comes through a thought. Sometimes it comes through a word that you hear in a still, small voice. Sometimes, it is an impression, a quickening, a feeling that you get.

Sometimes people say, "I have a bad feeling about this." What do they mean by that? They mean that they know something is wrong. That feeling can be the Holy Spirit speaking to them.

✦ You need to be able to **handle spiritual information.**

You need to know how to handle the information that you receive. There are some people whom the Holy Spirit cannot trust with certain information.

Jesus told His disciples, *"I still have many things to say to you, but you cannot bear them now."*

~ John 16 : 12

Some people can't receive from God because they can't handle the information. If you want to be used by God, you must have shelving ability. This means to have the ability to compartmentalize, or shelve information in such a way, that it does not affect what you are doing when God speaks to you. You have to be able to handle it.

Sometimes, God shows you things while you are ministering to a person. Just because God shows you something about a person, doesn't mean that you are supposed to say it to them. Maybe you are just supposed to pray about it. You have to learn these things. This is the school of the Spirit. The more you are able to be sensitive and pray about the secrets that the Holy Spirit gives you, the more He's going to entrust to you.

Before you get jealous about why someone else always gets the revelation and the words from God, you need to stop and think about it. Can you handle it? Some people would cause more damage than blessings to the kingdom if they had a special gift. When God gives you the ability to discern in the Spirit, you have to be able to exercise self-control and love. We don't need to show off. One of the things that has happened in some ministries is that they have moved from miracles into marketing. People try to prostitute their gifts. When they get these revelations, they want to sell them. They want to control people.

There is a Jezebel spirit – not just in the Church, but in the pulpits where preachers prostitute themselves. How? By using their gifts to make themselves rich and famous. God is not against you being blessed and prosperous. The real issue is: Can God trust you with more? Can He trust you with the healing gift? Are you going to build His kingdom, or are you going to build your own kingdom? You must keep a servant's heart because that's what you are there for. Do you get prideful thinking, "Do you know what kind of man is standing in your midst?" Be careful.

You must realize that it is not about you; it is about the people you have been called to reach. Be careful how you handle truth, and be careful how you share it.

If you want to be used by God, it's important that you hear from the Holy Spirit. Whenever you hear something, remember that there are three kinds of revelation, and that it doesn't necessarily come from God. If what you have heard is not confirmed through the Word of God, it's probably a flesh and blood revelation or a demonic inspired revelation. Be careful that what you receive is confirmed through the principles of the Word.

God has tied Himself to His Word. He has exalted His Word above His Name. So, anything you receive that is out of the boundaries and the principles of the Word is probably a work of the flesh or demonically inspired. Leave it alone. Spiritual exercise will help you grow in this area. It's like a muscle that you exercise. At first, you may just get little words, but the more you exercise, the more your gift will grow.

> *If you listen to the Holy Spirit,*
> *people will think that you are a genius!*

Chapter 6

You Can Cast It Down and Cast It Out

5 Spiritual Dimensions

The Spirit of the Lord is upon Me because He has anointed Me to preach the gospel to the poor; He has sent Me to heal the brokenhearted, to proclaim liberty to the captives and recovery of sight to the blind, to set at liberty those who are oppressed; to proclaim the acceptable year of the Lord.

~ Luke 4 : 18 - 19

When Jesus made His mission statement at the beginning of His ministry (in Luke 4), He expressed what I call the 5 Spiritual Dimensions – or 5 Levels of Operation – in the ministry. These are not discussed in numerical order. I believe that these dimensions are an important biblical blueprint for ministry. If you want to be used by God, you need to understand these 5 Spiritual Dimensions.

First Dimension: Teaching and Preaching

Verse 18 says, *"The Spirit of the Lord is upon Me, because He has anointed Me to preach the Gospel to the poor."*

> *Teaching is explaining, and preaching is proclaiming.*

That is the first dimension: to preach and teach the gospel – which also includes prophesying and proclaiming. We preach the Gospel to the poor, but the mission statement does not stop there. It goes further.

Second Dimension: Inner Healing

The second level of operation is found in the next statement Jesus made. He said, *"Because He has anointed Me to heal the brokenhearted."* The second level of operation in Jesus' ministry is inner healing. The inner healing dimension deals with inner, emotional pain. This inner pain may be present due to negative life experiences. The negative experiences can be the cause of emotional pain which the victim carries with them long after the damage occurred.

The Lord is near to those who have a broken heart, and saves such as have a contrite spirit.

~ Psalm 34 : 18

Jesus lifted the shame that was upon people. He allowed a prostitute to wash His feet, and He forgave a woman who was caught in the act of adultery. Inner healing ministry is important. There are many people who come to church who have broken hearts and a myriad of emotional issues. God wants to use us to minister inner healing to them.

Third Dimension: Physical Healing

The next statement Jesus made was that He had been anointed to bring recovery of sight to the blind. The third dimension of His ministry is physical healing. It is not enough to just preach the Gospel. When someone gets saved, they need to receive inner healing. If they are physically sick, they may need to experience the healing power of God. The third dimension is found in the next part of the verse where Jesus said, "He has sent me to bring *recovery of sight to the blind.*"

Fourth Dimension: Deliverance

The fourth dimension of Jesus' ministry is found in the statement, *"He has anointed Me to set at liberty those who are oppressed."* This is deliverance ministry.

Fifth Dimension: Restoration and Prosperity

And finally, the fifth dimension is found in Jesus' statement that He had been anointed, *"to proclaim the acceptable year of the Lord."* This is restoration and prosperity. God wants His people to prosper in every area of their lives: spiritually, emotionally, physically, financially, and relationally. Our God is also a redeemer. He can restore what was lost.

When Jesus ascended, He gave gifts to the Church. He gave some to be apostles, prophets, evangelists, teachers, and pastors. These apostles, prophets, evangelists, teachers and pastors (ministry gifts) are called to operate in the five dimensions... so are believers... and so are you. Some ministers only minister in one or two dimensions. That is okay; as long as the church leaders make sure that their church is exposed to all the dimensions, by inviting or bringing in guest speakers that operate in those dimensions in which the church leaders do not operate.

> *The preaching of a one-dimensional gospel creates dysfunctional Christians.*

One of the problems that we have in the body of Christ today is that there are so many ministries that major in only one level of operation. This is what I call the *one-dimensional gospel*. Some ministers take the message of prosperity, deliverance, healing, inner healing, or the prophetic, and that's all they teach. They do not understand that teaching only one part (prosperity, deliverance, healing, inner healing or the prophetic), *without* the rest of the puzzle, sounds awkward to the hearer.

Some ministers focus only on preaching an evangelistic Gospel. It is good to preach the Gospel. It is good to get people saved. But then, they need to get healed, delivered, restored, and begin prospering. We need to minister to spirit, soul, and body if we want to be effective. The lack of any of these dimensions creates spiritual malnourishment and dysfunction.

> *God does not want His Church*
> *to be full of people who are dysfunctional.*
> *God wants people to be complete.*
> *He wants them to be whole.*

It is not good that so many churches and ministries major in only one of the five dimensions. Why do people sometimes come to church with their problems, and return home in the same condition? It could be because the church service emphasizes only one dimension, and therefore, there is a spiritual lack in the ministry they receive. If you are going to be used by God, you need to understand the 5 dimensions of Jesus' ministry, and function in whatever capacity you feel the grace to minister.

Deliverance Ministry

In this part of the book, I am going to concentrate on discussing the fourth dimension: deliverance ministry. It is the desire of my heart that this level of operation of Jesus' ministry is studied more in-depth, so that you will be trained and equipped to stand your ground against the enemy in spiritual warfare.

The Church is supposed to be the moral authority of our society, but in many cases, we have not learned to fall back into the pattern of biblical truth. Instead, we find ourselves caught up in "religiosity" and religious systems. We, then, forget to return to the basics of Jesus' ministry, which is the dynamics of the power of God, and the manifestation of the gifts of the Spirit. That's why we sometimes find ourselves crippled, and instead of the world finding the answer through us, we are going to the world for answers.

> *Some churches are suffering from what I call,*
> *a "false advertisement syndrome."*
> *They advertise what they do not serve.*

Today, there are many people who have needs in the area of deliverance and inner healing, but cannot receive help because the church does not offer such a ministry. Some churches can be charged for "false advertisement", because they do not serve the Christianity that they advertise, and they do not serve what authentic Christianity has to offer. Can you imagine going to eat at a restaurant, and when they give you the menu, everything that you try to order from the menu is not available. They can't even serve you their specialty! This is called false advertisement.

The Bible is our menu. Jesus said:

Man shall not live by bread alone, but by every word that proceeds from the mouth of God.
                                                                    ~ Matthew 4 : 4

If it is **in** the Word, then we should experience it in our lives, in our ministry, and in the church.

> *God will never give us an assignment*
> *without giving us the power to match the assignment.*

If we are truly the Church that Jesus talks about in Matthew 16, then people should experience life and the fullness of the power of God:

On this rock I will build My church, and the gates of Hades shall not prevail against it.

~ Matthew 16 : 18

We need to realize that we live in the real world, with a real devil and real demons. But thank God, we have a real Savior, and His Name is Jesus Christ.

Sometimes in the body of Christ, we have confused people by trying to teach the Bible without appropriating the authority of the Bible.

The supernatural is real. There is such a thing as *God*. Jesus Christ is real. There is such a thing as the *Holy Spirit*. There are such things *as dreaming spiritual dreams, seeing visions, and prophecy.* There are such things as *angels and demons.* There are such things as *principalities, powers, and spiritual hosts of wickedness in the heavenly places.*

There is a hierarchy in the spirit realm which Paul graphically described in ~ Ephesians 6 : 12. Here, Paul gave us the structure of the enemy's battle plan. It says, *"For we do not wrestle against flesh and blood, but against principalities, against powers, against the rulers of the darkness of this age, against spiritual hosts of wickedness in the heavenly places."*

You need to understand that there is demonic activity at work. Satan operates under camouflage. He camouflages himself. He wants to get people to believe that he is not real, that demonic activity is not real, and that Satanism is not real. If he can do this, then he can win. That is his strategy. That's why Paul warned not to be ignorant of Satan's schemes.

So that no advantage would be taken of us by Satan, for we are not ignorant of his schemes.

2 Corinthians 2 : 11 (NASB)

The Greek word for "advantage" means, the upper hand. Paul is instructing us to not be ignorant of the way Satan works and operates, so that he cannot get the upper hand on us. If you want to be used by God, you should be awakened to the reality of Satan's strategies.

> *If Satan can get you to forget about him,*
> *or not believe in his existence,*
> *you have lost the battle before the fight begins.*

Demons like to operate in darkness... terrorizing people. Demons are afraid of the light of the Word, because the light exposes them in their places of darkness. When we receive Jesus Christ as our Lord and Savior, the Bible says in ~ Colossians 1 : 13, "*He has delivered us from the power of darkness and conveyed us into the kingdom of the Son of His love.*" This means that we have rebelled against Satan's kingdom. That action has opened us up to spiritual warfare, because we, now, represent a threat to his kingdom.

John 10 : 10a says, *"The thief does not come except to steal, and to kill, and to destroy."* Satan doesn't want us to understand that we are in a battle. He wants to fight us in darkness. You need to understand this very important principle: **Satan does not want anyone to understand how his kingdom operates.** He wants to remain in darkness. As long as he remains in darkness – as long as demons can oppress lives without anyone challenging him – he will not manifest himself. But, as soon as you push the "hot button" – as soon as you begin to shine the light on his activities – you will begin to see a reaction. In many of our crusades, conferences, and church meetings around the world, during the preaching and prayer, there are some demonic manifestations.

We need to stand up, because:

God has not given us a spirit of fear, but of power and of love and of a sound mind.

~ 2 Timothy 1 : 7

It is important to know that there is a demonic assignment against marriages, families, neighborhoods, and cities.

I thank God for hospitals, doctors, and medical institutions. We need them, and they are doing a good job. However, there are some problems that people are dealing with that have spiritual roots and cannot be dealt with by the intellect and medicine alone. Unfortunately, some people do not know or see the importance of deliverance. Because the natural man cannot understand the things of the Spirit, we sometimes have highly-educated people with degrees in medicine trying to diagnose people with psychological or pathological disorders, without understanding the true power that is operating in these people's lives. These medical professionals do not understand that the evil activity which is taking place sometimes has nothing to do with mental disorders, but has everything to do with satanic and demonic influence in our society.

> *Certain things cannot be counseled out;*
> *they can only be cast out.*

Deliverance is the practice of expelling demons by authoritative command in the name of Jesus.

Nature of Demons

If you want to be used by God, you need to understand how demons operate. Before you can fight your enemies, one of the things that you have to do is understand their strategy. Learn how they operate. If you are going to come against demonic powers and minister deliverance to people in need, the first thing that you have to understand is the nature of demons.

✦ Demons are Spiritual Beings.

Demons are spirit beings without bodies. They have an intense desire to live in a body so that they can carry out their own desires and use that body for their own purposes. Matthew 8 and Luke 10 : 17 tell us that Jesus cast out the spirits. When you travel, and the airplane is getting ready to land in certain countries, you can sense demonic oppression. I experienced this, strongly, in the Middle East. Just walking in the door of certain places – even in churches – you can sense a spiritual oppression. Sometimes, just driving through a city, you can sense it. You know in your spirit that something is not right. You can feel it. That is because you are not just a physical, natural being; you are also a spiritual being with spiritual senses.

> *The spiritual world is actually as real as the natural world.*

We live in two worlds: the supernatural world and the natural world. Sometimes, we do not know how to react when the Spirit moves, because our decisions are governed by our five natural senses. But, there is a supernatural dimension that supersedes our natural sight. The Holy Spirit will help us to walk in the supernatural and to understand what is happening in the spiritual world. The more you move into the supernatural dimension, the more you can sense it. The more you flow in it, the stronger and more real it becomes to you.

✦ Demonic Spirits Cannot Operate On The Earth Unless They Find A Body.

The devil cannot do anything on earth without human agreement. Demonic spirits need to find a person through whom they can operate. They want to occupy time and space in the material world, because without doing so, they are relegated to an abstract concept. To move from abstract to concrete, they must occupy time and space in the material world. They need a person to execute their will. Demon spirits refuse to live in a place where there is no man. Because they must have a human body in which to operate on the earth, they refuse to live in a place that I call "no man's land".

When an unclean spirit goes out of a man, he goes through dry places, seeking rest; and finding none, he says, "I will return to my house from which I came." And when he comes, he finds it swept and put in order. Then he goes and takes with him seven other spirits more wicked than himself, and they enter and dwell there; and the last state of that man is worse than the first.

~ Luke 11 : 24 – 26

The following scripture tells us that Satan's desire is to find a place or a person to execute his will.

And the Lord said to Satan, "From where do you come?" So Satan answered the Lord and said, "From going to and fro on the earth, and from walking back and forth on it."

~ Job 1 : 7

That's why many are oppressed, and many are possessed by demonic spirits today on the earth.

✦ Demons Speak.

Demons have an ability to speak, and for this purpose, they will use a person's voice. Demons spoke to Jesus and to the apostles. They asked Jesus a question.

And suddenly they cried out, saying, "What have we to do with You, Jesus, You Son of God? Have You come here to torment us before the time?"

~ Matthew 8 : 29b

✦ Demons Have Names.

The following evil spirits, or demons, are mentioned in the scriptures. Each one is a personality, and the word used expresses their nature:

Jealous spirit   (Numbers 5 : 14)

Familiar spirit   (Deuteronomy 18 : 11)

Spirit of fear   (2 Timothy 1 : 7)

Sorrowful spirit   (1 Samuel 1 : 15)

Spirit of harlotry   (Hosea 4 : 12)

Lying spirit   (2 Chronicles 18 : 21)

Spirit of Antichrist   (1 John 4 : 3)

Perverse spirit   (Isaiah 19 : 14)

Spirit of deep sleep   (Isaiah 29 : 20)

Spirit of infirmity   (Luke 13 : 11) (weakness)

Dumb spirit   (Mark 9 : 25)

Mute spirit   (Mark 9 : 25)

Foul spirit   (Revelation 18 : 2)

Spirit of divination   (Acts 16 : 16)

Spirit of error   (1 John 4 : 6)

Deceiving spirit   (1 Timothy 4 : 1)

Distressing spirit   (1 Samuel 16 : 14)

Unclean spirit   (Matthew 10 : 1)

Spirit of bondage   (Romans 8 : 15)

Spirit of the world   (1 Corinthians 2 : 12)

Different spirit   (2 Corinthians 11 : 4)

Demons Know Who Jesus Is.

The Bible says in Matthew 8 that demons said, "Son of God, have You come to torment us before our time?" They know Jesus.

Have You come here to torment us before the time?
~ Matthew 8 : 29b

Demons Know Their Fate.

Evil spirits know that they are doomed, and that they are going to burn for eternity.

Demons asked Jesus, "What have we to do with You, Jesus, You Son of God? Have You come here to torment us before the time?"
~ Matthew 8 : 29

Demons Understand and Experience Fear.

You believe that there is one God. You do well. Even the demons believe and tremble!
~ James 2 : 19

Demons are afraid of torment and of God's judgment. Not only do demons know and experience fear, but they also use it. Demons operate through fear. The spirit of fear is not of God. Have you ever found yourself walking in an area and suddenly fear grips you? Out of nowhere, you feel afraid. What happened to you? It could have been a demonic projection. Demons sometimes manifest themselves by releasing fear upon people.

✦ Demons Are In Direct Opposition to God's Program.

For the weapons of our warfare are not carnal but mighty in God for pulling down strongholds, casting down arguments and every high thing that exalts itself against the knowledge of God, bringing every thought into captivity to the obedience of Christ.

~ 2 Corinthians 10 : 4 - 5

When you are in the ministry, any form of ministry - you represent a threat to the kingdom of darkness. There are Satanists who pray and fast against the churches near them. They have assignments against the marriages and lives of pastors and church leaders. They are praying demonic curses over churches, because they represent the presence of God in their areas. Thank God that Jesus said:

On this rock I will build My church, and the gates of Hades shall not prevail against it.

~ Matthew 16 : 18

Demons are in direct opposition to God's program. That's why we need intercessors. You may say, "I'm just an intercessor. I can't preach." You may not feel that you are very important, but intercession is one of the most vital ministries of the Church. Guess what Jesus is doing right now? He is interceding. We need a praying church, because demonic forces are in direct opposition to God's program. An interceding force in a church ushers down the glory and the power of God, which manifests itself by blocking the assignments that come from hell to destroy the church.

✤ Demons Can Give A Person Supernatural Strength.

For He had commanded the unclean spirit to come out of the man. For it had often seized him, and he was kept under guard, bound with chains and shackles; and he broke the bonds and was driven by the demon into the wilderness.

~ Luke 8 : 29

This biblical story is about a man who had been bound with chains and shackles. He was so strong that he broke them, and was driven into the wilderness by the demonic spirit. Demons can give supernatural strength.

One time I was praying for a woman, who was a little over 4 feet tall. She had a demonic manifestation that was so strong, four ushers could not hold her. It was when I said, "Be still in Jesus' Name" that she became calm because of the authority of the Name of Jesus.

✤ Demons Deceive People.

Many people can be deceived today because of twisted doctrines that are demonically inspired. How do we recognize a doctrine that is demonically inspired? It usually exalts itself against the knowledge of God. Some of the doctrines will occasionally have a little truth in them, but are twisted with lies and deception.

Now the Spirit expressly says that in latter times some will depart from the faith, giving heed to deceiving spirits and doctrines of demons.

~ I Timothy 4 : I

Stages of Demonic Operation In a Person's Life

1) Oppression

"Oppression" means, *to exercise power over someone*. The word, "oppression", is a combination of two words: "oppose" and "press". According to the Oxford Dictionary, the word, "oppose", means, to *set oneself against*. The word, "press", can mean, to *enter violently*. With these definitions, we can gain a better understanding of the word, "oppression". It simply means, *to exercise power by setting one's self against another to enter violently*. In other words, Satan is setting himself against you in order to enter violently into your life.

How does oppression work? Satan operates by the power of suggestion. Have you ever wondered how you can be driving down the street and a weird idea just comes into your head? Sometimes we are bombarded by weird thoughts. That happens. You may be driving, or getting ready to go to sleep, and be bombarded in your thoughts. You may even be in prayer or in church when it happens. That's the power of suggestion. Satan is trying to gain a foothold in the minds of people. That's why people can do irrational things.

> *Our mind is a battleground, and we are going to be bombarded by the enemy with all kinds of thoughts.*

The enemy comes at them with negative thoughts. Sometimes people begin to agree with those negative thoughts, and do what their mind tells them to do.

> *Your mind is the gateway to your heart.*

If you are operating under guilt and condemnation, and if you feel like you will never make it and that you are a failure, that is probably the devil speaking to you. You need to tell him to be quiet, because this is the day and the hour for your freedom. That is the will of God.

Sometimes with the power of suggestion also comes a suspicious spirit. It can cause you to think, "Oh, sister so-and-so doesn't like me." Maybe, when you see two people talking, you think they are talking about you. Those thoughts can come from demonic influences operating through the power of suggestion. We need to pull down those strongholds – the demonic influence that is oppressing our minds. We need to take those thoughts captive to the obedience of Christ.

> *The enemy wants you to believe that his thoughts are your thoughts. Do not allow the enemy's thoughts to become part of your normal thought life. This is very important!*

> *To walk in victory, you need to know that the enemy's thoughts are his thoughts... not God's thoughts, and that your thoughts are your thoughts... not the enemy's thoughts! Know the difference!*

As a Christian, you need to understand that the Bible clearly says,

For the weapons of our warfare are not carnal but mighty in God for pulling down strongholds, casting down arguments and every high thing that exalts itself against the knowledge of God.

~ 2 Corinthians 10 : 4

We need to take those demonic thoughts into captivity in the Name of Jesus Christ. Those kinds of thoughts are not God speaking to you.

> *You cannot stop a bird from flying above your head, but you can surely stop it from making a nest in your hair.*
> ~ *Corrie ten Boom*

Bringing every thought into captivity to the obedience of Christ.

~ 2 Corinthians 10 : 5

Sometimes sin starts with your imagination.

> *Nothing threatens Christian character as do impure thoughts.*

We need to make a stand for righteous thinking. Many people need to give their minds a bath, because he who cannot control his thoughts will soon lose control of his actions.

> *Watch your thoughts; they are blueprints for actions.*

2)   Depression

After you have been successfully oppressed for a while, you become depressed. "Depression" means, *gloominess, defeatism, discouragement, heaviness.* When you are depressed, you have no strength to fight or stand your ground. Your mind focuses on all kinds of negative things. If you stay in that state long enough, it might lead you into the third stage of demonic operation, which is possession.

3)   Possession

"Possession" means, to *hold back the property.* When someone is in this state, that person is completely controlled by evil forces. This is the most dangerous and critical stage of demonic operation. Jesus dealt with every one of these stages, and He dealt with the roots of these problems. He healed all those who were oppressed.

Some Truths about Deliverance Ministry

There are several truths about deliverance ministry that are important to know if you are going to minister or receive deliverance:

1.   Some people are oppressed in this world.

We cannot argue against that. The Bible says that.

God anointed Jesus of Nazareth with the Holy Spirit and with power, who went about doing good and healing all who were oppressed by the devil, for God was with Him.

~ Acts 10 : 38

You can see oppressed people at your job, in your neighborhood, and on the streets. That's a reality. There are great needs for ministry. If you can just be sensitive enough, you will understand that people need help.

2. People are not oppressed by God; they are oppressed by the devil.

3. It is God's will for everyone to be delivered.

The Bible says that Jesus Christ went about healing all who were oppressed. The word for "all" means, *all.* That is the perfect will of God.

For this purpose the Son of God was manifested, that He might destroy the works of the devil.

~ I John 3 : 8b

Jesus said:

The Spirit of the Lord is upon Me, because He has anointed Me to proclaim liberty to the captives to set at liberty those who are oppressed.

~ Luke 4 : 18

Jesus died to set the captive free.

> *Christ's cleansing power can remove the most stubborn stain of sin on "all"!*

4.   People who operate in the deliverance ministry need the power of God.

You cannot minister deliverance in your own strength.

"It is not by might nor by power, but by My Spirit," says the Lord of hosts.

~ Zechariah 4 : 6b

For the weapons of our warfare are not carnal (earthly, natural, physical) but mighty in God for pulling down (destroying) strongholds (fortresses).

~ 2 Corinthians 10 : 4

We need the anointing of God. It was because God was with Him that Jesus was able to perform the miracles He did. In other words, if we are going to see people set free, we need the anointing. The anointing is the divine empowerment to accomplish Kingdom purposes. We are anointed so that God can release His healing power through us, and bring deliverance to people.

How do you get the anointing? Every believer is anointed. The Bible says:

But the anointing which you have received from Him abides in you, and you do not need that anyone teach you; but as the same anointing teaches you concerning all things, and is true, and is not a lie, and just as it has taught you, you will abide in Him.

~ 1 John 2 : 27

The anointing of God operates with the Spirit of God. Christ is the Anointed One, and He is the Word of God. When that Word abides in you, and you abide in that Word, God can release the anointing that breaks and destroys the yokes of bondage through your prayers.

In order to understand the schemes of the enemy and be strong in battle, we need to know how demons oppress lives. It is possible for demons to have access to a life by different activities the person is engaged in, and through generational curses.

How is it possible for demonic spirits to enter human beings? Demons are very legalistic beings. They must have a door, an avenue, by which to enter a person.

Doors of Demonic Influence

There are people in the world who are bound by evil spirits. They are suffering the way they are because they have a major door or avenue open in their life that is allowing Satan to operate. Satan can't really control a person's life unless the person opens a door. Someone can open a door by the things in which they are involved. There are a variety of ways and means by which demons can influence people.

Sin

One of the doors or avenues that exposes a person to demonic influence is sin. I know this is a very delicate subject, but when I say "sin", I'm not meaning to imply that we don't all sin. I'm talking about major, continual sin... a lifestyle of sin.

There are sins that can literally open doors for Satan to come into your life. I'm talking about, for instance, when someone is living in adultery. That behavior allows a spirit of lust to come into that person's life, and it affects their relationship with their wife or husband. A single person who is living in fornication or masturbation opens a door that creates an avenue allowing demons to begin to operate in his or her life. I'm talking about lifestyles that enslave us to sin - even such as homosexuality.

> *The chains of sin are too light to be felt until they are so strong you cannot break them.*

We always pay for the pleasure of sin with the coin of sorrow. Sin deceives, defiles, deadens, and destroys.

Unforgiveness and Bitterness

I have found that it is difficult for demons to be cast out of people when they have not forgiven other people. Unforgiveness is a very dangerous spiritual tool that can cause demonic oppression. We need to operate in forgiveness.

> *Everyone should have a large cemetery in which they bury the faults of others.*

It is far better to forgive and forget than to resent and remember. Getting revenge makes you even with your enemy, but forgiving him puts you above him. You will never get ahead of him as long as you are trying to get even with him! No one is ever stronger and stands higher than when he forgives.

> *Never does the human soul become so strong*
> *as when it dares to forgive an injury.*

Curse

Another door that can expose us to demonic influence can be through a curse.

The Bible says in ~ Galatians 3 : 13b - 14 *"Cursed is everyone who hangs on a tree,"* that the blessing of Abraham might come upon the Gentiles in Christ Jesus.

> *Christ became a curse for us to remove sin's curse from us.*

When you are born again, you have access to the blessings through the cross, the blood of Jesus, and by applying the principles of God in your life. A blessing means *an empowerment for success.* It is a system designed by God to bring forth the manifestation of the reality of His Kingdom. The opposite of the "blessing" is the "curse". It is a system designed by Satan to bring forth the manifestation of the reality of the kingdom of darkness into your life. What is a curse? It is a *repeated event in a generational line.*

…Visiting the iniquity of the fathers upon the children to the third and fourth generation….

~ Exodus 20 : 5

In a generational line, you can have a common pattern – a cycle of evil. It is something that repeats itself from the fathers or mothers to the children, and then, to the grandchildren. For instance, your grandparents divorced, your parents divorced, and you are currently struggling in your own marriage, and on the verge of a divorce. Chances are there is a generational curse on your family. Another sign of a generational curse is miscarriage. Perhaps your mother had a lot of miscarriages, you had several miscarriages, and now your children are having miscarriages.

Other generational curses can be diseases that show up one generation after another, such as heart disease or cancer. You can begin to look in your family line to see if there is a possibility of a generational curse. When you recognize a pattern or a cycle of evil in your family line that repeats itself in such a way, there is a great possibility that there is a generational curse that needs to be broken. Such curses are activated by demonic powers. Some demons feel that they have the right to oppress certain people because of generation curses.

The following conditions can indicate curses:

- Repeated mental and emotional breakdown.

- Repeated or chronic sickness.

- Repeated miscarriages.

- Repeated breakdown of marriage – family alienation.

- Repeated financial insufficiency, especially where the income appears sufficient.

- Repeated accidents.

Unholy Alliances

There shall not be found among you anyone who makes his son or his daughter pass through the fire, or one who practices witchcraft, or a soothsayer, or one who interprets omens, or a sorcerer, or one who conjures spells, or a medium, or a spiritist, or one who calls up the dead. For all who do these things are an abomination to the Lord, and because of these abominations the Lord your God drives them out from before you. You shall be blameless before the Lord your God. For these nations which you will dispossess listened to soothsayers and diviners; but as for you, the Lord your God has not appointed such for you.

~ Deuteronomy 18 : 10 - 14

People don't understand that in some parts of the world, there are people who consult witchdoctors for different reasons. This opens the door for demonic influences in their lives. Maybe they want good luck, or maybe they want protection because they don't know God. In America, there are people who go to see psychics, palm readers, fortune tellers, tarot card readers, etc. There are all kinds of programs on TV and sites on the Internet where you can get "predictions" about your future. These are demonic practices, and Satan will never give you anything for free. Every time you get involved in any form of occult activity (fortune-telling, contact with the dead, witchcraft, sorcery, yoga, reflexology, acupuncture, and other practices), a spiritual covenant between you and the kingdom of darkness is established. When you decide to partake of these demonic-inspired activities, legal ground is established for the devil to take a hold on your life. These things are evil, and if you are a Christian, you are not even supposed to come near those things.

Yoga

Some people cannot understand the problem that lies behind martial arts and practices such as acupuncture and yoga. We must always look at the philosophy which is behind a particular practice. For example, in the case of yoga, we may well do the exercises thinking there is no problem associated with them, but many of the exercises are positions of worship to demon gods. Behind the practice of yoga is the occult element of worship, and as we practice yoga, we invite these spirits to attach themselves to us.

Below is an email I received concerning yoga:

I attended a talk by an ex-yoga teacher, Mrs. Choy, who sold her yoga centre (where she earned lots of money giving yoga lessons) and severed all ties with yoga. She urged us to inform relatives, friends, family members, etc., NOT to get involved with yoga at all. She urged those who had taken up yoga lessons (hot yoga, power yoga, pe-la-tei, etc.) to repent and ask God for forgiveness.

Many claimed that they only joined to keep fit, that they were only doing the exercise poses and not the meditation. Christians think it is okay to be involved with yoga as long as they don't participate in the meditation part.

Mrs. Choy explained that central to the practice of yoga (which originated from Hinduism) is the spirit of Kundalini (spirit of the snake or cobra). Yoga poses are actually animal poses (e.g., camel, rabbit, snake). All of these stretches and exercises look very normal and harmless. The danger is, once a person forms such poses, the spirit of Kundalini (the snake, in a coiled position) is stimulated or aroused. As the person goes from basic to intermediate to advanced stages of yoga lessons (still not meditation yet), the coiled "snake" will be aroused further. It will rise further and further.

According to yoga, there are 7 centers in the human body, starting from the navel. The final center is the area between the eye brows (known to many as the third eye). When the spirit is aroused to the final centre, the third eye will be opened. This is what they call the *full enlightenment.* The first thing the person sees is demons. For some, they will become insane upon seeing such horrifying demons. For others, they are not afraid and will have the power to fore-tell other people's health, problems, luck, etc. (like a fortune-teller). In fact, they can become able to manipulate and control other people.

The meditation aspect of yoga will come in very subtly. Mrs. Choy said she was approached by a couple who found her contact information from the yellow pages and told her that they wanted to teach her new things about yoga. She was very keen and sat under their teaching. She learned how to meditate and how it had to be done during odd hours of the day (past midnight). So she tried it.

She actually felt a wriggling feeling in her stomach! She also mentioned that her third eye was opened. She could see her own aura (electric fields in all human beings). Her turning point came when God caused her spiritual eyes to open. She witnessed a lady being delivered by God, wriggling like a snake on the floor. Mrs. Choy thanked God for being gracious to her, and for allowing her to see, through spiritual eyes, what was actually happening to her as she participated in yoga.

There are some believers who still continue participating in yoga, saying that they find no harm in it after doing yoga for 3 years. It is a sad thing that there are even yoga lessons for children. Mrs. Choy said it is our soul that is in danger. The evil one will try all the ways he can to ensnare or trap Christians. God cannot be mocked. We are not against yoga teachers or yoga students. We are fighting against powers and principalities in the Spiritual realm. Let's be on guard. Be aware!

Acupuncture

Similarly, in the case of acupuncture, we find that it goes back to the Emperor Huang Ti who concluded, through a study of the stars, that harmony and balance exist in this practice. There is a definite input from astrology in this practice. There is a reference to an energy, or life force, called "Ch'i", which is supposed to go into the body at birth, and out again at death. This flows through the body in two systems, namely Yang (which is the male principle and represents the sun), and Yin (the female principle which represents the moon).

Yang and Yin are supposed to flow through the body by a system of canals called the *meridians,* which in turn, go under the skin around the body. There are fourteen main meridians linked by 15 luo canals and 46 subsidiary meridians, passing close to the skin at 365 points. It is not hard to see that just below this practice there is a philosophy involving the sun, the moon, and the days of the year.

I firmly believe there are psychic powers behind the practice of acupuncture, which even its most innocent form, can bring spiritual oppression. There can be a physical healing which takes place (as frequently happens when we use occult practices in medicine), and with that, comes a spiritual oppression.

Martial Arts

When we look at the philosophy behind practices of martial arts such as karate, kung-fu, and judo – and not the practice only – we will soon determine the philosophy is not Godly.

And no wonder! For Satan himself transforms himself into an angel of light.

~ 2 Corinthians 11 : 14

Cultural Practices

Many cultures, countries, and religions have different practices. Many cultural practices are, in fact, occult practices hidden under the design of a culture. This sort of cultural practice opens the door to the demonic powers that inspired them. Be careful of cultural practices because they can be open doors for demonic influence.

Sexual Abuse

Another way the enemy gains access to one's life is through child abuse. In some of the testimonies of people that received deliverance through our ministry, we discovered that the demonic oppression in their lives started after they were sexually abused.

A lot of people have been abused, and they are going through all kinds of turmoil on the inside, but nobody is talking about it. They think it's normal to keep it hidden. These people are walking around carrying a load that is dragging them down. They have no freedom or joy. God wants to set those people free!

Years ago, I remember watching the movie, "Finding Nemo". The story line of the movie is about how a father fish traveled the world to find his son that was lost. Watching this movie, you can ask yourself, "Do fish have a language or feelings? Can they communicate as we do?"

The following story is a perfect illustration of this world's current generation. It's a silent, suffering generation.

There was a family that had an aquarium in their house with a fish in it. One day the aquarium had a leak, and the water slowly leaked out. The people living in the house didn't realize it. Some of them were walking by, some were watching TV, and some were going in and out of the house. The next morning when they woke up, they found the fish dead with its mouth open. I asked myself the question, "If humans could communicate with fish, what would have been the conversation when the water was leaking out of the aquarium?" I think the fish's plea would have been, "Help! Somebody help me, please! Can't you see the water is leaking out? I am going to die! I am suffering! Please help me!" The fish would have a cry of desperation, a cry for help.

> *No entity that is alive can have life taken away from it without a cry for survival.*

Unfortunately, humans do not speak the language of fish. Even though the pain could have been real to the fish, it was silent to the people in the house. The cry of the fish could have been loud, but it was silent to the people. The fish suffered and died silently, even though it was crying and expressing itself loudly.

> *In the church today, we are sometimes dealing with a generation of silent sufferers.*

For people who have been sexually abused or emotionally damaged, their behavior (and sometimes their addiction) is a cry for help, but often, it is silent to the church because we do not always understand the language of pain and trauma. As a result, many times, people who are attending church – maybe even for years – never receive ministry in this area, so they go off the deep end... and everybody is surprised. There was a problem all along in their lives, but nobody could see their desperation or hear their cries for help. We need to talk about these things and expose them. Somebody needs to stand and tell the people the truth.

There are people in church who are bound with all kinds of problems, but they put on happy faces when they come on Sunday morning. They have problems in their hearts, but, sometimes, all the preacher does is scratch the surface without really touching the root of their problem. That's why deliverance and inner healing ministry are important and necessary today in the church: so that those who are suffering silently because of trauma and abuse can be helped.

Pride

Another avenue that allows demonic spirits to operate is pride. One of the reasons Satan was thrown out of heaven was his pride. He wanted to take over the throne of God.

The Bible tells us, "God resists the proud but gives grace to the humble."

~ James 4 : 6

We have to pray every day for God to help us in this area, because it's a thing that many people struggle with – sometimes without even realizing it. This happens especially to those who are talented, gifted, or used by God. Once you begin to walk in spiritual pride, you open yourself up to demonic influence. There are famous, seasoned preachers who start very well in the ministry. They have great ministries. Some of them have a healing anointing, and see great breakthroughs in their ministries. Suddenly, because they begin to walk in spiritual pride, they fall into deception – thinking they are something special – and they begin to develop their own doctrines. A lot of cults begin in this way as people begin to drift away from God's revelation.

When you are anointed and used by God, you need to be very careful not to fall for the temptation to believe that you are the only one, that you are the anointed one, and that you are the only one who is needed.

You can't glorify self and Christ at the same time.

When the "I" becomes dominant, the "spiritual eye" sees the entire world in distortion. The greatest barrier between some Christians and God's omnipotent power, is their own supposed strength. If you have begun to slip into that kind of spiritual pride, you need a heart check, because before you realize it, you could step over the line and be lost.

Be careful that you don't start out on fire for God, sincere, with a heart for God, and willing to pay the price, but end up like Saul... without God and rejected. Be careful of pride.

Soul Ties

There are Godly relationships, but there are also relationships that have an ungodly soul tie. The ungodly soul tie is a counterfeit for the Godly covenant. God calls us to have Godly, healthy relationships. In a Godly covenant, your soul is naturally involved, but there is a great amount of individuality, peace, and freedom to be the person God created you to be. An ungodly soul tie is when the emotions, the mind, and the will of more than one person become so intertwined, that the thoughts of the individuals are no longer their own. In other words, someone is unnaturally and inordinately affected by the will, the emotions, and the desires of another person. This tie occurs when the soul is improperly influenced, misdirected, and altered by a relationship with someone.

> *A soul tie is an improper, inappropriate influence.*

God never wanted our soul to be tied to or controlled by a relationship.

> *If everything you think about,*
> *everything you relate to, every place you go,*
> *everything you say, and every way you dress*
> *is based upon another person, your soul is*
> *more than involved. Your soul is tied.*

When you've developed a soul tie, you've lost your individuality, and that makes your response ungodly. The ungodly soul tie is in direct opposition to the way God intended for your soul to be involved in a relationship. Soul ties also allow demonic influences to enter.

Shock or Trauma

Traumas such as death, the breakdown of a marriage, or an accident, can often release demonic influences that bring fear and depression.

Music

Music is a universal language, and its popularity – particularly among young people – makes it one of the primary vehicles for shaping their beliefs, values, and worldview. We cannot underestimate the role of music in the lives and culture of today's youth. For this reason, Satan seeks to infuse into their music his godless message of anger, anti-establishment, promiscuity, hatred, hopelessness, depression, and despair. Is it any surprise, then, that suicide, violence, sexual license, and addictions of all kinds afflict so many of the young people today? It is stirring up things within them, and consciously or unconsciously influencing them.

Few communication media affect the human spirit the way music does.

> *Lyrics affect the mind, rhythm affects the will, and melody affects the emotions.*

Show me the kind of music someone listens to, and I can tell you a lot about that person's lifestyle. If you fill your mind with songs about broken relationships, don't be surprised when it comes true in your own life. If your daughter listens day and night to songs about being sexy, don't be surprised when she has a baby out of wedlock. If your son immerses himself in sad songs of suicidal despair, and angry songs of tough living, don't be surprised when he commits suicide or takes a gun to school to shoot some of his classmates.

> *Music creates an atmosphere conducive to behavior that reflects the spirit of music.*

One has only to be present at Rock Festivals to realize the spirit of violence and hatred which can come through many forms of rock music today. The term "Rock and Roll" has its origins in the sexual act, and the beat of rock music draws the demon powers. Satan himself loves music. He was the anointed cherub created by God, and was involved with timbrels and pipes, which signify music.

Today, through the medium of rock music and eastern religion, much heresy is entering our homes. We must stand against it. You have to be very selective in your choices of the music that you and your kids listen to. Music has a spirit. There is satanic music. Rock-n-roll is used a lot in the cult of Satan. Some people think that because they are Christians, they can listen to any kind of music, but you need to understand that music has a spirit. We could be walking down the street together, and I could be singing a song. Five minutes after we part ways, you might find yourself singing the same song. What happened? The song influenced you.

> *It is human nature... eventually we become what we continually fill our minds with.*

The same thing happens when you listen to a CD, or a song on the radio. A few minutes later, when you are by yourself, you find yourself singing the same song. What has happened? You have been influenced, for the good, or for the bad. There is influence behind music. A lot of people do not think that music really matters – that the words of the song are all that matters. But you have to understand that there is satanic music out there, and if you are not careful about what you are listening to, what you are doing is feeding your soul with satanic influence. On some records today, we find that if they are played backwards, we can hear voices encouraging us to worship Satan, or to commit suicide, or violence, or rape or some similar crime. These voices cannot be heard at the normal hearing level when music is being played. But it is just below that level, so that it is a subliminal advertising for demonic influence.

One of the great dangers of music is the spirit of pride attached to it. We must always be mindful that we worship God, and not the spirit of music. A spirit of pride seems to come as the music itself is worshipped, rather than the Lord.

> *We must be very careful that the music we listen to edifies both our spirit and the Spirit of the Living God, rather than the sensual areas of our emotions, which stir up desires that are not of God.*

I believe that God is calling Christians to be creative. We need to have awesome music that glorifies God, so that our young people will not turn to ungodly music, but towards the music of God. This will create a righteous atmosphere, and godly behavior.

Books and Literature

Beware lest anyone cheat you through philosophy and empty deceit, according to the tradition of men, according to the basic principles of the world, and not according to Christ.

~ Colossians 2 : 8

I am not against education or the reading of books, but sometimes, the legal ground for Satan to have access into someone's life is related to the types of books and literature they read. There are satanic books out there that allow demonic influences into someone's life.

Also, many of those who had practiced magic brought their books together and burned them in the sight of all. And they counted up the value of them, and it totaled fifty thousand pieces of silver.

~ Acts 19 : 19

Movies

Another way the enemy attempts to influence our lives is through violent, horror, and sexually explicit movies. When you watch movies that, literally, *demonstrate* fear, a door can be opened for fear to begin to operate in your life through dreams, imagination, and irrational thinking.

Possessions

Sometimes people possess occult objects in their homes, and this is an abomination in the eyes of God.

You shall burn the carved images of their gods with fire; you shall not covet the silver or gold that is on them, nor take it for yourselves, lest you be snared by it; for it is an abomination to the Lord your God. Nor shall you bring an abomination into your house, lest you be doomed to destruction like it. You shall utterly detest it and utterly abhor it, for it is an accursed thing.

~ Deuteronomy 7 : 25 - 26

This became known both to all Jews and Greeks dwelling in Ephesus; and fear fell on them all, and the name of the Lord Jesus was magnified. And many who had believed came confessing and telling their deeds. Also, many of those who had practiced magic brought their books together and burned them in the sight of all. And they counted up the value of them, and it totaled fifty thousand pieces of silver.

~Acts 19 : 17 - 19

It is important to remove lucky charms, fetishes, Buddha carvings, African masks, and anything which relates to witchcraft.

Addiction

> *Bad habits (man's mortal enemies),*
> *must be slain or they will slay him.*

Another area of demonic activity is addictions. Some people are addicted to smoking, drugs, alcohol, gambling, television, soap operas, sleeping aids, pain killers, over-eating, and many other behaviors or substances. Sometimes these arise from sheer habit. But at other times, they develop because of a sense of unworthiness or frustration. The root of so many of these addictions is frustration. So, many people feel frustrated and allow this attitude to develop into a spiritual problem.

> *If we deal with the frustration,*
> *then we deal with the addiction.*

But the fruit of the Spirit is... self-control.

~ Galatians 5 : 22 - 23a

> *Bad habits are like comfortable beds,*
> *easy to get into, but hard to get out of.*

One of the best freedoms is freedom from bad habits, because we build our lives each day with the bricks of habits that we have.

Pornography

The same is true with pornography. When you watch pornography, a door is opened for lust and unclean influences in your mind and emotions. When you see those things, the next thing you know, you are bound by them. There is something about how viewing a little will draw you to viewing more and more. The spirit behind pornography is pulling you into more and deeper forms of what you're viewing.

> *Sin is an ever-increasing desire*
> *with a never-ending satisfaction.*

Many people today, even leaders, are struggling with some of these issues. If you are one of them, you need to get some help before it takes over and destroys your life, your marriage, and your ministry. Eventually, secret sins make the headlines.

> *It's easier to prevent bad habits than to break them.*

If you want to be used by God, you need to have your roots deep in the Word of God. You need to be strong. You need to be courageous. You need to take a stand!

How can we be used by God to help people that struggle with the different legal grounds we just discussed? To help people, we must learn how to destroy the enemy's legal ground which gives him access into their lives. The person ministering deliverance must be free from the issue they are trying to help the other person with.

> *I personally believe that deliverance is 20% counseling, 30% prayer, and 50% discipline.*

30% is Prayer

Spiritual preparation is important to minister deliverance. This includes fasting, knowing the Word, listening to the Holy Spirit, and knowing how to use your authority in Christ.

> *You can expect God to intervene when you have taken time to intercede.*

Prayer is not a last extremity, it's a first necessity.

Some Important Things to Know When Ministering Deliverance:

• While praying for deliverance, you can use the Word of God.

It is good to pray or quote scriptures with belief.

For the word of God is living and powerful, and sharper than any two-edged sword, piercing even to the division of soul and spirit, and of joints and marrow, and is a discerner of the thoughts and intents of the heart.   ~ Hebrews 4 : 12

• While praying for deliverance, you can use your prayer language.

As we are praying in tongues, our spirit is praying with the help of the Holy Spirit, and we are using an authority far beyond the understanding or knowledge of our natural mind.

For if I pray in a tongue, my spirit prays, but my understanding is unfruitful.   ~ 1 Corinthians 14 : 14

• While praying for deliverance, you must command with authority.

On several occasions, Jesus simply commanded the demons to go. He knew He had authority over them, and He has given you that same authority. A simple command to a demon to "go in Jesus' name" will always be effective when the demon knows that you are aware that you are operating under God's authority through Jesus Christ. You do not need to use lengthy phrases to command demons to leave, but can simply command them to go. If we do so with authority, they will begin to leave.

• While praying for deliverance, praise God and let the person you pray for praise God.

God lives in the praises of His people, and as we praise God, the Spirit of God comes and drives out the demon power.

But You are holy, enthroned in the praises of Israel.
                                                    ~ Psalm 22: 3

> *When the praises go up, deliverance, healing, breakthrough, and blessings come down.*

• While praying for deliverance, listen to the Holy Spirit.

While praying, be sensitive to the Holy Spirit. He can direct you in how you should pray through the word of knowledge and word of wisdom.

…Those who are led by the Spirit of God are sons of God.
                                                    ~ Romans 8 : 14

• While praying for deliverance, you can lay hands on the person you are ministering to.

It is absolutely scriptural to lay hands on people during the course of deliverance. Jesus did so.

And behold, there was a woman who had a spirit of infirmity eighteen years, and was bent over and could in no way raise herself up. But when Jesus saw her, He called her to Him and said to her, "Woman, you are loosed from your infirmity." And He laid His hands on her, and immediately she was made straight, and glorified God.

~ Luke 13 : 11 - 13

- While praying for deliverance, plead the blood of Jesus.

There is great power in the blood of Jesus. While praying for deliverance, it can be good to let the person repeat some scriptures about the blood. The demon hates for the person to confess the Word of God. It is the confession of their mouth and belief in their heart which sets them free and drives the demon power out.

You can use the scriptures and confessions below:

In Him we have redemption through His blood, the forgiveness of sins, according to the riches of His grace.

~ Ephesians 1 : 7

Let the redeemed of the Lord say so, whom He has redeemed from the hand of the enemy.

~ Psalms 107 : 2

Therefore I can say: through the blood of Jesus, I am redeemed out of the hand of the Devil. Through the blood of Jesus, all my sins are forgiven.

Much more then, having now been justified by His blood, we shall be saved from wrath through Him.

~ Romans 5 : 9

Therefore I can say: through the blood of Jesus, I am justified, made righteous... just as though I had never sinned.

Therefore Jesus also, that He might sanctify the people with His own blood, suffered outside the gate.

~ Hebrews 13 : 12

Therefore I can say: through the blood of Jesus, I am sanctified, made Holy, set apart to God.

Or do you not know that your body is the temple of the Holy Spirit who is in you, whom you have from God, and you are not your own? For you were bought at a price; therefore glorify God in your body and in your spirit, which are God's.

~ 1 Corinthians 6 : 19 - 20

And they overcame him by the blood of the Lamb and by the word of their testimony, and they did not love their lives to the death.

~ Revelation 12 : 11

Therefore I can say: my body is a temple of the Holy Spirit. I am redeemed, cleansed, and sanctified by the blood of Jesus. Therefore, the devil has no more place in me and no more power over me. Through the blood of Jesus, I overcome Satan by the blood of the lamb and the word of my testimony.

• While praying for deliverance, it is important to know that we have ministering angels surrounding us. It's most reassuring to know that we have the presence of God's angels around us as we fight these spiritual battles.

Are they not all ministering spirits sent forth to minister for those who will inherit salvation?

~ Hebrews 1 : 14

• While praying for deliverance, some manifestations might take place.

There are manifestations that sometimes occur during the course of deliverance. Sometimes, there is no manifestation whatsoever, because the spirit goes quietly. In whichever way it occurs, we are to have faith to believe that deliverance is taking place. We must not be disappointed if there is no physical sign of deliverance, because quite frequently, spirits do leave without any sound. However, we must always have a witness in our spirit that they have, in fact, left. On other occasions, there are clear manifestations as they go. This is confirmed in the Book of Acts:

or unclean spirits, crying with a loud voice, came out of many who were possessed; and many who were paralyzed and lame were healed.

~ Acts 8 : 7

Here are some manifestations that can take place during a deliverance: hissing, coughing, screaming, spitting, belching, roaring, vomiting, sobbing, trembling, violent shaking, vile smells, barking, feigning death, yawning, and other miscellaneous manifestations.

You shouldn't be afraid of manifestations. Use your God-given authority!

• After praying for deliverance, it is important that those who received deliverance are followed-up.

Follow-up is very important because they can slip back into their old sin, or if pride enters, then there can be deception. There are 4 downward steps: pride, rebellion, deception, and perversion of the flesh and the spirit. Once someone allows pride to enter, then rebellion will soon follow. When they do not listen to anybody, or do not want to be corrected by anybody, the spirit of deception will come in. Finally, they begin to allow perversion of the flesh and of the spirit to take hold. Perversion of the spirit involves occult activity and following other spirits, while perversion of the flesh can take the form of sexual immorality.

20% is Counseling

Before praying for the person to be delivered, we should seek (either through discernment by the Holy Spirit or from their own testimony) the area of problem in their life. This may require some time for counseling and prayer together. Diagnose the problem, and ask the right questions. How long ago did the problem start? How did it start? Where did it start? Once you know the roots of the problem, give wise advise, and follow-up. Sometimes we can cast out a demon directly without asking the person questions. However, when there is a resistance to authority, we must stop and ask the right questions in order to know the roots of the problem so that we can direct our prayers and authority effectively.

In the story below, we see that even Jesus asked questions:

So He asked his father, "How long has this been happening to him?" And he said, "From childhood."

~ Mark 9 : 21

He wanted to attack the problem at its root. That is how Jesus operated. It is important to know what the root of the problem is, and then, you can cast out the spirit.

> *When confession is made and forgiveness is released,*
> *the enemy's legal ground is destroyed,*
> *and the demon has no choice but to come out of the person.*

You can discern the root(s) of the problem by asking the right questions using this check-list:

Place a circle around any area which applies.

Before proceeding, ask the Holy Spirit to bring to their remembrance all that the person needs to remember.

Do you have:
unforgiveness – bitterness – rebellion – jealousy – violence.

Do you frequently:
lie – steal – cheat – get mad – argue.

Have you been:
emotionally abused – physically abused – sexually abused – raped – molested – rejected – abandoned – traumatized.

Are you addicted to:
nicotine – alcohol – sleeping aids – food – pain killers – pornography – drugs – anti-depressives – shopping – TV.

Have you been involved in or have the tendency toward:

homosexuality – adultery – masturbation – fornication – sadomasochism.

Do you fear:

death – people - heights – enclosed places – outdoors and open spaces – dogs – thieves – water – thunderstorms – dentists – shadows – heart disease – number 13 – riding in vehicles – staying single – blood – poverty – changes – crossing bridges – snakes – the police – anxiety – spiders – elevators – divorce – injury – tornados – loud noises – strangers – the dark – being bullied – being not accepted – flying – catching a specific illness – of leaving your home – contamination – social embarrassment – men - women.

Are there any repeated cycles of evil in your family tree:

adultery – sickness – anger – alcohol addiction – drug addiction – fear – homosexuality – poverty – fornication – greed – pride – rebellion – lying – unforgiveness – bitterness – stealing – cheating.

Did you have:

an abortion.

Do you have a soul tie with your:

mom – dad – uncle – ex-boyfriend – ex-girlfriend – ex-husband – ex-wife - boss at work – pastor – minister.

Do you:
speak to the dead – pray for the dead

Have you been into:
black magic (invoking hidden powers for bad ends) - kabbala (occult lure) – magic – mental suggestion – mesmerism – black mass - white magic (invoking powers for good ends) – self hypnosis (self-induced trance states) – hypnosis (whether magical or medical) - Gypsy curses put on you (death, injury, or trance states) – Pk (parakineses, control of objects by the power of the mind and will) – Tk (Telekinesis, movement of objects around the room, instruments play by themselves, engines start, etc.) - witchcraft – hex signs.

Do you carry an ankh (a cross with a ring top, used in satanic rites and are dangerous).

Have you taken part in:
Ouija boards – planchette (glass on the table) – seances – mediums – floating trumpets – disembodied voices – consulted people who have clairvoyance (the ability to see objects or events spontaneously and super-normally beyond the natural range of vision, second sight) – clairaudience (ability to hear voices and sounds super-normally, spirited voices alleging to be that of dead people giving advice or warnings).

Have you engaged in:
activities involving mind reading – ESP (extra sensory perception) – mental telepathy – thought transference

– dream interpretation (as with the Edgar Cayce book) – eckenkar or mind dynamics (Silva Mind Control) or touch for health.

Have you been into:

fortune telling by palm reading – tea leaf readings – astrology – horoscopes - phrenology (reading character, or one's future, by the conformations of a person's skull), crystal ball, cartomancy (using playing cards) – tarot cards (22 picture cards for fortune-telling) – handwriting analysis – numerology (reducing the letters of one's name to numbers) – psychometry (telling fortunes by lifting or holding object belonging to the enquirer) – transcendental meditation.

Have you tried or practiced:

divining – dowsing – or witching for water – minerals – underground cables – finding out the sex of an unborn child using a divining rod – pendulum – twig or planchette – using a pendulum, divining rod or a mechanical pendulum, called a motot skopua, for diagnosing illness and its treatment by color therapy and screening.

Have you sought:

acupuncture – acupressure - healings through magic practices using charms and charming for wart removal, death magic (where the name of the sickness plus a written spell is cast into a coffin or grave) – conjuration (summoning up a spirit by incantation) – psychic healing – psychic surgery – concept therapy – the use of a trance condition – clairsentience (supernatural sense perception) – iridology (eye diagnosis to diagnose illness) – sonar puncture – radionics - astrologic medicine – chromo therapy – sound therapy – orgonomy.

Have you participated in:

levitation (body lifting by demonic power) – table tipping – spirit knockings – rappings – automatic (spirit) writing – bad Halloween parties.

Have you been involved in:

yoga (exercises and meditation) – karate – kung-fu – aikido judo (martial arts) – out-of-the-body (astral) travel of the soul.

Have you been trusting in:

amulets (tiger's claw, shark's tooth, horse shoes over the door, mascots, gold earring man) – talisman (magic picture) – letters (occult) of protection – zodiac charms (birthdates) – pagan fetishes (objects charged with magical powers and carried about as a means of protection or luck) – relics and artifacts which have been used in pagan temples or pagan religious rites – omens – significant days – moon-mancy – chain letters and numerical symbolism – African masks.

Have you been on:

hallucinogenic drugs (LSD, heroin, marijuana) – sniffing thinners.

Have you been into:

heavy acid rock – painting under hallucinogenic stimulus.

Have you visited pagan rites such as:
Voodoo (West Indies) – Sing Sings (New Guinea) – Fire Walking (Fiji) – Corroborees (Australian Aboriginals) - Umbahda and Macumba (Brazil), etc.

Do you possess:
occult literature – horror movies.
The following is a list of cults and non-Christian religions which fall into the above category:

Jehovah's Witnesses (Dawn Bible Students) – Mormons (Church of Jesus Christ of the latter day Saints) – Brahnamism (worship of William Brahnam) – Worldwide Church of God (Hebert W. Armstrong) – Children of God – The Unification Church (Moonies, One World Crusade) – Unitarian Church – Christadelphians – Freemasonry – Spiritualism – Scientology – Christian Science – Rangatuism – Religious Science – Anthrosophy – Theosophy – Rosecrucianism – Inner Peace Movement – Spiritual Frontiers Fellowship – Eastern religions such as: Hare Krishna – Buddhism – Hinduism – Islam – Shintoism – Confucianism – Japanese Flower Arranging (sun worship), Bahai.

Do you participate or practice any cultural practice:
a special ritual or tradition when someone is born – a special ritual or tradition when somebody dies – a special ritual or tradition when a child becomes an adult – a special ritual or tradition before you come to church or before you pray.

50% is Discipline

Often, after a person receives deliverance, they will be tempted to go back to the same things.

Resist the devil and he will flee from you.

~ James 4 : 7b

It is important that the delivered person cleans their house from occult objects, alcohol, drugs, pornographic movies, or any things that can be a stumbling block. They will have to choose not to go to certain places or to be with certain people. They will have to renew their mind, study the Word, and pray daily.

Necessary Steps That One Must Take To Experience Deliverance:

1. They must receive Jesus Christ as their savior.

> *Because if Christ is kept outside, something must be wrong inside.*

2. They must recognize that they have a problem.

As long as they do not recognize that they have a problem, it will be hard for them to be delivered. Because of a lack of knowledge, people sometimes don't recognize that their problem comes from a demonic influence. (~ Hosea 4 : 6)

> *They must make what they recognize*
> *as a problem, their enemy.*

3.   They must take responsibility for what they recognize.

> *They cannot put their sins behind*
> *until they are willing to face them.*

4.   They must repent and ask God to forgive them.

Repentance is an important key that opens doors, and before we can expect a lasting deliverance, *true* repentance must take place. Unless there is true repentance, there will be no lasting deliverance.

To be able to receive deliverance, people need to have Godly sorrow. They must realize that Jesus died for their sins, and that they can have a new life through Him.

> *There are none so good that they can save themselves,*
> *and none so bad that God cannot save them.*

God accepted us while we were still sinners by allowing Jesus to die on the cross for us. Therefore, people should realize and be taught that God accepts them. This is a great release point for many people. When people are taught that God accepts and loves them, then they can also be taught to accept themselves.

> *When a person is ready to confess their sins,*
> *God is always ready to cover them with His blood.*
> *Sin brings fear; confession brings freedom.*

Reasons Why People are Not Delivered:

- They do not repent.
- They fail to confess specific sins.
- They fail to forgive.
- They fail to break with the occult and false religion.
- They fail to repent from pride.
- There are circumstances around them that make it very hard to retain their deliverance (home, friends, parents, etc.).

5.   They must renounce all the legal grounds listed above.

In order to destroy a demon's legal ground and receive deliverance, a person needs to renounce the activities that gave the demon access in the first place. There is power in confession. It is how you become saved. You activate the gift of salvation by confessing the Lord Jesus Christ as your personal Lord and Savior.

If we confess our sins, He is faithful and just to forgive us our sins and to cleanse us from all unrighteousness.

~ 1 John 1 : 9

For with the heart one believes unto righteousness, and with the mouth confession is made unto salvation.

~ Romans 10 : 10

Confession is a powerful element in our theology, because what comes out of your mouth can affect your spirituality. It can make you either alive or dead spiritually.

Death and life are in the power of the tongue.

~ Proverbs 18 : 21a

Demonic spirits can come into someone's life through what that person speaks, and those spirits can also come out when the person confesses their sin. Remember that Jesus said that it's not what goes into the mouth of the man that defiles him, but what comes out of his mouth that defiles him. Confession has the power to neutralize any demonic activity. That's why renunciation is very strategic in destroying the legal ground of the enemy in a person's life.

> *Confession nullifies the demon's right to habitation.*

The enemy's biblical, legal ground in someone's life is like a bird holding onto the branch of a tree. That branch is the bird's "ground". If you break that branch, what happens? The bird falls.

Spiritually, when the enemy has found legal ground to enter a person's life, confession destroys those doors and avenues, and the enemy has nothing left to hold onto in that person's life. At that point, he can be cast out immediately.

6.   They can receive prayer or pray for themselves.

It is important when you pray for someone that you lead them through all the steps discussed above. Then, you can cast out the evil spirit in the name of Jesus. We must be open to the

Holy Spirit, and let Him lead us during the ministry time and the follow-up.

> *Prayer is the spiritual laboratory that supplies on earth what heaven has prepared: their deliverance.*

7.   They must learn how to keep their deliverance.

• They must love God.

> *Their love for God will be made visible through their actions.*

• They must take the necessary actions.

Once someone is delivered, they must "clean their house", choose not to go to that certain place or person, and have the right friends and fellowship. This is important because:

> *Association brings manifestation.*
> *The wrong association will bring the wrong manifestation.*
> *The right association will bring the right manifestation.*

• They must associate with the right people because:

> *Some people are around them that are connected to their history, but God will bring people around them that are connected to their destiny.*

They will have to know that they cannot do God's will and please everyone.

- They must live a holy life.

> *They must know that there is a high cost for low living!*

Because Christ died for their sin, they can die to sin.

> *They gain the victory when they give up sin's pleasure in exchange for Christ's power.*

- They must read the Word of God daily.

The Word of God will reveal God's heart.

> *When they know God's heart, they will never question His will.*

- They must pray daily.

> *Either prayer will make a person stop sinning, or sin will make him stop praying.*

- They must be disciples of Christ.

> *A disciple is a disciplined follower of Jesus Christ.*

True freedom is not having their own way, but yielding to God's way.

- They must learn how to rejoice and give God thanks.

They will add to their joy when they count their blessings. Joy is the best proof of having the presence of God.

> *Joy is the by-product of obedience.*
> *Joy oils the machinery of life.*

It is easy to sing when we walk with the King.

> *Laughter is a sound of celebration.*
> *Laughter is a sound of triumph.*
> *Laughter is a sound of deliverance.*

This type of joy does not deal with emotions or feelings, but with the revelation of who our God is, and how able He is. Having joy doesn't mean that there is absence of trouble, but it is the presence of Christ. The world will know that you don't rejoice based on what you see, but that you rejoice based on what you know.

> *A thankful heart enjoys blessings twice:*
> *when they're received and when they're remembered.*

He who laughs… lasts!

- They must be filled with the Holy Spirit.

- They must learn how to resist the enemy by putting on the whole armor of God.

Conclusion: Use Me Lord!

In this book, we have learned how to have the right thinking and the right mindset, how to exercise your authority, how to pray for the sick, how to flow in the gifts of the Spirit, how to minister deliverance, and much more. Maybe you are saying to yourself, "Am I called to do these things?" You need to understand that:

> *The call is how God sees you,*
> *the gift is how you see God.*
> *God will gift you because of your calling,*
> *but men will call you because of your gift.*

A man's gift makes room for him.

~ Proverbs 18 : 16b

- God uses people who are **ordinary.**

> *When God looks around for someone to use,*
> *He does not choose people the way that we typically do.*

God never sees what men see. This is great news for us! He doesn't necessarily go for the most eloquent or top of the class. He can use regular, ordinary people.

What makes our work extraordinary is not us... it's God!

> *"All God's giants have been weak men, who did great*
> *things for God, because they relied on His being with them."*
> *~ Hudson Taylor, missionary to China*

The next time you feel like God can't use you, just remember:

Noah was a drunk... Abraham was too old... Isaac was a daydreamer... Jacob was a liar... Leah was ugly... Joseph was abused... Moses had a stuttering problem... Gideon was afraid... Samson had long hair and was a womanizer... Rahab was a prostitute... Jeremiah and Timothy were too young... David had an affair and was a murderer... Elijah was suicidal... Isaiah preached naked... Jonah ran from God... Naomi was a widow... Job went bankrupt... John the Baptist ate bugs... Peter denied Christ... The Disciples fell asleep while praying... Martha worried about everything... Mary Magdalene was, well, you know... The Samaritan woman was divorced, more than once... Zacheus was too small... Paul was too religious... Timothy had an ulcer... and... Lazarus was dead!

> *God can use you to your full potential.*
> *You aren't the message, you are just the messenger.*

- God uses people who are **available.**

> *What you are is God's gift to you.*
> *What you make of yourself is your gift to God.*

There are many things to learn from the story of the Good Samaritan. (Luke 10) What is apparent to me is how the Samaritan was able to respond to a need because he had an openness in his schedule, and an awareness to respond to the need as he saw it. Unfortunately, a great many of us are too strapped with our time or money to be able to respond when God brings needs our way.

> *When you are ready, open, and willing to be used*
> *however God chooses, you'll be amazed at how*
> *many opportunities come your way.*

- God uses people who have **failed.**

This is one of the great story lines of the entire Bible. God chooses to use people who are not perfect, and who, in many cases, have failed miserably. It is the story of David, who followed one horrible decision by a series of other horrible decisions, and soon found his life to be a complete wreck. Yet, among other things, he became an essential part of the family tree of

Jesus. It was the story of Peter who replied, "Man, I don't know what you're talking about!" Just as he was speaking, the rooster crowed. Jesus turned and looked straight at Peter. Then Peter remembered the word Jesus had spoken to him: "Before the rooster crows today, you will disown me three times." Then Peter went outside and wept bitterly. Yet, after that, he repented and preached the gospel and was a martyr.

No matter what you have done in your life or how you have failed, God can still use you to accomplish great things.

But God has chosen the foolish things of the world to put to shame the wise, and God has chosen the weak things of the world to put to shame the things which are mighty; and the base things of the world and the things which are despised God has chosen, and the things which are not, to bring to nothing the things that are, that no flesh should glory in His presence.... As it is written, "He who glories, let him glory in the Lord."

~ I Corinthians I : 27 - 31

God doesn't use the strong only. He uses the weak and the lowly, too. He wants us to be dependent on Him – not on our strengths, our talents, or our experiences.

> *When you think you are indispensable,*
> *you are probably not usable.*
> *But, when you think you are not useable or*
> *not indispensable, you are probably usable.*

Did you ever stop to think that when Moses thought he was usable, he wasn't?

Now it came to pass in those days, when Moses was grown, that he went out to his brethren and looked at their burdens. And he saw an Egyptian beating a Hebrew, one of his brethren. So he looked this way and that way, and when he saw no one, he killed the Egyptian and hid him in the sand. And when he went out the second day, behold, two Hebrew men were fighting, and he said to the one who did the wrong, "Why are you striking your companion?" Then he said, "Who made you a prince and a judge over us? Do you intend to kill me as you killed the Egyptian?" So Moses feared and said, "Surely this thing is known!" When Pharaoh heard of this matter, he sought to kill Moses. But Moses fled from the face of Pharaoh and dwelt in the land of Midian; and he sat down by a well.

~ Exodus 2 : 11 – 15

And when Moses thought he wasn't, he was! After 40 years out of the spotlight, God decided Moses was usable.

- God uses people who are **insecure.**

When God called on Moses to serve Him, Moses offered nothing but excuses:

• I'm nobody!
But Moses said to God, "Who am I that I should go to Pharaoh, and that I should bring the children of Israel out of Egypt?"

~ Exodus 3 : 11

• I have no authority!
Then Moses said to God, "Indeed, when I come to the children of Israel and say to them, 'The God of your fathers has sent me to you,' and they say to me, 'What is His name?' what shall I say to them?"

~ Exodus 3 : 13

• I'm not persuasive!

Then Moses answered and said, "But suppose they will not believe me or listen to my voice; suppose they say, 'The Lord has not appeared to you.'"

~ Exodus 4 : 1

• I have no speaking skills!

Then Moses said to the Lord, "O my Lord, I am not eloquent, neither before nor since You have spoken to Your servant; but I am slow of speech and slow of tongue."

~ Exodus 4 : 10

• I'd just rather not do it!

But he said, "O my Lord, please send by the hand of whomever else You may send."

~ Exodus 4 : 13

Moses was inadequate for the task and knew it... just the kind of man God was looking for.

- God uses people who are **unlikely.**

But the Lord said to Samuel, "Do not look at his appearance or at his physical stature, because I have refused him."

~ 1 Samuel 16 : 7a

The Lord does not look at the things men look at.

Man looks at the outward appearance, but the Lord looks at the heart."

~ 1 Samuel 16 : 7b

Samuel had made this mistake before:

…And when he [Saul] stood among the people, he was taller than any of the people from his shoulders upward. And Samuel said to all the people, "Do you see him whom the Lord has chosen, that there is no one like him among all the people?"

~ I Samuel 10 : 23- 24

And Samuel said to Jesse, "Are all the young men here?" Then he said, "There remains yet the youngest, and there he is, keeping the sheep."

~ I Samuel 16 : 11

Even David's father didn't believe he was qualified to be king.

Jesus was an unlikely Messiah:

He was in the world, and the world was made through Him, and the world did not know Him. He came to His own, and His own did not receive Him.

~ John 1 : 10 – 11

He had no beauty or majesty to attract us to him, nothing in his appearance that we should desire him. He was despised and rejected by men, a man of sorrows, and familiar with suffering. Like one from whom men hide their faces he was despised, and we esteemed him not.

~ Isaiah 53 : 2 – 3 NIV

And he said to the Jews, "Behold your King!" But they cried out, "Away with Him, away with Him! Crucify Him!"

~ John 19 : 14b – 15a

You are God's Masterpiece

I can almost hear someone saying, "I am not fit for the Master's use." While some are saying, "I am not ready, yet."

Do you know what? That is a trick of the devil, to delay the fulfillment of your destiny. Say to the enemy, "It will not work!" Say to Satan, "I cannot be fooled again!" What is that thing that you have done, or the sin you have committed that you think is unpardonable? Why do you think God does not want you or can't use you? Let me tell you something. Satan is a liar and a deceiver! He is the father of lies. The devil has tried his tricks on other people before you, but they overcame his tricks, and God did mighty things in their lives afterwards.

We may believe God can use people, but sometimes we doubt that God can use us. We come up with many reasons why God couldn't use us. *"I'm not talented." "I'm a new Christian." "I don't know enough about the Bible." "I'm not outgoing." "I'm too young." "I'm too old." "I believe God can use him/her, but I don't believe He can use me."*

If you doubt God can use you, read this:

For we are God's masterpiece, He has created us anew in Christ Jesus, so we can do the good things he planned for us long ago.

~ Ephesians 2 : 10 NLT

Who are we?
"God's masterpiece."

What are we created to do?
"The good things He planned for us long ago."

"masterpiece" = "poiema", a product with a designated purpose; workmanship.

> *I don't care who you are, how much education you have,*
> *how knowledgeable of the Bible you are,*
> *how shy you can be, or how unprepared you feel.*
> *God can – and will – use you to further His kingdom.*

God isn't only looking for super-spiritual Christians, or for those who seem to have it all together. He wants to use you!

I know that in reality, this is hard to comprehend – especially when it seems like everything around us is saying the exact opposite. But the truth is, God wants to use you now… wherever you are.

> *We didn't become Christians in order to*
> *just sit on the bench or be a cheerleader,*
> *God wants every one of us in the game.*

If you are reading this book right now, I can guarantee that it is true for you, because if God didn't have something for you to do, you would already be in heaven.

Today I know that there are some people reading, who are thinking, "Guy Peh, you have absolutely no clue. God cannot use me because of my shyness, or my lack of abilities, or my family circumstances, or "_____" (fill in the blank). If that's you that I just described, let me say that I am not here to condemn you, but I am here to encourage you. If you were to talk to most Christians out there who are serving God, I am sure they would tell you, that on their own, they are inadequate to serve God. They will also tell you that as soon as they stepped out and started serving, those inadequacies no longer mattered, because it was then that God stepped in and gave them more strength than they needed to cover their weaknesses.

As God told Paul, and says to each and every one of us:

And He said to me [Paul], "My grace is sufficient for you, for My strength is made perfect in weakness."
~ 2 Corinthians 12 : 9a

You see, God could use those who feel confident in their abilities, but many times He doesn't... so that His power can be seen. Then there is no way we can let pride seep in, because it really isn't us doing the job. So, no matter where you are today, let me encourage you to not be afraid to let God use you.

There is nothing that serves as a better faith builder than to allow God to move through you. And through that, the world around you will come to know Him.

Often we think we aren't ready to be used by God. We think we need to be someone else or somewhere else for God to use us. We think we need a certain talent, or a certain skill for God to use us.

> *We think it's about the gifts in us and not the God in us.*
> *We forget that His indwelling is the only reason He can use us.*

God gives each individual singular gifts, but those talents can, sometimes, only be poured out onto the world through the cracks in our lives. Why do we think we need to be in a better place spiritually, geographically, financially, or professionally before God can use us? Sometimes, out of our own brokenness in this place, God pours out of us and into the world. It's part of the divine paradox.

> *God gives us gifts, and we offer our talents*
> *(the work we do with our hands, and our minds) back to God.*

This act is one of the ways God, Himself, meets the needs of our world. It may be an encouraging word to a colleague, or a hearty handshake when meeting a neighbor. It may be a project well done at work, a warm tone of voice when answering the phone, or a line of gratitude in an email. He hides Himself in all we do so that even the simple, the daily, is enough.

> *Human gifts ebb and flow and fail,*
> *and we really only have one true Gift to offer.*
> *That gift is to offer in our work, our words,*
> *and our daily ways, "Here, all I have to give is Christ."*

The truth is, God may never choose to bestow that talent we yearn for, or that valued position we jockey for. But isn't that the point?

> *God has a plan, and it's His... not ours.*

We may be very receptive to God using us in the ways we imagine, but are we open to the way God wants to use us? He has a unique and distinctive vision for each of us. It involves using us today, exactly as we are, where we are, and doing what we do.

> *If we can't serve God in this day, in this work,*
> *in this brokenness, when will we?*

Start where you are. Start now! You are God's masterpiece. My prayer is that this book is not a one-time read. It is a reference guide to be used over and over again, as you grow in God's Word to be used in His Kingdom, for His Glory.

The lyrics of the song "Use Me" from Ron Kenoly's album, God is Able, are the heartbeat of the cry of someone who wants to be used by God.

If You can use anything Lord, You can use me.
If You can use anything Lord, You can use me.
Take my hands Lord and my feet.
Touch my heart Lord, speak through me.
If You can use anything Lord, You can use me.

Lord, You called Moses from the wilderness and You put a rod in his hand.
You used him to lead Your people over to the Promised Land.
Lord, I'm willing to trust in You, so take my life Lord and use it too.
Yes, if You can use anything Lord, come on and use me.

If You can use anything Lord, You can use me.
If You can use anything Lord, You can use me.
Take my hands Lord and my feet.
Touch my heart Lord, speak through me.
If You can use anything Lord, You can use me.

When David fought Goliath and that mighty giant fell.
He proved to his people that God was alive in Israel.
Lord, I'm available to You and I'm waiting to be used.
Yes I am, Lord.

If You can use anything Lord, You can use me.
If You can use anything Lord, You can use me.
Take my hands Lord and my feet.
Touch my heart Lord, speak through me.
If You can use anything Lord, You can use me.

After the multitudes heard the words that Jesus said,
He took two fish and five loaves, and the multitude was fed Lord.
What I have may not be much but I know it can multiply by Your touch.
So if You can use anything Lord come on and use me.

If You can use anything Lord, You can use me.
If You can use anything Lord, You can use me.
Take my hands Lord and my feet.
Touch my heart Lord, speak through me.
If You can use anything Lord, You can use me.

Do you want to help build a
Bridge of *Hope?*

People, wasn't it Jesus' teaching to feed the poor, to care for the sick and hurting? Only 6% of evangelical churches believe it's necessary to be concerned for the world's issues!

Many people around the world today are disadvantaged economically, socially, educationally and physically by their circumstances.

With your financial contribution, Bridge of Hope, an outreach of Reconciliation Ministries International (RMI), is dedicated to build a bridge that will give an opportunity to disadvantaged people around the world to have a better life by providing food, support for orphanages, assistance in disasters, to dig water wells, to help pastors and ministers in need and anything that we feel is necessary.

As missionaries to the nations, we need to have more than just the language of words. We also need the language of actions.

Matthew 25 : 35-36
Jesus said: I was hungry, you gave me food.
I was thirsty, you gave me drink.
I was a stranger, you took me in.
I was naked, you clothed me.
I was sick and you visited me.
I was in prison and you came to me.

Verse 40b
I say to you, inasmuch as you did it to one of the least of these, My brethren, you did it to Me.

James 1 : 27 says:
Pure and undefiled religion before God and the Father is this: to visit orphans and widows in their trouble.

Do you want to make their lives different?

You can change this boy's live

Bridge of HOPE *

A child dies of a water-related illness every 15 seconds. In a world of unprecedented wealth, almost 2 million children die each year due to lack of clean water.

You can change the *life* of a *child*, his or her family and an entire village with $1,700.

Build a water well! Make the difference!

Clean water from the new well

The old well

The new well

As missionaries to the nations, we need to have more than just the language of words. We also need the language of actions.

Prayer Shield Network

Prayer is not a way of getting what we want, but the way to become what God wants us to be.

Amazing things can happen when people come into agreement. It's a principle from God's word and the Prayer Shield Network is dedicated to praying with people who desire to see the Holy Spirit's miracle working power unleashed.

We couldn't have done what the Lord has done through us in the nations of the world without the prayer support of the body of Christ around the world.

To be part of the Prayer Shield Network, a group of people that prays for Guy & Ilke and for prayer requests from around the world, you can sign up at www.guypeh.com on the prayer shield network link.

If you have a <u>prayer request</u> and would like the prayer shield network to intercede for you, email your prayer request at prayer7@guypeh.com

Watch

Dr. Guy Peh

on web TV at

www.tvguypeh.com

Book: Keys to Receiving Your Miracles

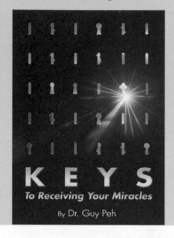

There was never a day of miracles, only a God of miracles.

A man with a genuine experience with God is never at the mercy of a man with an argument against God. Without faith in the miraculous, people subscribe to a mentality of pessimism and defeat.

You will always know what God will do tomorrow because of what He has already done.

God wants you to enjoy miracle living. His plan for you is to dominate sickness, evil spirits and destruction just as Jesus did. What Jesus started you can continue.

In this book Dr. Guy Peh gives you practical keys that will unlock your understanding about the miracle realm and how to receive your miracle.

Purchasing and Contact Information:

Reconciliation Ministries International

P.O. Box 763174

Dallas TX 75376

USA

Phone: 214 – 808 7218

Email: guyandilke@guypeh.com

Visit us on the web:

www.guypeh.com

Notes:

Notes:

Notes:

Notes: